# Africa and the Discovery of America

# AFRICA

## AND THE

# DISCOVERY *of* AMERICA

### VOLUME II

## *By* LEO WIENER

PROFESSOR OF SLAVIC LANGUAGES AND LITERATURES AT
HARVARD UNIVERSITY; AUTHOR OF "A COMMENTARY TO
THE GERMANIC LAWS AND MEDIAEVAL DOCUMENTS,"
"CONTRIBUTIONS TOWARD A HISTORY OF ARABICO-
GOTHIC CULTURE," "HISTORY OF YIDDISH LITERATURE,"
"HISTORY OF THE CONTEMPORARY RUSSIAN DRAMA,"
"ANTHOLOGY OF RUSSIAN LITERATURE," "INTERPRETA-
TION OF THE RUSSIAN PEOPLE;" TRANSLATOR OF THE
WORKS OF TOLSTOY; CONTRIBUTOR TO GERMAN, RUSSIAN
FRENCH, ENGLISH, AND AMERICAN PHILOLOGICAL
PERIODICALS, ETC., ETC.

INNES & SONS
129-135 N. TWELFTH ST., PHILADELPHIA, PA.
MCMXXII

# TABLE OF CONTENTS

ⴰ

# LIST OF ILLUSTRATIONS.

# FOREWORD

In the present volume I muster the information accessible as to the presence in America of tobacco, cotton, and shell-money, previous to the so-called discovery of America by Columbus. I have not knowingly omitted any statement made by an early writer, whether in favor of my argument or against it, but the mass of material that had to be waded through was so great, that I may have overlooked some passages. The accumulated evidence is overwhelmingly in favor of an introduction of the articles under discussion from Africa, by European and Negro traders, decades earlier than 1492. Unfortunately certain archaeologists insist upon denying all but the archaeological evidence and shower upon an objective investigator a veritable deluge of abuse. Upon these I shall urge the admirable concluding words of J. Batalha-Reis in an article entitled *The Supposed Discovery of South America before 1448, and the Critical Methods of the Historians of Geographical Discovery:* "The greater probability is, therefore, in my opinion, in favour of the supposition that the north-east corner of South America had been seen on or before 1448, although this cannot be affirmed with the same historical certainty with which we can affirm that, in 1492, Columbus landed on some of the Antilles.

"It appears to me (if I dare express my whole feeling on the subject) that to answer questions like this with an unconditional affirmative or a rigid negative, is not to realize, in all their true conditions, historical problems—not to realize, in fact, what real life is, and how history ought to be studied and written.

"Almost all the historians of geographical discoveries consider it their absolute duty to arrive at a radical conclusion in the study of problematical questions, answering with a *yes* what only deserves a *perhaps*, or, more frequently, dismissing with a *no* what ought to be held as probable."[1]

Wherever I have occasion, in this volume, to censure the archaeologists I have in mind the vociferous Philistines who conspicuously pretend to talk for all the archaeologists, and not the fairminded scholars of the profession, the lineal descendants of Bandelier, Squier, Davis, Cyrus Thomas, Holmes, and many more, but who unfortunately have been conspicuously silent and so cannot be quoted, reverently or otherwise. The vast amount of new matter that has turned up since I began this investigation compels me to relegate the conclusive proof of Mandingo influence upon pre-Columbian America through its fetishism to a third volume. I take this occasion of thanking Mr. John B. Stetson, Jr. for communicating to me from time to time important points bearing on my subject, as they occurred to him in his wide and judicious readings of early authors on South America.

The Author.

[1] In *The Geographical Journal*, London 1897, vol. IX, p. 210.

# SOURCES QUOTED

Acosta, J. de      Historia natural y moral de las Indias, vol. I, Madrid 1894.

Alvares d'Almada, A.      Tratado breve dos rios de Guine' do Cabo-Verde, ed. by D. Köpke, Porto 1841.

American Anthropolcgist, The, vol. XXIII.

Andagoya, P. de      Narrative of the Proceedings of Pedrarias Davila, trans. and ed. by C. R. Markham (The Hakluyt Society), London 1865.

Arriaga, P. J. de      Extirpación de la idolatria del Pirú, Buenos Aires 1910.

Arrian.      'Ινδικά.

Artemidori Daldiani &      Oneirocritica, Lutetiae 1603.
Achmetis Sereimi F.

Athenaeus.

Atti della Società Ligure di Storia Patria, vol. IV, Genoa 1866.

Avezac, A. d'      Bref récit et succincte narration de la navigation faite en MDXXXV et MDXXXVI par le capitaine Jacques Cartier aus îles de Canada, Hochelaga, Saguenay et autres, Paris 1863.

Avicenna.      See Ibn-Sīnā.


Baessler, A.      Peruanische Mumien, Untersuchungen mit X-Strahlen, Berlin 1906.

Baldelli-Boni, G. B.      Il Milione di Marco Polo, vols. I, II, Firenze 1827.

Bandelier, A. F.      The Journey of Alvar Nuñez Cabeza de Vaca, New York 1905.

Barbosa, Duarte      Collecção de noticias para a historia e geografia das nações ultramarinas, vol. II, Lisboa 1867.

Barbot, J.      See Churchill, vol. V.

Barré, N.      Copie de quelques letres sur la navigation du chevallier de Villegaignon es terres de l'Amérique oultre l'Aequinoctial, iusques soulz le tropique de Capricorne, Paris 1558.

Batalha-Reis, J.      The Supposed Discovery of South America before 1448, and the Critical Methods of the Historians of Geographical Discovery, in The Geographical Journal, vol. IX, London 1897.

Baxter, J. P.      A Memoir of Jacques Cartier, Sieur de Limoilou, New York 1906.

Beauchamp, W. M.      Wampum and Shell Articles Used by the New York Indians, in Bulletin of the New York State Museum, No. 41, vol. 8.

Belon du Mans, P.      Les observations de plusieurs singularitez & choses memorables, trouvées en Grece, Asie, Judée, Egypte, Arabie, & autres pays estranges, Paris 1555.

Bentley, W. H.          Dictionary and Grammar of the Kongo Language,
                        London 1887, 1895.
Benton, P. A.           Notes on some Languages of the Western Sudan,
                        London, New York 1912.
Berthelot, M.           Collection des anciens alchimistes grecs, vols. II,
                        III, Paris 1888.
Beverley, R.            The History and Present State of Virginia, Book
                        III, London 1705.
Binger, G.              Du Niger au Golfe de Guinée, vol. II, Paris 1892.
Bleek, W. H. J.         The Languages of Mosambique, London 1856.
Blochmann, H.           Āīn i Akbarī, in Bibliotheca Indica, published by
                        the Asiatic Society of Bengal, new series, No.
                        149.
Boban, E.               Documents pour servir à l'histoire du Mexique,
                        Catalogue raisonné de la collection E. Eugène
                        Goupil, Paris 1891.
Boletim do conselho ultramarino, Legislação antiga, vol. I, Lisboa 1867.
Bosman, W.              A New and Accurate Description of the Coast of
                        Guinea, London 1721.
Bostock, J. and         The Natural History of Pliny, London 1855.
  Riley, H. T.
Botanical Gazette, vol. LXI.
Botanisches Centralblatt, vol. III.
Bowdich, T. E.          Mission from Cape Coast Castle to Ashantee,
                        London 1819.
Brandes, H.             Ueber die antiken Namen und die geographische
                        Verbreitung der Baumwolle im Alterthum, in 5.
                        Jahresbericht des Vereins von Freunden der
                        Erdkunde zu Leipzig, 1866.
Breton, R. P. R.        Dictionaire caraibe-français, Leipzig 1892.
Brodhead, J. R.         History of the State of New York, vol. I, New
                        York 1853.
Bry, Th. de             Admiranda narratis fida tamen, de commodis et
                        incolarum ritibus Virginiae, Francofurti ad
                        Moenum 1590.
Butaye, R.              Dictionnaire kikongo-français, français-kikongo,
                        Roulers [1909].


Camerarius, J.          De plantis epytome utilissima, Francofurti ad
                        Moenum 1586.
Candolle, A. de         Origine des plantes cultivées, Paris 1883.
                        Origin of Cultivated Plants, New York 1885.
Cartier, J.             See Avezac.
Catholic Historical Review, The, vol. VI, (April 1920).
Cavazzi, A.             Istorica descrizione de' tre' regni, Congo, Matamba,
                        et Angola, Bologna 1687.
Champlain, J. de        See Laverdière.
Chavannes, E.           Documents sur les Tou-Kiue (Turcs) occidentaux,
                        St. Pétersbourg 1903.
Cherbonneau, M. A.      Définition lexicographique de plusieurs mots usités
                        dans le langage de l'Afrique septentrionale, in
                        Journal Asiatique, IV. ser., vol. XIII.

Christopher, W. — Vocabulary of the Maldivian Language, in The Journal of the Royal Asiatic Society of Great Britain and Ireland, vol. VI (1841).

Churchill, J. — A Collection of Voyages and Travels, vols. I, V, London 1704, 1732.

Cobo, P. B. — Historia del Nuevo Mundo, vols. II, IV, Sevilla 1890-93.

Colección de documentos inéditos del archivo de Indias, vol. II.

Colección de documentos inéditos, para la historia de España, vol. V, Madrid 1844.

Colección de documentos inéditos, relativos al descubrimiento, conquista y organización de las antiguas posesiones españolas de América y Oceanía, vol. XIV, 1. ser., Madrid 1870.

Colección de documentos inéditos, relativos al descubrimiento, conquista y organización de las antiguas posesiones españolas de Ultramar, vol. V, 2. ser., Madrid 1890.

Colección de libros y documentos referentes á la historia del Perú, vol. III, Lima 1916.

Comes, O. — Histoire, géographie, statistique du tabac, Naples 1900.

Cook, McLachlan and Meade. — A Study of Diversity in Egyptian Cotton, in U. S. Dept. of Agriculture, Bureau of Plant Industry, Washington 1909, Bulletin No. 156.

Cordeiro, L. — Memorias do Ultramar. Viagens, explorações, e conquistas dos Portuguezes, part 2 (of 1574-1620), Da Mina ao Cabo Negro, part 5 (of 1607), Estabelecimentos e resgates portuguezes na costa occidental de Africa, Lisboa 1881.

Cordeiro da Matta, J. — Ensaio de diccionario kimbúndu-portuguez, Lisboa 1893.

Cortes, H. — See Gayangos and MacNutt.

Cotgrave, R. — A Dictionarie of the French and English Tongues, London 1632.

Crooke, W. — The Popular Religion and Folk-Lore of Northern India, vol. I, Westminster 1896.

Ctesias. — Ἰνδικά.

Cuevas, M. — Documentos inéditos del siglo XVI, para la historia de México, México 1914.

Curtis's Botanical Magazine, No. 8006.


Dames, M. L. — The Book of Duarte Barbosa (The Hakluyt Society), vol. I, London 1918.

Dapper, O. — Naukeurige Beschrijvinge der Afrikaensche Gewesten van Egypten, Barbaryen, Lybien, Biledulgerid, Negroslant, Guinea, Ethiopiën, Abyssinie, Amsterdam 1676.

Daumas, E. — Le Sahara algérien, Paris 1845.

Defrémery, C. and Sanguinetti, B. R. — Voyages d'Ibn Batoutah, vol. IV, Paris 1879.

Delafosse, M. — Manuel dahoméen, Paris 1894.
Sur des traces probables de civilisation égyptienne et d'hommes de race blanche à la Côte d'Ivoire, in L'Anthropologie, vol. XI, Paris 1900.

Dictionnaire français-fiote, dialecte du Kakongo, Paris 1890.
Dioscorides.
Doutté, E.                    Magie et religion dans l'Afrique du Nord, Alger
                              1909.
Ducange.                      Glossarium mediae et infimae latinitatis, ed. by
                              Léopold Favre, Niort 1883-87.


Elliott, W. A.                Notes for a Sindebele Dictionary and Grammar,
                              Bristol [19--].
Engler, E.                    Die Pflanzenwelt Ost-Afrikas und der Nachbar-
                              gebiete, Th. B., Berlin 1895.
                              Ueber floristische Verwandtschaft zwischen dem
                              tropischen Afrika und Amerika, in Sitzungs-
                              berichte der Königlichen Preussischen Akademie
                              der Wissenschaften, Berlin 1905.
Escalona y Agüero, G. de Gazophilatium regium perubicum, parte II, lib. II,
                              Matriti 1675.
Extracts from a work called Breeden Raedt aen de vereenighde Neder-
    landsche Provitien, printed in Antwerp in 1649, translated from the
    Dutch original by Mr. C., in E. B. O'Callaghan's The Documentary
    History of the State of New York, vol. IV, Albany 1851.


Falgairolle, Ed.              Jean Nicot, Ambassadeur de France en Portugal
                              au XVIe siècle, Paris 1897.
Focke, W. O.                  Die Pflanzen-Mischlinge, ein Beitrag zur Biologie
                              der Gewächse, Berlin 1881.
Foster, W.                    The English Factories in India, 1618-21, 1622-23,
                              1624-29, 1630-33, 1634-36, 1637-41, A Calendar
                              of Documents in the India Office, British
                              Museum and Public Record Office, Oxford
                              1906-1912.
Fürst, J.                     Hebräisches und chaldäisches Handwörterbuch,
                              Leipzig 1876.


García Icazbalceta, J.        Bibliografía mexicana del siglo XVI, vol. I,
                              México 1886.
                              Colección de documentos para la historia de
                              México, vols. I, II, México 1858-66.
                              Memoriales de Fray Toribio de Motolinia, Méjico
                              1903.
Garcilasso de la Vega.        Historia general del Peru, Cordova 1617.
Gayangos, P. de               Cartas y relaciones de Hernan Cortés al Emperador
                              Carlos V, Paris 1866.
Gazetteer of the Bombay Presidency, vols. VI, XI.
Giacosa, P.                   Magistri Salernitani, Torino 1901.
Gómara, F. López de           Conquista de Méjico, vol. II, Barcelona 1887-88.
                              La historia general delas Indias, Anvers 1554.
González de la Rosa.          Estudio de las antiguedades peruanas halladas
                              bajo el huano, in Revista Histórica, órgano del
                              Instituto Histórico del Perú, vol. III, Lima 1908.

Granada, D.    Vocabulario rioplatense razonado, Montevideo 1890.

Gray, A. and Bell, H. C. P.    The Voyage of François Pyrard (The Hakluyt Society), vols. I, II², London 1887-90.

Grünbaum, M.    Neue Beiträge zur semitischen Sagenkunde, Leiden 1893.

Guernsey, S. J. and Kidder, A. V.    Basket-Maker Caves of Northeastern Arizona, Report on the Explorations, 1916-17, in Papers of the Peabody Museum of American Archaeology and Ethnology, Harvard University, vol. VIII, No. 2.

Guerreiro, F.    Relaçam annal das cousas que fizeram os padres da Companhia de Jesus, nas partes da India Oriental, Lisboa 1611.

Haller, A. de    Artis medicae principes, vol. XI, Lausannae 1774.

Helmreich, G.    Marcelli de medicamentis, Lipsiae 1889.
Scribonii Largi compositiones, Lipsiae 1887.

Henning, G.    Samuel Braun, der erste deutsche wissenschaftliche Afrikareisende, Beitrag zur Erforschungsgeschichte von Westafrika, Basel 1900.

Henslow, G.    Medical Works of the Fourteenth Century, London 1899.

Hernández, F.    Nova plantarum, animalium et mineralium mexicanorum historia, Romae 1651.

Herodotus.

Herrera, A. de    Descripción de las Indias occidentales, Decada I, libro III.

Heyd, W.    Geschichte des Levantehandels im Mittelalter, vol. II, Stuttgart 1879.
Histoire du commerce, etc., vol. II, Leipzig 1886.

Hiern, W. P.    Catalogue of the African Plants Collected by Dr. Friedrich Welwitsch in 1853-61, vol. I, London 1896.

Hirth, F. and Rockhill, W. W.    Chau Ju-Kua: His Work on the Chinese and Arab Trade in the twelfth and thirteenth Centuries, entitled Chu-fan-chï, St. Petersburg 1911.

Holmes, W. H.    Aboriginal Pottery of the Eastern United States, in Twentieth Annual Report of the Bureau of American Ethnology to the Secretary of the Smithsonian Institution, 1898-99, Washington 1903.
Textile Fabrics of Ancient Peru, in Smithsonian Institution, Bureau of Ethnology, Washington 1889.

Homburger, L.    Étude sur la phonétique historique du Bantou, in Bibliothèque de l'École des hautes études, Paris 1913.

Hort, A.    Theophrastus, Enquiry into Plants and Minor Works on Odours and Weather Signs, vol. I, London, New York 1916.

Houdas, O.    Histoire de la dynastie Saadienne au Maroc, (1511-1670), Paris 1889.

Hümmerich, F.      Quellen und Untersuchungen zur Fahrt der ersten
Deutschen nach dem portugiesischen Indien,
1505-6, in Abhandlungen der Kgl. Bayerischen
Akademie der Wissenschaften, philosophisch-
philologische und historische Klasse, vol. XXX,
part 3.

Hutchinson, M.      See Lopez.


Ibn-al-Awam.      Le livre de l'agriculture d'Ibn-al-Awam, trans.
and ed. by J.-J. Clément-Mullet, vol. II, Paris
1866.

Ibn-Sīnā.      Avicennae Liber Canonis, Venetiis 1582.

Informes sobre la existencia de huano en las Islas de Chincha presentados
por la comision nombrada por el Gobierno peruano, con los planos levantados por la misma comision, Lima 1854.


Jerez, F. de y      Las relaciones de la conquista del Perú, in Colec-
    Sancho, P.      ción de libros y documentos referentes á la
historia del Perú, vol. V, Lima 1917.

Jiménez de la      Relaciones geográficas de Indias, vols. I, III, IV,
    Espada, M.      Madrid 1881-97.

Jobson, R.      The Golden Trade: or, A discouery of the Riuer
Gambra, and the Golden Trade of the Aethio-
pians, London 1623.

Johnson, Th.      The Workes of that famous Chirurgian Ambrose
Parey, London 1634.

Josephus Flavius.      Antiquitates Judaicae.

Journal of the Royal Asiatic Society of Great Britain and Ireland, The,
vol. XX.

Jully, A.      Manuel des dialectes malgaches, Paris 1901.


Kidder, A. V. and      Archeological Explorations in Northeastern Ari-
    Guernsey, S. J.      zona, in Smithsonian Institution, Bureau of
American Ethnology, Washington 1919, Bulletin
65.

King, L. W.      An Early Mention of Cotton: The Cultivation of
Gossypium Arboreum, or Tree-Cotton, in Assyria
in the Seventh Century B. C., in Proceedings of
the Society of Biblical Archaeology, vol. XXXI.

Kingsborough, E.      Antiquities in Mexico, London 1830.

Knust, H.      El libro de Marco Polo, ed. by R. Stuebe, Leipzig
1902.

Krapf, J. L.      A Dictionary of the Suahili Language, London
1882.

Kühn, D.      Medicorum graecorum opera, vol. II, Lipsiae 1830.

Kuntze.      Plantae Pechuelianae Hereroenses, in Jahrbuch
des Königlichen Botanischen Gartens (1886),
Berlin 1886.
Revisio generum plantarum, pars II.

Labat, J.-B. Nouvelle relation de l'Afrique occidentale, Paris 1728.

Lagarde, P. de (Petri Hispani) de lingua arabica libri duo, Gottingae 1883.

Lamer, H. Das Rauchen im Altertume, in Jahresberichte des philologischen Vereins, vol. XLIV.

Lane, E. W. An Account of the Manners and Customs of the Modern Egyptians, vol. II, London 1871.

Lane-Poole, S. Coins and Medals, London 1894.

Laufer, B. The Beginnings of Porcelain in China, in Field Museum of Natural History, Publication 192 (Anthropological ser.), vol. XV, No. 2.

Laverdière, C. H. Oeuvres de Champlain, Québec 1870.

Leclerc, L. Traité des simples par Ibn El-Beïthar, in Notices et extraits des manuscrits de la Bibliothèque Nationale, vols. XXV, XXVI.

León, N. Códice Mariano Jiménez, Nómina de tributos de los pueblos Otlazpan y Tepexic en geroglífico Azteca y lenguas Castellana y Nahuatl, 1549, Mexico [1904].

Cuatro libros de la naturaleza, extracto de las obras del Dr. Francisco Hernández, Morelia 1888.

Studies on the Archaeology of Michoacan (Mexico), in Smithsonian Report, 1886, Washington 1889.

Léry, J. de Histoire d'un voyage faict en la terre du Brésil, vol. I, Paris 1880.

Lescarbot, M. Histoire de la Nouvelle-France, vol. III, Paris 1866.

Letters Received by the East India Company from its Servants in the East, vol. I, London 1896.

Levy, E. Provenzalisches Supplement-Wörterbuch, Leipzig 1892-1915.

Liebaut, J. L'agriculture et maison rustique de M. Charles Estienne docteur en medecine, Paris 1570.

Lippmann, E. von Der Leidener und Stockholmer Papyrus, in Entstehung und Ausbreitung der Alchemie, Berlin 1919.

Littmann, E. Bibliotheca abessinica: The Legend of the Queen of Sheba in the Tradition of Axum, Leyden, Princeton, N. J. 1904.

Lopez, Duarte A Report of the Kingdom of Congo and of the Surrounding Countries; drawn out of the Writings and Discourses of the Portuguese, Duarte Lopez, by Filippo Pigafetta, trans. and ed. by M. Hutchinson, London 1881.

MacDougal, D. T. The Reactions of Plants to New Habitats, in Ecology, vol. II (1921).

MacNutt, F. A. Letters of Cortes, vol. I, New York 1908.

Madan, A. C. Lala-Lamba-Wisa and English, English and Lala-Lamba-Wisa Dictionary, Oxford 1913.

Swahili-English Dictionary, Oxford 1903.

Malgaigne, J.-F.        Oeuvres complètes d'Ambroise Paré, vol. II, Paris 1840.

Marees, P. de          Beschryvinghe ende historische verhael van het gout koninckrijck van Gunea, 's-Gravenhage 1912.

Marie.                 La producción de algodón en el Perú, in Boletin del Ministerio de Fomento, primer trimestre de 1916, Lima 1916.

Marin, C. A.           Storia civile e politica del commercio de' Veneziani, vol. V, Vinegia 1800.

Markham, C. R.         The Incas of Peru, New York 1910.
                       The Travels of Pedro de Cieza de Leon (The Hakluyt Society), London 1864.

Mas'ūdī.               Les prairies d'or, ed. by C. B. de Meynard and P. de Courteille, Paris 1861-77.

Matthiolus, P. A.      Commentarii in sex libros Pedacii Dioscoridis Anazarbei de medica materia, Venetiis 1565.

Means, P. A.           A Survey of Ancient Peruvian Art, in Transactions of the Connecticut Academy of Arts and Sciences, vol. XXI.

Mendieta, G. de        Historia eclesiástica indiana, México 1870.
Middendorf, E. W.      Das Muchik oder die Chimu-Sprache, Leipzig 1892.
Monardes, N.           Joyfull Newes Out of the New-found Worlde, London 1596.

Moore, C. B.           Antiquities of the St. Francis, White, and Black Rivers, Arkansas, Philadelphia 1910.

Moore, F.              Travels into the Inland Parts of Africa, London 1738.

Moraes é Silva, A. de  Diccionario da lingua portugueza, Lisboa 1877-78.
Motolinia, Fray Toribio See García Icazbalceta.

Nieuwenhuis, A. W.     Kunstperlen und ihre kulturelle Bedeutung, in Internationales Archiv für Ethnographie, vol. XVI (1904).

Novisima recopilacion.

Ogilby, J.             Africa: Being an accurate Description of the Regions of Aegypt, Barbary, Lybia, and Bille-dulgerid, the Land of Negroes, Guinee, Aethiopia, and the Abyssines, London 1670.

Orozco y Berra, M.     Historia antigua y de la conquista de México, México 1880.

Oviedo, G. F. de       Historia general y natural de las Indias, vols. I, II, III, IV, Madrid 1851-55.
                       Sumario dela natural y general istoria delas Indias, Toledo 1526.

Pacheco Pereira, D.    Esmeraldo de situ orbis, in Boletim da Sociedade de Geographia de Lisboa, 22ª ser., Lisboa 1904.
Paré, A.               See Malgaigne and Johnson.
Parkinson, J.          Paradisi in Sole Paradisus Terrestris, London 1904.

Pauthier, G.                  Le livre de Marco Polo, 2 vols., Paris 1865.

Pearce, F. B.             Zanzibar, the Island Metropolis of Eastern Africa, London 1920.

Peñafiel, A.              Monumentos del arte mexicano antiguo, Berlin 1890.

Philostratus.            Vita Apollonii.

Pizarro, P.              Descubrimiento y conquista del Perú, in Colección de libros y documentos referentes á la historia del Perú, vol. VI, Lima 1917.

Pliny.                     Historia Naturalis. See Bostock.

Plutarch.               De Iside et Osiride.

Pobéguin, H.             Côte occidentale d'Afrique, Paris 1906.

Pollux.

Polo, Marco             See Baldelli-Boni, Knust, Pauthier and Yule.

Pomar, J. B. y          Relación de Tezcoco, in Nueva colección de docu-
  Zurita, A. de        mentos para la historia de México, vol. III, México 1891.

Portugaliae monumenta historica, vol. I, Olisipone 1856.

Primera parte de las noticias historiales de las conquistas de Tierra Firme en las Indias, [Cuenca 1627].

Purchas, S.              Hakluytus Posthumus or Purchas His Pilgrimes, vol. VI, Glasgow 1905.

Pyrard, F.              See Gray.


Raccolta di documenti e studi pubblicati dalla R. Commissione Colombiana, part I, vols. I, II, Roma 1892-96.

Ramos i Duarte, F.     Diccionario de Mejicanismos, Méjico 1895.

Ramusio, G. B.        Delle navigationi et viaggi, vol. I, Venetia 1588.

Ravenstein, E. G.     The Strange Adventures of Andrew Battell of Leigh, in Angola and the Adjoining Regions (The Hakluyt Society), London 1901.

Reber, B.              Les pipes antiques de la Suisse, in Anzeiger für schweizerische Altertumskunde, N. F., vols. XVI, XVII.

Recchi, N. A.          See Hernández.

Reiss, W. and         The Necropolis of Ancon, vol. I, Berlin 1880-87.
  Stübel, A.

Renzi, S. de            Collectio Salernitana, vols. I, II, III, V, Napoli 1852-1859.

Revista de Archivos, Bibliotecas y Museos, vol. XXVII, Madrid 1913.

Revista do Instituto historico e geographico de São Paulo, vol. III.

Ritter, K.              Ueber die geographische Verbreitung der Baum-wolle und ihr Verhältnis zur Industrie der Völker alter und neuer Zeit, in Abhandlungen der Kgl. Akademie der Wissenschaften zu Berlin, 1851.

Robertson, W. G.     An Introductory Handbook to the Language of the Bemba-People, London 1904.

Rolland, E.           Faune populaire de la France, vol. III, Paris 1881.

Roth, H. L.            Great Benin, its Customs, Art, and Horrors, Halifax 1903.

Rouffaer, G. P.            Waar kwamen de raadselachtige Moetisalah's
                          (Aggri-Kralen) in de Timor-groep oorspronkelijk
                          van daan?, in Bijdragen tot de Taal-, Land- en
                          Volkenkunde van Nederlandsch-Indië, vol. VI,
                          's-Gravenhage 1899.


Sagard-Théodat, F. G.      Histoire du Canada et voyages que les Frères
                          Mineurs Recollects y ont faicts pour la conver-
                          sion des infidèles, vol. I, Paris 1866.
                          Le grand voyage du pays des Hurons, vol. I,
                          Paris 1865.
Sahagun, B. de             Historia general de las cosas de Nueva España, in
                          Biblioteca Mexicana, México 1890-96.
Schoff, W. H.              The Periplus of the Erythraean Sea, New York
                          1912.
Schulze, F.                Balthasar Springers Indienfahrt, 1505-06, Strass-
                          burg 1902.
Schweinfurth, G.           The Heart of Africa, vol. I, London 1873.
Seler, E.                  Die alten Bewohner der Landschaft Michuacan,
                          in Gesammelte Abhandlungen zur amerikan-
                          ischen Sprach- und Alterthumskunde, vol. III,
                          Berlin 1908.
                          Die mexikanischen Bilderhandschriften Alexander
                          von Humboldt's in der Kgl. Bibliothek zu Berlin,
                          in Gesammelte Abhandlungen zur amerikan-
                          ischen Sprach- und Alterthumskunde, vol. I,
                          Berlin 1902.
Serrano y Sanz, M.         Historiadores de Indias, Apologética historia de
                          las Indias, de Fr. Bartolomé de las Casas, in
                          Nueva Biblioteca de autores españoles, vol. I,
                          Madrid 1909.
Smith, B.                  Narratives of the Career of Hernando de Soto in
                          the Conquest of Florida, New York 1866.
Smith, H. I.               The Archaeological Collection from the Southern
                          Interior of British Columbia, Ottawa 1913.
Soares de Sousa, G.        Tratado descriptivo do Brasil em 1587, Rio de
                          Janeiro 1879.
Solorzano Pereira, J. de   Politica indiana, Madrid 1648.
Steinen, K. von den        Unter den Naturvolkern Zentral-Brasiliens, Berlin
                          1894.
Steingass, F.              A  Comprehensive  Persian-English  Dictionary,
                          London [1892].
Stevens, J.                A New Dictionary, Spanish and English, and Eng-
                          lish and Spanish, London 1726.
Strabo.
Stubel, A., Reiss, W.      Kultur und Industrie sudamerikanischer Volker,
  and Koppel, B.           vol. I, Berlin 1889.
Sudhoff, K.                Beitrage zur Geschichte der Chirurgie im Mittel-
                          alter, in Studien zur Geschichte der Medizin,
                          vol. II, Leipzig 1918.

Tello, J. C.                 Los antiguos cementerios del Valle de Nasca, in
                             Proceedings of the Second Pan-American Scien-
                             tific Congress, vol. I (1917).
Terrien de Lacouperie,       The Metallic Cowries of Ancient China, in Journal
   A.                        of the Royal Asiatic Society, vol. XX, London
                             1888.
Thacher, J. B.               Christopher   Columbus,   New   York,   London
                             1903-04.
Theal, G. McC.               Records of South-Eastern Africa, [London] 1898-
                             1903.
Theophrastus.                See Hort.
Thesaurus syriacus.
Thevet, A.                   La cosmographie universelle, Paris 1575
Thomas, G. M.                Capitular des deutschen Hauses in Venedig,
                             Berlin 1874.
Tootal, A.                   The Captivity of Hans Stade of Hesse in A. D.
                             1547-1555, among the Wild Tribes of Eastern
                             Brazil (The Hakluyt Society), London 1874.
Torrend, J.                  A Comparative Grammar of the South-African
                             Bantu Languages, London 1891.
Torres Saldamando, E.        Libro primero de Cabildos de Lima, segunda parte,
                             Paris 1900.
Trumbull, J. H.              Natick Dictionary, in Smithsonian Institution,
                             Bureau of American Ethnology, Washington
                             1903, Bulletin 25.
Twenty-eighth Annual Report of the Bureau of American Ethnology to
   the Secretary of the Smithsonian Institution (1906-1907), Washington
   1912.


Uhle, M.                     La esfera de influencias del país de los Incas, in
                             Revista histórica, órgano del Instituto Histórico
                             del Perú, vol. IV, Lima 1909.
Uricoechea, E.               Gramática, vocabulario, catecismo i confesionario
                             de la lengua chibcha, Paris 1871.


Vieira, A.                   Arte de furtar, in Historia do futuro, Lisboa 1855.
Visseq, A.                   Dictionnaire fiot-français, Paris 1890.
Vries, D. P. de              Korte historiael ende journaels aenteyckeninge van
                             verscheyden voyagiens in de vier deelen des
                             wereldts-ronde, als Europa, Africa, Asia, ende
                             Amerika gedaen, 's-Gravenhage 1911.


Watt, G.                     The Wild and Cultivated Cotton Plants of the
                             World, London 1907.
Welwitsch, F.                See Hiern.
Wieger, L.                   Chinese Characters, trans. by L. Davrout, vol. I,
                             Ho-kien-fu 1915.

Wiener, L.                    Africa and the Discovery of America, vol. I,
                                  Philadelphia 1920.
                              Contributions toward a History of Arabico-Gothic
                                  Culture, vol. IV, Philadelphia 1921.
                              Economic History and Philology, in The Quarterly
                                  Journal of Economics, vol. XXV.
                              German Loan-Words and the Second Sound
                                  Shifting, in Modern Language Notes, vol. X.
                              Pseudo-Karaibisches, in Zeitschrift für Roma-
                                  nische Philologie, vol. XXXIII.


Yule, H.                      Hobson-Jobson, a Glossary of Colloquial Anglo-
                                  Indian Words and Phrases, new ed. by William
                                  Crooke, London 1903.
                              The Book of Ser Marco Polo, vol. II, London 1871.


Zimmermann, J.                A Grammatical Sketch of the Akra- or Gã-Lan-
                                  guage, Stuttgart 1858.
Zorita, A. de                 Historia de la Nueva España, vol. I, Madrid 1909.
                              See Pomar.

# PART I:  COTTON.

# CHAPTER I.

## The Prehistory of Cotton.

The earliest datable references to *cotton* are found in two inscriptions of the Assyrian Sennacherib, of the year 694 B. C.[1] "A great park, like one on Mt. Amanus, wherein were included all kinds of herbs, and fruit trees, and trees, the products of the mountains and of Chaldea, together with trees that bear wool (*işê na-aš šipâti*), I planted beside it." "The miskannu-trees and cypresses that grew in the plantations, and the reed-beds that were in the swamp, I cut down and used for work, when required, in my lordly palaces. The trees that bear wool they sheared, and they shredded it for garments."

It is a curious fact that neither here nor for centuries later in Greek literature do we get the name of the cotton-tree, but only the descriptive title "the tree that bears wool or linen." Herodotus tells of a corselet which Amasis, King of Egypt, had sent to the Lacedaemonians, and which was embroidered with gold and tree wool (εἰρίοισι ἀπὸ ξύλου).[2] However, minute microscopical investigations of the mummy bands have failed to show the presence of cotton in any of the ancient Egyptian graves.[3] Herodotus similarly speaks of the Indians in Xerxes' army as wearing cotton

---

[1] L. W. King, *An Early Mention of Cotton: The Cultivation of Gossypium arboreum, or Tree-Cotton, in Assyria in the Seventh Century B. C.*, in *Proceedings of the Society of Biblical Archaeology*, vol. XXXI, p. 339 ff.

[2] III. 47.

[3] K. Ritter, *Ueber die geographische Verbreitung der Baumwolle und ihr Verhältnis zur Industrie der Völker alter und neuer Zeit*, in *Abhandlungen der Kgl. Akademie der Wissenschaften zu Berlin*, 1851, p. 317.

dresses (εἵματα ἀπὸ ξύλων πεποιημένα)[1] and of the wild-
growing trees of India which bear wool finer in beauty
and goodness than that of sheep.[2]   There can be little
doubt that in the V. century B. C. India was already
manufacturing cotton cloth, even as Ctesias refers to
cotton cloth (ξύλινα ἱμάτια) in India.[3]   This is confirmed in the IV. century by Theophrastus, who says
that the island of Tylos, the modern Bahrein, in the
Persian gulf "produces the 'wool-bearing' tree (τὰ
δένδρα τὰ ἐριοφόρα) in abundance.   This has a leaf
like that of the vine, but small, and bears no fruit; but
the vessel in which the 'wool' is contained is as large as
a spring apple, and closed, but when it is ripe, it unfolds
and puts forth the 'wool,' of which they weave their
fabrics, some of which are cheap and some very expensive.   This tree is also found, as was said, in India as
well as in Arabia."[4]   But we are also specifically informed by him that the Indians cultivated these trees.
"The trees from which they make their clothes have a
leaf like the mulberry, but the whole tree resembles the
wild rose.   They plant them in the plains in rows,
wherefore, when seen from a distance, they look like
vines."[5]   There is no mistaking the description: we
have here a correct characterization of the *Gossypium
arboreum.*

There is no further reference to cotton in Greek literature until after the beginning of the Christian era.   In
the very valuable *Periplus of the Erythraean Sea*,[6] of
the end of the I. century, raw cotton is mentioned as
κάρπασος, while the cheap manufactured goods are

[1] VII. 65.
[2] «Τὰ δὲ δένδρεα τὰ ἄγρια αὐτόθι φέρει καρπὸν εἴρια, καλλονῇ
τε προφέροντα καὶ ἀρετῇ τῶν ἀπὸ τῶν ὄϊων· καὶ ἐσθῆτι οἱ Ἰνδοί, ἀπὸ
τούτων τῶν δενδρέων χρέωνται.» III. 106.
[3] Ἰνδικά, XXII.
[4] *Enquiry into Plants*, IV. 7. 7., in A. Hort's translation, London 1916.
[5] IV. 4. 8.
[6] W. H. Schoff, *The Periplus of the Erythraean Sea*, London 1912.

ὀθόνια.[1] This is the more remarkable since both terms occur in Greek only as the designation for linen or some costly textile, while ὀθόνιον also occurs in the sense of "ship's sail," even as the Latin *carbasus* refers to linen or a sail. One cannot trust, especially in the *Belles Lettres*, any denomination of fabrics, because they are easily confused, and there is a general tendency to apply the same name to some substitute or cheaper material. The author of the *Periplus* was a merchant, and his transfer of ὀθόνιον to cotton shows that just such a deterioration of the Eastern textiles was in progress and that they were manufactured in India from cotton, which in India was known as *kārpāsa;* hence he is the only one of the Greek writers who uses κάρπασος in the proper sense.

Strabo knew of the wool-growing trees of the Indians, and quoted Nearchus to the effect that their webs of fine cotton (σινδόνες) were made from this wool, and that the Macedonians used it for stuffing mattresses and the padding of saddles.[2] This Nearchus was the Admiral of Alexander's Indian fleet, but there is some doubt about the genuineness of his work. He is also mentioned by Arrian: "The dress worn by the Indians is made of tree-linen (λίνον ἀπὸ τῶν δενδρέων). But this cotton is either of a brighter white color than any cotton found elsewhere, or the darkness of the Indian complexion makes their apparel look so much whiter."[3]

At a later time Philostratus called the cotton βύσσος and described the plant as a tree: "They describe the peoples beyond the Indus as dressed in indigenous flax, with shoes of papyrus and a hat for wet weather; distinguished persons wear cotton, which grows on a tree

---

[1] ‹Πολυφόρος δὲ ἡ χώρα . . . καρπάσου καὶ τῶν ἐξ αὐτῆς 'Ινδικῶν ὀθονίων τῶν χυδαίων,› sec. 41; ὀθόνια is also mentioned in secs. 6, 14, 39, 49.

[2] XV. 1. 20.

[3] 'Ινδικά. XVI.

resembling a poplar in the stump, and about corresponding to the willow in the leaf.  Apollonius says he
was pleased with the cotton, because it looked like the
sad-colored habit of a philosopher.  Cotton from India
finds its way into many a temple in Egypt."[1]  However fanciful the work of Philostratus may be, we have
here the very important and unquestionably genuine
statement that cotton was imported into Egypt, which
may account for its absence in the mummy wrapping
where the native product was used.  It was this imported article in Egypt, which, no doubt, Philostratus
knew from an older source, that had caused Pollux before him to call the Indian cotton βύσσος, while in
Egypt he placed tree-wool, ἔριον ἀπὸ ξύλου, whereas
in Egypt the only substance resembling cotton was
obtained from the papyrus plant.[2]

Cotton was unquestionably cultivated long before
Sennacherib; but in Egypt and China substitutes in
the form of linen and silk were early introduced, and
in some cases the ancient appellation was transferred
to the new products, even as the designation of "linen,"
whatever its origin, and "wool" was transferred back
to cotton.  For this reason it is not always easy to
determine whether a particular textile was made of
cotton or linen.  In Egyptian, "flax" and, possibly,
"linen" are represented by *pesht*, while a garment made
of fine linen, "byssus," is called *peg*, and "linen cloth,
threads of flax" is *pir*.  There can be no doubt as to
the origin of the words, not only from a study of these
terms in Egyptian, but in all other languages in which
they occur.  In Egyptian we have the roots *pek*, *peg*,
*petch*, *pest* "to spread out," which, as the final con-

---

[1] *Vita Apollonii*, 62.
[2] VII. 75. For a fuller account of cotton in Greek literature, see H.
Brandes, *Ueber die antiken Namen und die geographische Verbreitung der
Baumwolle im Alterthum*, in *5. Jahresbericht des Vereins von Freunden der
Erdkunde zu Leipzig*, 1866, p. 91 ff.

sonant and a comparison with a vast number of languages show, go back to a root with a final cerebral *r*,
namely *par*, *per* "to spread, cover."

The Egyptian terms for "linen," etc. are found in
other languages which, no doubt, borrowed them from
Egyptian, although even here the relation to the older
"spread out" remains unimpaired. We have Hebrew
פֵּשֶׁת *pēšet*, פִּשְׁתָּה *pištāh*, Talmudic פִּשְׁתָּן פִּשְׁתִּים *pištān*,
*pištīm*, Punic φοιστ "linen," while for "to spread out"
we have Hebrew פָּרַשׂ *pāraš*, פָּרַץ *paraṣ*, פָּשָׂה *pāsāh*,
etc. Just as Egyptian *pesht* has produced Greek
βύσσος, so it led to Hebrew בּוּץ *būṣ*, which was some
kind of fine linen, but may also have referred to cotton,
even as Syriac ܒܘܨܐ *būṣd* not only refers to linen but also
to silk, since the term apparently indicated a fine textile of whatever origin. We have also Hebrew בַּד *bad*
"linen." In Arabic the forms of the word and the
meanings run riot. Here we find بَزّ *bazz* "cloths or
stuffs of linen or cotton," برس *birs*,[1] بجوز *baǧūz*[2]
"cotton," برش *birš* "linen."[3] This even developed
the meaning "white," at least in برش *baraš* "white
specks in the skin," برص *barṣ* "leprosy, a certain disease which is a whiteness." Here, too, فرش *faraša* "he
spread out" bears witness to the original meaning,
while in Assyrian we have *piṣū*, *paṣū* "white," and
*parš* "to fly," that is, "to spread the wings." In
Sumerian we get the simple *bara*, *par* "to spread out,"
which is represented in Assyrian in the compound *šu-
paruru* "to spread out."

---

[1] *Thesaurus syriacus*, cols. 2923, 1857.
[2] *Ibid.*, col. 3134.
[3] *Ibid.*, col. 1857.

In the Dravidian languages the original root-forms of
the Asiatic languages are best preserved.  Here we
have Kannada *parĕ, pari, harĕ, hari* "to spread, scatter, run, flow," *pāṛu* "to leap up, run, fly about," *pīṛ,
pēṛu* "to scatter, spread in different directions," Tamil,
Malayalam *paṛa* "to fly, run very swiftly," and similarly
in all the other Dravidian languages.  It is not necessary here to give the enormous mass of such derivatives, but Kannada *parĕ* "a scale or coat of an onion,
the skin or slough of a snake, the web of a spider" at
once shows how the idea of cloth was deduced from
this root.  In Kannada *parti, patti, paḷti, hañji, hatti,*
Tamil *pari, pañji, pañju, parutti, paratie,* Malayalam
*paññi, parutti,* Telugu *pauttie, paratti, paritt* "cotton
in the pod, cotton in general" we have, just as is the
case in Egyptian, derivatives from the root which
means "to spread out," but here the original meaning
of "cotton" has not changed and bears witness to
the antiquity of the term, which is older than the corresponding Egyptian, Semitic or Greek terms.  In
Persian and Turki *pakhta* "cotton" we have a survival
of the Dravidian word, possibly through the Dravidian
Brahui colony which preserved the memory of the
ancient word.  But this is not necessarily so, for various
forms of this are scattered, as we have seen, from
Egypt to India.

The Dravidian *paratie, pauttie* found their way into
China.  In the first or second century of our era the
Hóu-Han-shu says that the Ai-lau aborigines in Yün-
nan manufactured 白氎 *po-tié* or 帛疊 *pai-tié,*
but a later history (Weï-shu) tells that it was a textile
fabric of hemp.[1]  In the VI. century the Liang-shu

---

[1] F. Hirth and W. W. Rockhill, *Chau Ju-Kua: His Work on the Chinese
and Arab Trade in the twelfth and thirteenth Centuries, entitled Chu-fan-chï,*
St. Petersburg 1911, p. 218.

says that "in K'au-chang (Turfan) there grew in great abundance a plant the fruit of which resembled a silk cocoon. In the cocoon is a silky substance like fine hemp which is called *po-tié-tzi*. The natives weave it into a cloth which is soft and white, and which they send to the markets (of China)."[1] A little later we read for the same region, "there is here a plant called *pe-tie;* they pluck its flower, from which cloth can be woven."[2] In the V. century Fa-hién, who traveled in India, called the cotton fabrics there *po-tié.*[3] There can be thus no doubt that originally cotton was introduced into China from India or from Turfan, and that it was at home in southern India. In Ceylon, cotton is called *pichu*, which is obviously a corruption of the Dravidian word, and the plant is called *pichawya.* It is interesting to observe that here *pichu* also means "a cutaneous eruption, leprosy," as in the corresponding word in Arabic.

## II.

Josephus, in describing the vestments of the priest, says that over his nether clothes "he wore a linen coat of fine flax (σινδόνος βυσσίνης) doubled: it is called *Chethomene* (χεθομένη), which denotes linen, for we call linen by the name of *Chethon* (χεθόν)."[4] Here "linen" and "linen flax" are as general as in previous cases, but the name *chethomene* leaves no doubt behind that we are dealing here with an Egyptian name for a garment. *Chethomene* is the Egyptian *ketn meni* or *het en meni* "linen tunic."

*Meni* has not entered into any other languages, though it seems to be identical with Chinese *mien* "soft, downy

[1] *Ibid.*
[2] E. Chavannes, *Documents sur les Tou-Kiue (Turcs) occidentaux*, St. Pétersbourg 1903, p. 102.
[3] Hirth and Rockhill, *op. cit.*, p. 218.
[4] *Antiquitates Judaicae*, III. 7. 2.

cotton;" but other forms of it, *māḫ, m'ḫi* "flax," *meḫi* "flax, linen" have had interesting developments. The usual Coptic form of this is *mahi* "linen," *mahe* "linen, girdle," and this also is recorded in a Coptic Bible translation as *mbai* "spindle," and as *mpai, empai, empa*, with the article as *pempai* "linen," and the Lord's cloth is translated as "sudarion *mpempa*," that is, *mpempa* means "linens, linen." This leads at once to Persian *pambah* "cotton," whence it made its way into India. The Persians got this word from their mercantile colonies along the east coast of Africa, wherefore it is also found in Zanzibar as *pamba* "cotton," *mpamba* "the cotton shrub," hence *pomba* "to adorn with fine dress, gold rings, to put a piece of cotton into the nose, etc., of a deceased," *pombo* "finery, attire." This word is found in many Bantu languages: Sotho *fapa* "to wrap around," Pédi *fap'a*, Swahili *pambaja*, Ganda *wambatira* "to embrace," Bondei *hamba* "to adorn," Herero *pamba* "to weave," Tabwa *ipamba* "to roll around one."[1] The European developments of Coptic *pempai* need not detain us long. It is first recorded in Greek in the beginning of the IX. century, in Ahmad's *Oneirocritica*,[2] after which it is very common.

So far I have touched only on such *par* words as lead to "cotton," leaving the enormous mass of derivatives for a separate work. It is now necessary to direct the attention to another "enclosure, cover" word, which leads to important results. By the side of *par* there is a pre-Sumerian *kar* word, which is widely represented. Here again I quote only such forms as will ultimately bear upon the determination of cotton in Asia, Africa, and Europe.

[1] L. Homburger, *Étude sur la phonétique historique du Bantou*, in *Bibliothèque de l'École des hautes études*, Paris 1913, p. 379.
[2] «Τὸ φυτὸν ἐξ οὗ ἡ βάμβαξ,» cap. 200; «ἱμάτιον ἔχον ἀντὶ βάμβακος μετάξην,» cap. 222, *Artemidori Daldiani & Achmetis Sereimi F. Oneirocritica*, Lutetiae 1603.

The Dravidian languages have only a few reminiscences of these "cover" words, namely Kannada *kiḍ* "to make close, shut, cover as darkness does, envelop," which is an umlaut form of Kannada *kaṟ*, *kār*, *kaṟĕ*, *karĕ*, etc., which has preserved here and throughout a vast number of other languages the meaning "to cover as darkness does, black," and departs too far from our immediate connotation. In the Sumerian, "enclosure" is expressed by *gid*, *gil*, *kil*, *kir*, *kur*, *kuru*, but the original meaning is not well preserved in them; but *ku* "clothing," *gad*, *kid* "some kind of cloth" are, in all probability, reduced forms from this group. The *kaṟ* forms are merely reductions of an older *qwaṟ* or *qbaṟ* root, from which *paṟ* is itself a reduction. This can be shown by a large number of cases in the languages under discussion.

In Hebrew we have a vast number of "cover, wrap" words of the type *qbar*. Some of these are: *kābar* "to bind," *kābal* "to wind around, wrap," *kāban* "to bind," *kāpar* "to cover," *kāpal* "to bind," *kāpas* "to bind together," *kāpat* "to wrap around," *qābal* "to cover," *gābal* "to bind," *ḥābar* "to unite, tie together," *ḥābal* "to unite, wind around," *ḥabaš* "to cover, wind around," *ḥāpaš* "to surround, cover," *ḥōpeš* "coverlet," *ḥāpā*, *ḥāpāh*, *ḥāpap* "to cover." The list is not by any means exhausted, since a study of the corresponding Dravidian words shows that "strong" through "to extend the arm" is generally derived from the "cover" words, as in the case of Kannada *kara* "great, extensive" by the side of *kara* "black." This brings Hebrew *gābar* "to be strong" into our group. The relationship of all of these words in Hebrew was long ago recognized by J. Fürst,[1] who tried to explain them as arising from a root *bar*, *baš*, etc., by means of an epenthetic *k*, *g*, *q*, *ḥ*. The other Semitic languages have the same profusion of derivatives, obviously from an original *qbar*.

---

[1] *Hebräisches und chaldaisches Handwörterbuch*, Leipzig 1876.

In the Dravidian languages we have a *pu* derivative from *kaᵣ*, but which originally must have been *kaᵣ-paᵣ* or *kpaᵣ*, as a study of the Semitic forms shows. We have Kannada *kaᵣpu*, *kappu* "to cover, extend, black," which has further been reduced to universal Dravidian *kavi* "to cover, spread, rush upon, attack." This is unquestionably at the foundation of Sanskrit *kurpāsa* "bodice, coat of mail," which is represented in Assyrian *lubāra*, *lubašu*, Hebrew *lĕbūš*, Arabic *libās* "garment," Arabic *libs* "cuirass," Egyptian *rebasha* "to be clothed in armor," *rebeshaiu* "cuirass, trapping." The universality of this root may be illustrated by Chinese *kiah*, old pronunciation *kap*, "covering, cuirass," to which are related the meanings "to clasp under the arm, a lined dress, breast plate, undershirt." The Dravidian languages have similarly derivatives from *kavi*, namely Kannada *kavadi*, *kavidi* "quilted cover," and the relation of Sanskrit *kurpāsa* to this is seen from the fact that Sanskrit also has *kavača* "cuirass, coat of mail, bodice," which is still nearer to the Dravidian.

The Sanskrit *kurpāsa* and Assyrian *lubašu* indicate a compound *kur-paša*, and this is shown to be the case from the Sumerian denomination *ku*, which precedes the name of any particular garment, that is, an old *kuᵣpaᵣ* was divided up into *ku-rpaᵣ*, from the usual association of *ku* with "garment," and thus arose the anomalous Assyrian *lubāru*, *lubašu*, etc. The second part, it appears from the former discussion, referred to cotton, from which such protective armor would be formed; hence Sanskrit *kārpāsa* "cotton" is only an extension of the term for "bodice" to the material itself, a process met with constantly. The Greek κάρπασος, Latin *carbasus* referred to some fine eastern wares, not necessarily of cotton, though the original meaning was quite surely "cotton," as in Sanskrit.

The usual designation for "cotton" in the Syrio-Arabic vocabularies is, for Arabic, بـرس القطن *al-qutn bars*, in which we have already found *bars* as the designation for "cotton." The first part, like Sanskrit *kurpāsa*, originally referred to "garment," as in the case of Egyptian *ketn*, Greek χιτών. In Arabic, قطن *qutn* frequently varies with كتان *kattān* "linen," as the material in *qutn* and *kattān* was not sufficiently clear without the addition of *bars*, which is the true word for "cotton;" hence we have in the Arabic not only a parallel with a pre-Sumerian *kur-par*, but apparently a development of the same word, for Assyrian *kittu* "garment," from which the Arabic *qutn* is derived, through its Sumerian equivalent *gad, gid,* goes back to the same *kar* origin.

The philological discussion leads to the same results as the historical data: Assyria and India were the homes of cotton in dim antiquity, and there is no evidence of any early introduction of the plant into Egypt and Europe. Even in the VI. century Coptic *pempai* seems to refer exclusively to linen, and not to cotton, and all the new designations for the plant and the product, as we shall soon see, proceed from Egypt after the Arabic conquest. There seems to be an exception to the historical evidence in the direct reference to cotton in Pliny, but it will be easy to show that we are dealing there with interpolations.[1]

| | |
|---|---|
| "Tylos insula in eodem sinu est, repleta silvis qua spectat orientem quaque et ipsa aestu maris perfunditur. magnitudo singulis arboribus fici, flos suavitate | «Ἐν Τύλῳ δὲ τῇ νήσῳ, κεῖται δ' αὕτη ἐν τῷ Ἀραβίῳ κόλπῳ, τὰ μὲν πρὸς ἔω τοσοῦτο πλῆθος εἶναί φασι δένδρων ὅτ' ἐκβαίνει ἡ πλημμυρὶς ὥστ' ἀπωχυρῶσθαι. |

[1] For interpolations in Pliny see my *Contributions toward a History of Arabico-Gothic Culture*, Philadelphia 1921, vol. IV.

inenarrabili, pomum lupino simile, propter asperitatem intactum omnibus animalibus. eiusdem insulae excelsiore suggestu lanigerae arbores, alio modo quam Serum: his folia infecunda, quae ni minora essent, vitium poterant videri. ferunt mali cotonei amplitudine cucurbitas, quae maturitate ruptae ostendunt lanuginis pilas, ex quibus vestes pretioso linteo faciunt. arborem vocant gossypinum, fertiliore etiam Tylo minore, quae distat X p.

"Iuba circa fruticem lanugines esse tradit linteaque ea Indicis praestantiora, Arabiae autem arborem, ex qua vestes faciant, cynas vocari, folio palmae simili. sic Indos suae arbores vestiunt. in Tylis autem et alia arbor floret albae violae specie, sed magnitudine quadriplici, sine odore, quod miremur in eo tractu." Pliny, XII. 38, 39.

πάντα δὲ ταῦτα μεγέθη μὲν ἔχειν ἡλίκα συκῆ, τὸ δὲ ἄνθος ὑπερβάλλον τῇ εὐωδίᾳ, καρπὸν δὲ ἄβρωτον ὅμοιον τῇ ὄψει τῷ θέρμῳ. φέρειν δὲ τὴν νῆσον καὶ τὰ δένδρα τὰ ἐριοφόρα πολλά. ταῦτα δὲ φύλλον μὲν ἔχειν παρόμοιον τῇ ἀμπέλῳ πλὴν μικρόν, καρπὸν δὲ οὐδένα φέρειν· ἐν ᾧ δὲ τὸ ἔριον ἡλίκον μῆλον ἐαρινὸν συμμεμυκός· ὅταν δὲ ὡραῖον ᾖ, ἐκπετάννυσθαι καὶ ἐξείρειν τὸ ἔριον, ἐξ οὗ τὰς σινδόνας ὑφαίνουσι, τὰς μὲν εὐτελεῖς τὰς δὲ πολυτελεστάτας.

«Γίνεται δὲ τοῦτο καὶ ἐν Ἰνδοῖς, ὥσπερ ἐλέχθη, καὶ ἐν Ἀραβίᾳ. εἶναι δὲ ἄλλα δένδρα τὸ ἄνθος ἔχοντα ὅμοιον τῷ λευκοΐῳ, πλὴν ἄοδμον καὶ τῷ μεγέθει τετραπλάσιον τῶν ἴων.» Theophrastus, IV. 7. 7, 8.

The relation of Pliny to Theophrastus may equally be observed from the English translation of the two passages:

"In the same gulf, there is the island of Tylos, covered with a forest on the side which looks towards the East, where it is washed also by the sea at high tides. Each of the trees is in size as large as the fig; the blossoms are of an indescribable sweetness, and the fruit is similar in shape to a lupine, but so rough and prickly, that it is never touched by any animal. On a more elevated plateau of the same island, we find trees that bear wool, but of a different nature from those of the Seres; as in these trees the leaves produce nothing at all, and, indeed, might very readily be taken for those of the vine, were it not that they are of smaller size. They bear a kind of gourd, about the size of a quince; which, when arrived at maturity, bursts asunder and discloses a ball of down, from which a costly kind of linen cloth is made.

"In the island of Tylos, which is situated in the Arabian gulf, they say that on the east side there is such a number of trees when the tide goes out that they make a regular fence. All these are in size as large as a fig-tree, the flower is exceedingly fragrant, and the fruit, which is not edible, is like in appearance to the lupin. They say that the island also produces the 'wool-bearing' tree (cotton-plant) in abundance. This has a leaf like that of the vine, but small, and bears no fruit; but the vessel in which the 'wool' is contained is as large as a spring apple, and closed, but when it is ripe, it unfolds and puts forth the 'wool,' of which they weave their fabrics, some of which are cheap and some very expensive.

"This tree is known by the name of gossypinus: the smaller island of Tylos, which is ten miles distant from the larger one, produces it in even greater abundance.

"Juba states, that about a certain shrub there grows a woolly down, from which a fabric is manufactured, preferable even to those of India. He adds, too, that certain trees of Arabia, from which vestments are made, are called cynae, and that they have a leaf similar to that of the palm. Thus do their very trees afford clothing for the people of India. In the islands of Tylos, there is also another tree, with a blossom like the white violet in appearance, though four times as large, but it is destitute of smell, a very remarkable fact in these climates." J. Bostock and H. T. Riley, *The Natural History of Pliny,* London 1855, vol. III, p. 117 f.

"This tree is also found, as was said, in India as well as in Arabia. They say that there are other trees with a flower like the gilliflower, but scentless and in size four times as large as that flower." A. Hort, *op. cit.*, p. 343 f.

The part which is in Pliny, and not in Theophrastus, is an interpolation and partly a forgery. What is purported to be taken from Juba is really taken from Theophrastus, IV. 4. 8: « Ἐξ ὧν δὲ τὰ ἱμάτια ποιοῦσι τὸ μὲν φύλλον ὅμοιον ἔχει τῇ συκαμίνῳ, τὸ δὲ ὅλον φυτὸν τοῖς κ υ ν ο ϱ ό δ ο ι ς ὅμοιον. φυτεύουσι δὲ ἐν τοῖς πεδίοις αὐτὸ κατ' ὄρχους, δι' ὃ καὶ πόρρωθεν ἀφορῶσι ἄμπελοι φαίνονται. ἔχει δὲ καὶ φοίνικας ἔνια μέρη πολ-λούς. καὶ ταῦτα μὲν ἐν δένδρου φύσει.» "The trees from which they make their clothes have a leaf like the mulberry, but the whole tree resembles the wild rose. They plant them in the plains in rows, wherefore, when seen from a distance, they look like vines. Some parts also have many date-palms. So much for what comes under the heading of 'trees.'" "Some parts also have many date-palms" was con-fused with the cotton-plant; κυνοϱόδοις ὅμοιον pro-duced "cynas vocari" and "so much for the nature of trees," which in Theophrastus refers to India, pro-duced "sic Indos suae arbores vestiunt." The sen-tence "arborem vocant gossypinum" is merely an Arabic gloss for "wood," namely حشب ḥašbun, pl. ḥušbun, in the oblique case ḥušbin, which produced gossypinus. The interpolator went even further and changed Theophrastus' μῆλον ἐαρινόν "spring apple" to "malum cotoneum," as though it were "a quince apple;" but in reality this is a reminiscence of the Arabic quṭn "cotton." In another place we find in Pliny: "Superior pars Aegypti in Arabiam vergens gignit fruticem, quem aliqui gossypion vocant, plures xylon et ideo lina inde facta xylina. parvus est similem-que barbatae nucis fructum defert, cuius ex interiore bombyce lanugo netur. nec ulla sunt cum candore mol-liora pexiorave. vestes inde sacerdotibus Aegypti gra-tissimae."[1] "The upper part of Egypt, in the vicinity of Arabia, produces a shrub, known by some as 'gossy-pium,' but by most persons as 'xylon;' hence the name of 'xylina,' given to the tissues that are manufactured

[1] XIX. 14.

from it. The shrub is small, and bears a fruit, similar in appearance to a nut with a beard, and containing in the inside a silky substance, the down of which is spun into threads.   There is no tissue known, that is superior to those made from this thread, either for whiteness, softness, or dressing: the most esteemed vestments worn by the priests of Egypt are made of it."[1]   Here we have a reminiscence of Greek βόμβαξ, Coptic *pempai*, which now assumes the name of "cotton," and once more we get the Arabic word for ξύλον.   The interpolator goes on to say that cotton garments were most acceptable to the Egyptian priests, whereas we have the specific statements in Herodotus[2] and in Plutarch[3] that the priests were allowed to wear linen garments only.   Thus we are once more confronted with the fact that no cotton is recorded in Egypt before the arrival of the Arabs.

## III.

In Africa we can trace the overwhelming Arabic influence upon the cotton industry through the geographical distribution of the Arabic terms for cotton.

The ancient Egyptian conception of purification was connected with the use of water; hence *uāb* "to be innocent, clean, purified, wash clean, pure, holy" has for its denominative water flowing from a vessel.   The enormous significance of this term upon the religious conceptions of the Egyptians is found in the derivatives from this term.   We not only have *uāb* "holy man, priest, libationer," but also *uābu* "those who are ceremonially clean," *uābtiu* "the holy ones, that is, the dead," *uāb* "holy raiment or vestment, apparel which is ceremonially pure," *uābt* "the chamber in a

---

[1] Bostock and Riley, *op. cit.*, p. 134 f.
[2] II. 37.
[3] *De Iside et Osiride*, 3, 4.

temple in which the ceremonies symbolic of the mum-
mification of Osiris were performed," *ṭa-uāb-t* "to
purify." This latter factitive lies at the foundation of
a large number of "purification" words in Coptic: *tbbe*
"to purify, be clean," *tbbēu* "pure, sanctified, holy,"
*teba* "purity," *etouab, ettbbēu* "pure."

The Arabs took over this term as referring to death;
hence we have Arab. عطب *'ataba* "he died, perished,
became spoiled," عطب *'atbah* "perdition, gangrene,
pest," and, since the Mohammedan purification of the
dead consisted in cleaning the body with cotton, we get
Arab. عطب *'utb* "cotton," though this and عطبة *'utbah* may
also mean "a portion of wool." "The ordinary ablution
preparatory to prayer having been performed upon the
corpse, with the exception of the washing of the mouth
and nose, the whole body is well washed, from head to
foot, with warm water and soap, and with 'leef' (or
fibres of the palm-tree); or, more properly, with water
in which some leaves of the lote-tree ('nabk' or 'sidr')
have been boiled. The nostrils, ears, etc., are stuffed
with *cotton*; and the corpse is sprinkled with a mixture
of water, pounded camphor, and dried and pounded
leaves of the nabk, and with rose-water. Sometimes,
other dried and pounded leaves are added to those of the
nabk. The ankles are bound together, and the hands
placed upon the breast.

"The 'kefen,' or grave-clothing, of a poor man consists of a piece, or two pieces, of *cotton*; or is merely a
kind of bag. The corpse of a man of wealth is generally
wrapped first in muslin; then in *cotton* cloth of thicker
texture; next in a piece of striped stuff of silk and *cotton*
intermixed, or in a ḳuftán of similar stuff, merely stitched
together; and over these is wrapped a Kashmeer shawl."[1]

[1] E. W. Lane, *An Account of the Manners and Customs of the Modern
Egyptians,* London 1871, vol. II, p. 253 f.

It may be that the Arabs took the word over from
the Egyptians before reaching Egypt, but this is not
likely, because we have no record of the Egyptian use
of cotton for purification.    It is far more likely that the
Arabs got the custom from the Christian Copts who
employed cotton in their burial ceremony and in mon-
astic vestments.    In any case the distribution of the
Arabic word among neighboring races shows that the
"cotton" words of this type are posterior to the Arabic
invasion.    We have Saho 'oṭbe, Afar 'oṭbi, Bedauye tēb,
Somali udbi, Galla jirbi "cotton," and here there are
no derivatives from the meaning "purify."    Swahili
has the Egyptian uāb as eupe "clean, clear, white," but,
as we have seen, "cotton" is derived from a Coptic
"linen" word.    Like the Arabs, the Swahili do not
bury without having adorned the apertures of the body
of the deceased, by stuffing cotton into the nose, mouth,
eyes, ears, vagina, buttocks, and under the nails of the
deceased person.    "The Suahili take out the excrements
from the bowels of a dead man by putting the hand
skilfully through the fundament.    When the head can be
brought to touch the great toe they consider all dirt to
be gone, and the fumigations begin, in order to clear the
room from the bad smell which the operation has produced.    It must be remarked that the corpse is put
upon a bedstead under which a pit has been dug in the
ground, to receive all the filth.    The reason why the
Muhammedans take so much trouble is because the
Angel Gabriel will come to the dead man in the grave,
to examine him."[1]    Some of the African languages
seem to have derivatives of the Egyptian uābt, namely
Tuareg abduya, Hausa abduga, audiga, Bagirmi oudega,
Kandin abdiga, but these, which are much further
away from Egypt than the first, are more likely trans-

[1] J. L. Krapf, *A Dictionary of the Suahili Language*, London 1882, p. 205.

positions of *adbuya*, etc., especially since none of them
has preserved the meaning "purity."

There is another Arabic word used for the ceremonial purification, namely وضو *wudū'* "the act of ablution," also referring to the washing of the dead body.
This has gone into a large number of African languages.
We have Somali *'adai* "brighten, whiten," *maïd* "to
wash clean," Swahili *uthu*, Bedauye *wada*, Kabyl *uḍu*
"religious ablution before prayer," but in the west
strange changes have taken place. In Kanuri we get
*wolongin* "ceremonial washing," while in one of the
Kabyl dialects in Tamazirt the word has united with
the Arabic article, producing *ludhu*, and this has gone
into Hausa as *luḷlo*, *aḷlowa* "purification," leading to
Peul *lōṭi* "to wash." But in the Niger valley and
beyond, this has produced the "cotton" words, just as
the Coptic "ablution" word produced the "cotton"
words in the west. Here we find Nupe, Basa, Gbari
*lulu*, Pika *lōlo*, Sobo, Egbele, Bini, Ihewe, Oloma *olulu*,
Goali *lulo*, Esitoko *lolu*, Puka *līlu*, Kupa *eōru*, Okuloma
*ōūrō*, Isoama, Aro *ōro*, Aku *ōwu*, Yoruba *owuh*, Ekantulufu *newū*, Udom *lewu*, which are all, no doubt, due to
Hausa influence.

In the oases and the Mandingo countries and about
Timbuktu, Arabic *quṭn* words prevail for "cotton."
In the oases we have *goṭun*, *kuṭan*, and, as Kabyl *qṭen*,
it has spread over a large territory. In the Peul languages it produced *hoṭollo*, given also as *poṭollo*, Wolof
*wuṭen*, *wiṭen*. This is found as *koṭole* in Soninke, while
in Bornu we get the compound *kal-gudan*, Kanuri *kal-
guṭan*. But to us the most important forms are those
which appear in the Mande languages. Bambara has
the successive deteriorations *koṭondo*, *korandi*, *kori*,
*kuori* "cotton." We have similarly Malinke *koṭōdīn*,
Mandingo *koṭondo*, *korandē*, Kalumga *kuṭandō*, Toronka *koyondyī* "cotton," Dyula *korho* "cotton,"

*korho-nde* "cotton-tree." We have also Akra *odonti*, and the scattered Bulonda *fkotūn*, Landoma *akūtan*, Buduma *kundēra*, Gurma *kunkuntu*, Padsadse *pakonde*, Gabun, Fan *okondo*, Koama *kunkun*, Bagbalan *gungun*. In the Mandingo region there is also another "cotton" word, namely Soso *gese-fute*, Toma *geze*, Kra, Gbe *gesē*, Gio, Dewoi *gie*, Mano *īye*, but Soso, Bambara, Malinke *gese* "thread in the loom" show that the origin is Arabic غزل *gazl* "cotton thread." It is significant that so many of the "spin, weave" words in the African languages are of Arabic origin. Thus, for example, we have Hausa *ẓarre*, *ẓari* "thread," *mazari* "spindle," *zaria* "to dance" from Arabic در *ḍarra* "he ran vehemently," مدره *miḍarrah* "spindle with which a woman spins cotton or wool." In the other African languages, where the Mohammedan influence is less apparent, there is a large variety of names for "cotton," where the connection with "ablution" is not noticeable. It is, therefore, obvious that the Arabs popularized cotton in Africa, even if the plant existed there before, in connection with the ceremonial purification of the dead, and that cotton steadily advanced in cultivation from Central and Southern Asia westwards, to the Western Sudan.

# CHAPTER II.

## Cotton and Columbus.

In the Middle Ages the western cotton could not compete in quality with that which came from the east,[1] hence Columbus included cotton among the things he hoped to find in his discovery of India by a western route, and in his *Letter* he promised the King to furnish from America all the cotton demanded of him.[2] But the *Journal of the First Voyage* does not bear out his statement that he had found any cotton in the islands visited by him.

We hear of cotton in America the very first day Columbus landed in Guanahani. Under the date of October 11, 1492, we read: "That they might be very friendly to us and because I saw that they were people who would more easily be freed and converted to our Holy Faith by love than by force, I gave some of them red caps and some glass beads, which they placed around their necks, and many other things of little value, which pleased them greatly, and they became wonderfully friendly with us. They later came swimming to the ships' boats, where we were, and *brought us parrots and cotton thread in balls*, and spears and many other things, and traded them with us for other things which we gave them, such as small

[1] W. Heyd, *Geschichte des Levantehandels im Mittelalter*, Stuttgart 1879, vol. II, p. 572 ff.

[2] "En conclusión, á fablar d'esto solamente que se a fecho este viage, que fué así de corrida, pueden ver Sus Altezas que yo les daré oro quanto ovieren menester, con muy poquita ayuda que Sus Altezas me darán; agora, especiería y *algodón* quanto Sus Altezas mandarán." *Raccolta di documenti e studi pubblicati dalla R. Commissione Colombiana*, Roma 1892, part I, vol. I, p. 132.

glass beads and hawk's bells.   Indeed, they took everything and gladly gave whatever they had, but it
seemed to me that they were very poor people in everything.   They all go naked, just as their mothers bore
them, even the women, but I saw only one who was
very young."[1]

If Columbus told the truth, then it is exceedingly
curious that the Indians should have known the value
of parrots and cotton to the Spaniards, instead of offering them their native maguey, maize or dozens of other
things which are more common in the West Indies.   Let
us assume that "many other things" included just
these native products which Columbus did not mention.
It is still remarkable that Columbus should have singled
out those articles which Alviso Cada Mosto nearly half
a century earlier referred to as coming from Africa,
whence he brought more than 150 parrots.[2]   He, too,
speaks of the swimming properties of the Negroes[3] and of
the mass of cotton which they raised.[4]  Even the canoes,
so characteristic of the American Indians, are fully
described by Cada Mosto.   Columbus is made to say:
"They came to the ship with almadías, which are made
of the trunk of a tree, as long as a barque, and all of one
piece, and marvellously wrought, according to the
country, and large, in some of which came forty and

---

[1] "Yo, porque nos tuviesen mucha amistad, porque cognoscí que era gente
que mejor se libraría y convertiría á nuestra santa fe con amor que no por
fuerça, les dí á algunos d'ellos unos bonetes colorados y unas cuentas de
vidro, que se ponían al pescueço, y otras cosas muchas de poco valor, con
que ovieron mucho plazer;  y quedaron tanto nuestros que era maravilla.
los quales, después, venían á las barcas de los navíos, adonde nos estávamos,
nadando, y nos trayan papagayos y hylo de *algodón* en ovillos, y azagayas,
y otras cosas muchas, y nos las trocavan por otras cosas que nos les dávamos,
como cuentezillas de vidro y cascaveles. en fin, todo tomavan y davan, de
aquello que tenían, de buena voluntad;  mas me pareçió que era gente muy
pobre de todo. ellos andan todos desnudos, como su madre los parió;  y
también las mugeres, aunque no vide más de una farto moça," *ibid.*, vol. I,
p. 16.
[2] G. B. Ramusio, *Delle navigationi et viaggi*, Venetia 1588, vol. I, fol. 104b.
[3] *Ibid.*, fol. 102a.
[4] *Ibid.*, fol. 104b.

fifty men, and others smaller, down to the size holding
but one man. They rowed with something resembling
a baker's shovel, and the boat went wonderfully, and
if it turned over they all started swimming, until it
was righted and bailed out with the calabashes, which
they carried. They brought skeins of spun cotton and
azagays and other little things too tedious to enumerate.
And these they gave for anything given to them."[1]
This is only a modification of Cada Mosto's account of
the Negroes' canoes and of their manner of barter. Of
the first he says: "They have certain boats, that is,
almadías, all of one piece of wood, with three or four
men at most in the larger ones, and with these they
fish, cross the river, and go from place to place. These
Negroes are the best swimmers in the world."[2] Of the
Negro market Cada Mosto says: "In these market
places I saw plainly that those people were very poor,
considering the things which they brought to the market
for sale, namely cottons, but not in quantity, and spun
cotton, and cotton cloth, vegetables, oil, millet, wooden
dishes . . . . . . . . . . They sell everything by barter, and
not for money, for they have none, and they are not
accustomed to money purchases but only to barter,
that is, one thing for another, two for one, three for
two."[3]

Columbus gave the Indians, in return for the objects
obtained from them, glass beads and hawk's bells. As
we shall later find the hawk's bells in a presumably pre-
Columbian village, it is necessary to point out the importance of these hawk's bells in the trading with the
Indians. The Spanish *cascavel* "sleigh bell, small
round brass bell, with a little clapper inside" is originally a Coptic word, *kašabel*, hence was introduced into

[1] *Ibid.*, fol. 17 f.
[2] *Ibid.*, fol. 102.
[3] *Ibid.*, fol. 104b.

Spain by the Arabs.[1]   Columbus carried such bells
specifically for the purpose of trading with the Indians,
no doubt, because voyagers to Africa had found them
acceptable to the Negroes, who used rattles and bells
in their fetish ceremonies.   Columbus showed the
Indians that such bells could be worn in the ear,[2] hence
they were comparatively small.   They were generally
attached to the legs of a sparrow hawk.[3]   Another time
he calls them "brass timbrels, worth a maravedi
apiece."[4]   At every meeting he distributed these to the
Indians,[5] who were crazy for them and ready to give
much gold for the hawk's bells.[6]

On October 13, the Indians again brought spun cotton, parrots, and spears, and the Spaniards exchanged
three ceotis of Portugal for sixteen balls of cotton,
which would be more than an arroba of spun cotton.[7]
Columbus sent the cotton, which grew on this island,
to the King of Spain.[8]   On October 16, Columbus for
the first time saw veils woven from cotton and clouts

[1] See my *Contributions*, vol. IV, p. 114.
[2] "Dos cascaveles, que le puse á las orejas," *Raccolta*, vol. I, p. 20.
[3] "Algunos d'ellos trayán algunos pedaços de oro colgado al nariz, el qual
de buena gana davan por un cascavel d'estos de pie de gavilano," *ibid.*, p. 28.
[4] "Algunas sonagas de latón, d'estas que valen en Castilla un maravedí
cada una," *ibid.*, p. 22.
[5] *Ibid.*, pp. 27, 53, 54, 61, 158.
[6] "Vino otra canoa de otro lugar, que traya çiertos pedaços de oro, los
quales quería dar por un cascavel, porque otra cosa tanto no deseavan como
cascaveles, que aun no llega la canoa á bordo, quando llamavan y mostrava[n]
los pedaços de oro, diziendo "chuque chuque" por cascaveles, que están
en puntos de se tornar locos por ellos. después de aver visto esto, y partién-
dose estas canoas, que eran de los otros lugares, llamaron al almirante, y le
rogaron que les mandase guardar un cascavel hasta otro día, porqu' el[los]
traería[n] quatro pedaços de oro tan grandes como la mano," *ibid.*, p. 80 f.
[7] "Trayán ovillos de algodón filado, y papagayos, y azagayas, y otras
cositas que sería tedio de escrevir, y todo davan por qualquiera cosa que se
los diese. . . . mas todo lo que tienen lo dan por qualquiera cosa que les
den que fasta los pedaços de las escudillas y de las taças de vidro rotas res-
catavan, fasta que ví dar .16. ovillos de algodón por tres çeotis de Portugal,
que es una blanca de Castilla, y en ellos avría más de un' arrova de algodón
filado," *ibid.*, p. 18.
[8] "Esto defendiera y no dexara tomar á nadie, salvo que yo lo mandara
tomar todo para Vuestras Altezas, si oviera en cantidad. aquí naçe en esta
isla; mas por el poco tiempo no pude dar así del todo fe," *ibid.*, p. 18.

worn by women.[1] Similar breech-cloths and ham-
mocks made of cotton were seen on October 17.[2] A
vast amount of spun cotton was brought by Indian
canoes on November 1,[3] and five days later the Spaniards saw more than five hundred arrobas of picked,
spun, and woven cotton in one house, and more than
four thousand quintals could be obtained there in one
year. Columbus expressed the opinion that it was not
sowed and that it bore fruit the whole year.[4] Columbus was convinced that the very large quantity of cotton
which was raised in the islands would not have to be
taken to Spain, but could be sold in the large cities of
the Great Khan.[5] But under November fourth, we
have Columbus' own statement that the cotton, which

[1] "Esta gente es semejante á aquella de las dichas islas, y una fabla y unas
costumbres, salvo qu'estos ya me pareçen algún tanto más doméstica gente,
y de tracto, y más sotiles, porque veo que an traýdo algodón aquí á la nao,
y otras cositas, que saben mejor refe[r]tar el pagamento que no hazían los
otros. y aun en esta isla vide paños de algodón fechos como mantillos, y la
gente más dispuesta, y las mugeres traen por delante su cuerpo una cosita
de algodón, que escassamente le cobija su natura," ibid., pp. 22, 38.
[2] "Aquí vide que unos moços de los navíos les trocaron azagayas, unos
pedaçuelos de escudillas rotas y de vidro. y los otros que fueron por el agua
me dixeron como avían estado en sus casas, y que eran de dentro muy
barridas y limpias, y sus camas y paramentos de cosas que son como redes
de algodón. ellas, scilicet las casas, son todas á manera de alfaneques, y muy
altas y buenas chimeneas, mas no vide entre muchas poblaçiones, que yo
vide, ninguna que passasse de doze hasta quinze casas. aquí fallaron que las
mugeres casadas traýan bragas de algodón," ibid., p. 24.
[3] "Vinieron luego á los navíos más de diez y seis almadías ó canoas, con
algodón hylado, y otras cosillas suyas, de las quales mandó el almirante que
no se tomase nada," ibid., p. 33.
[4] "La tierra muy fértil y muy labrada de aquellas mames y fexoes y habas
muy diversas de las nuestras, eso mismo panizo, y mucha cantidad de
algodón cogido, y filado, y obrado, y que en una sola casa avían visto más
de quinientas arrobas, y que se pudiera aver allí cada año quatro mill
quintales. dize el almirante que le parecía que no lo senbravan, y que da
fruto todo el año; es muy fino, tiene el capillo grande. todo lo que aquella
gente tenía diz que dava por muy vil precio, y que una gran espuerta de
algodón dava por cabo de agujeta ó otra cosa que se le dé," ibid., p. 37 f.
[5] "Tanbién aquí se avría grande suma de algodón, y creo que se vendería
muy bien acá, sin le llevar á España, salvo á las grandes ciudades del gran
can, que se descubrirán sin duda, y otras muchas de otros señores que avrán
en dicha servir á Vuestras Altezas, y adonde se les darán de otras cosas de
España y de las tierras de oriente, pues estas son á nos en poniente," ibid.,
p. 39.

the Indians did not sow, grew in the mountains, on high trees, which he saw in flower and with ripe bolls at the same time.[1]

If Columbus did not make up his account of cotton he found in the West Indies, he did not see any cotton at all, but only silk-cotton, the product of the *Bombax ceiba*, which grows in all tropical America. He specifically tells us that the cotton was not sowed, but grew on high trees. As the *Gossypium arboreum*, mentioned in Arabia in the twelfth century[2] by Ibn-al-Awam and known to exist from India to the Senegal, is totally unknown to America, Columbus' reference to high cotton trees puts it beyond any possible doubt that he saw only ceibas, but the silk-cotton of these trees does not twist and cannot be used by itself as a textile. It is known in trade under the Javanese name of *kapok*, and is used as a stuffing for mattresses and life belts.

The Franciscan monks who were in Hispaniola in 1500 apparently refer to ceiba cotton from which cloth was made: "The Indians have a great abundance of wool which grows on trees, and yet they go naked. From this wool a certain Brother from necessity spun threads and made garments for himself and his companion."[3] "Lana arboribus procreata" may be a translation of the German "Baumwolle" and so may refer to real cotton, but the fact that the monk out of necessity had to spin his own threads and weave his

[1] "Estas tierras son muy fértiles, ellos las tienen llenas de mames, que son como çanahorias, que tienen sabor de castañas, y tienen faxones y favas muy diversas de las nuestras, y mucho algodón, el qual no siembran, y nace por los montes, árboles grandes; y creo que en todo tiempo lo aya para coger, porque ví los cogujos abiertos, y otros que se abrían, y flores, todo en un árbol, y otras mill maneras de frutas, que me no es possible escrevir; y todo deve ser cosa provechosa," *ibid.*, p. 35 f.

[2] Ibn-al-Awam, *Le livre de l'agriculture d'Ibn-al-Awam*, trans. and ed. by J.-J. Clément-Mullet, Paris 1866, vol. II.

[3] "Lanam arboribus procreatam in copia habent et tamen ab antea nudi incedebant; ex qua lana quidam Frater compulsus, filando ipsam, sibi et confratri suo habitum fecit," *The Catholic Historical Review*, April 1920, vol. VI, p. 64.

own cloth, while the Indians went naked, shows conclusively that the Franciscans found no cotton cloth in use in Hispaniola.

Cotton is frequently mentioned afterwards, but that is of no consequence since we have the definite statement that in 1493 Columbus loaded his ships in the Canaries with animals and seeds,[1] which may have included cotton seed as well. Three years later the Indians who did not work in the gold mines were compelled to pay their tribute in cotton, twenty-five pounds per person, that is, the Indians were compelled to raise cotton for the white man.[2] Authors from Oviedo until the present time unanimously assert that under the Spaniards the cultivation of cotton declined very rapidly, but this is contradicted by Columbus' law of 1496, which made every effort to introduce cotton on a large scale, but completely failed because the Indians had not been used to it.

In 1498 Columbus, according to the *Journal of the Third Voyage*, wrote to the King of Spain that he sent him "açul, lacar, ámbar, algodón, pimienta, canela, brasil infinito, estoraque, sándalos blancos y cetrinos, lino, áloes, gengibre, incensio, mirabolanos de toda especie."[3] As most of these products do not grow in America, Columbus simply applied the names of spices to similar plants, hence it is not certain that

---

[1] *Op. cit.*, p. 140.
[2] "Impuso el almirante á todos los vezinos de la provinçia de Çybao y á los de la Vega Real y á todos los çercanos á las minas, todos los de catorze años arriba, de tres en tres meses, un cascabel de los de Flandes . . . lleno de oro . ; toda la otra gente, no vezina de las minas, contribuyese con una arroba de algodón cada persona . ordenóse después de hazer una çierta moneda de cobre ó de latón, en la qual se hiziese una señal, y esta se mudase á cada tributo, para que cada Yndio de los tributarios la trayese al cuello, porque se cognosçiese quién la abía pagado, y quién no; por manera qu'el que no la truxese abía de ser castigado, aunque, diz que, moderadamente, por no aber pagado el tributo. pero esta invençión . . . no pasó adelante por las novedades y turbaçiones que luego succedieron. . ," *ibid.*, p. 207 f.
[3] *Ibid.*, vol. II, p. 24.

*algodon* refers to "cotton."   It may have been ceiba or
any other textile fiber, such as maguey.  This is made the
more certain by the letter itself, which is lost, but which
Herrera apparently quotes more fully, when he says:
"se hallaua azul, ambar, *algodon*, pimienta, canela, brasil,
estoraque, sandalos blancos, y cetrinos, linaloes, gengibre,
encienso, mirabolanos de toda especie, y la *Cabuya*, que
es una yerua que haze pencas como cardo, de que
es puede hazer muy buena tela, por el buen hilo que
deella se saca."[1]  The addition *cabuya*, that is, "a
variety of maguey, an herb producing spiny leaves like
a thistle, from which a very fine cloth can be made, on
account of the fine thread which is gotten from it,"
shows that by that time Columbus knew that the
Indians made their cloth from the maguey, and not
from cotton.  But, having committed himself to cotton, he or his editor cut out the damaging sentence in
his letter when the *Journal of the Third Voyage* was
made up.

In 1526 Oviedo wrote: "(The Indians of the mainland) fish with nets, for they have very good ones, of
cotton, with which nature has provided them abundantly, and many woods are full of them; but the whitest
and best is that which they plant in their settlement
close to their houses or places, where they live."[2]  In
1535 we have a different story: "There is much wild
cotton in Hispaniola, and there are also cultivated
fields, and here it is better than in the open, and whiter
and taller, and some of these plants grow one cubit and
a half or two and send out new shoots from the ground.
And thus it continues to produce cotton without being
taken care of.  But since people do not cultivate it in
this island, it does not grow as in Indian times.  The

[1] A. de Herrera, *Descripción de las Indias occidentales*, decada I, libro
III, cap. 12.
[2] G. F. de Oviedo, *Sumario dela natural y general istoria delas Indias*,
Toledo 1526, fol. XIIa.

Christians do not busy themselves on their farms, although it is very good and would increase as well as on the mainland, where it produces ordinary shoots every year, and where it is sowed and reaped; hence it is small in comparison with the cotton there, although I have seen there some high plants." It is the old story: Where we are not, things do well; where we are, we cannot verify what has become a conviction, namely that cotton was grown by the Indians. From Oviedo's statement only this can be concluded, that the plant deteriorated when it was not cultivated, and that the so-called wild species were plants escaped from cultivation. If the commercially valuable cotton plant were really wild, no such rapid deterioration could have been observed as implied by Oviedo.

This is amply borne out by everything we know of the wild species of cotton in America. De Candolle regretted that next to nothing was known of it, and Watt confirms this absence of any definite knowledge as to wild cotton in America: "De Vica is reported to have, in 1536, discovered a wild cotton in Texas and Louisiana. Similar reports have subsequently been spasmodically made, but no qualified botanist has critically studied the wild species of *Gossypium* that exist in the American Continent and Islands, and thus the stories of travellers have not been confirmed. When first made known to Europe, the American Continent as also the West Indies, possessed not only a cotton industry but both wild and cultivated cottons, independent of those of the Old World. It is most unfortunate that no botanical specimens, no drawings, no descriptions exist of the plant or plants seen by Columbus and his associates. And, moreover, there is no record of these plants having been conveyed to Europe, so that we know nothing for certain of the species of American cottons until approximately two centuries after their

original discovery.   In fact we know more of the foreign
stocks supplied to America than of the influences of its
indigenous  plants on the modern staple."[1] But the case
is much worse yet, for when we turn to the specific localities from which cotton is recorded in literature since the
discovery of America, we do not get a single case of
wild-growing cotton which is not also recorded as growing wild in Asia and Africa, so that the best that can be
said of these varieties is that they have escaped from
cultivation.   Of *Gossypium vitifolium*, which is supposed to be the American cotton *par excellence*, Watt
says: "Possibly originally a native of Central and
South America to the Amazon basin, as also of the Les-
ser Antilles; recently distributed under cultivation to
the Southern States of North America, the West Indies,
and Africa; occasionally met with in Egypt, India,
the Celebes, Madagascar, Mauritius, &c.   Frequently
mentioned as seen in a wild condition, but it is possible
that with better and more extensive material there may
be found to be two or more perfectly distinct species
included under the present form."[2]    But it is not certain
that this kind of cotton has been found in a wild state,
and it may have been confused with *Gossypium barbadense:*   "If *G. vitifolium* has any claim to having been
seen in a truly wild condition, and I am disposed to
think it has, then it is highly likely that *G. barbadense*
is but one of its many cultivated states."[3]   Of the latter
he says: "Hemsley says of this species, 'Cultivated and
wild, probably indigenous in America;' and Schumann
(Martius, 'Fl. Bras.') remarks, 'specially cultivated in
the islands of the Antilles and in Central America, more
rarely in N. America and the tropics of the Old World.'"[4]

[1] G. Watt, *The Wild and Cultivated Cotton Plants of the World*, London
1907, p. 17 f.
[2] *Ibid.*, p. 257.
[3] *Ibid.*, p. 261.
[4] *Ibid.*, p. 267.

No. 37. GOSSYPIUM PERUVIANUM, C.V.

(A) Reproduces Cavanilles' original plate (Diss. t. 168); (B) shows a typical specimen from Herb. J. Gay.

From Watt's *The Wild and Cultivated Cotton Plants of the World.*

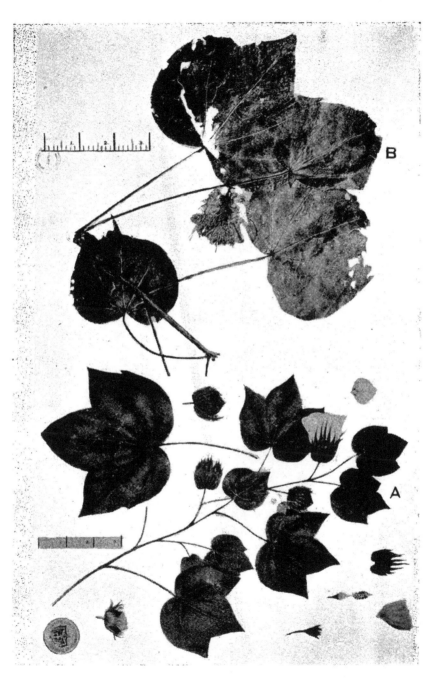

GOSSYPIUM BRASILIENSE, from Watt's *The Wild and Cultivated Cotton Plants of the World.*

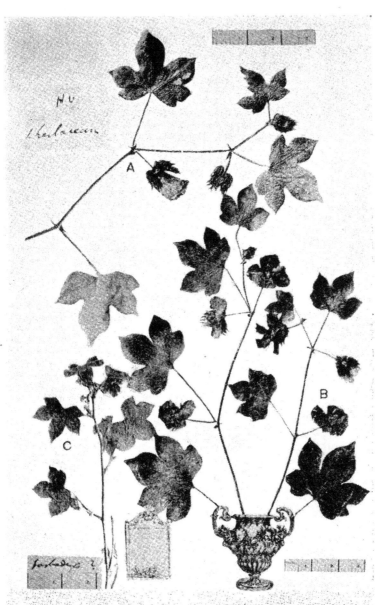

No. 24. GOSSYPIUM HERBACEUM, *LINN.*

(A) Type of species in Linn. Herb. Lond. named by Linnæus ' *I. herbaceum*' and the letters H. U. (Hortus Upsl.); (B) type specimen of Hort. Cliff. preserved in B. M.; (C) specimen in Linn. Herb. named by himself as ' *barbadense*'; see remarks, Plate No. 19.

From Watt's *The Wild and Cultivated Cotton Plants of the World.*

It would seem that at least in Mexico there were genuinely native varieties of cotton growing wild. Watt records *Gossypium Palmerii* in Mexico as having "all the appearance of being a wild species."[1] So too, *Gossypium lanceolatum* grows in Mexico by roadsides,[2] and *Gossypium microcarpum* "probably originated in Mexico;"[3] but the fatal admission that "the existence of an extensive assortment of specimens collected in Africa shows that its cultivation must be fairly ancient, seeing that it had got distributed so widely, long anterior to its recognition botanically,"[4] at once invalidates the last assumption, while the previous species and a few others, by Watt's own admission, have been variously associated with other forms, and no conclusion can be drawn as to the original home of the wild or *ferine* species.

Nor are we better off in regard to the Peruvian cotton. Marie[5] recognizes only one wild species there, the *Gossypium religiosum* of Linné; but, according to Watt,[6] this is the *Gossypium hirsutum* of modern botany, and this is "reported from Europe, Persia, China, Java, India, Africa, throughout America etc."[7] Similarly the distinctly South American cotton, *Gossypium brasiliense*, is, even by Watt's discussion, of uncertain origin: "Indigenous to South America, more especially Brazil and Guiana. Marcgraf speaks of it as growing in damp and warm places, but especially on cultivated ground. Spruce (see under *G. peruvianum*, p. 215) says he had never seen it wild, and that it is nowhere the common cotton of the Indians. Cultivated in China,

[1] *Ibid.*, p. 205.
[2] *Ibid.*, p. 210.
[3] *Ibid.*, p. 211.
[4] *Ibid.*, p. 213.
[5] *La producción de algodón en el Perú*, in *Boletin del Ministerio de Fomento, primer trimestre de 1916*, Lima 1916, p. 32.
[6] *Op. cit.*, p. 204.
[7] *Ibid.*, p. 184.

Japan, India (twice mentioned as wild), Malaya, Poly-
nesia, Africa (often spoken of as wild), Mascarene
Islands, Central and South America and the West Indies.
Koster ('Travels in Brazil,' 1816, p. 368) says 'I have
seen some species of wild cotton, of which, however,
as I have neither note nor specimen I cannot pretend to
give a description.'"[1]   Hiern[2] says that *Gossypium
barbadense* and *vitifolium* "are met with wild in the
neighborhood of villages" in Angola in Africa, and, similarly, "*Gossypium peruvianum* is abundant and wild in
depressions and on the drier slopes" in Golungo Alto.
This excludes the presence of cotton in a wild form in
America as a proof that it is *native* in America.   In a
pamphlet of the U. S. Department of Agriculture,
which is *A Study of Diversity in Egyptian Cotton*,[3] we
read: "The cultivated varieties of cotton appear to fall
into two series.   Varieties native in America find their
nearest relatives in other New World varieties, and all
*appear to be widely distinct from the indigenous species of
Asia and Africa.*   Though very different from the Upland varieties of the United States, the Egyptian cotton
and the Sea Island cottons are also native of tropical
America and are not so fundamentally different from
the Upland cottons as is often supposed.

"No varieties have as yet been discovered which are
exactly intermediate between the Egyptian and the
Upland types, but many of the Central American and
West Indian varieties which are obviously related to
our Upland cottons show some of the characteristics of
the Egyptian and the Sea Island series.   At the same
time it has been found that the West Indian and Central
American relatives of the Sea Island and Egyptian cot-

---

[1] *Ibid.*, p. 298.
[2] W. P. Hiern, *Catalogue of the African Plants Collected by Dr. Friedrich
Welwitsch in 1853-61*, London 1896, vol. I, p. 77 ff.
[3] By Cook, McLachlan, and Meade, Washington 1909, Bureau of Plant
Industry, Bulletin No. 156, p. 8.

tons show many Upland characters. *Only a little additional evidence is needed* to prove that the native American types of cotton form a continuous series, without any larger breaks than those which serve to separate the very numerous local varieties still kept in cultivation among the agricultural Indians of tropical America. The results of the present study of diversity in Egyptian cotton tend to emphasize the relationships of the American varieties and make it evident that the Egyptian cottons have the same wide range of variation that other American cottons have been known to display." The words italicized by me show how uncertain the knowledge of the so-called indigenous American varieties is, and even if the Egyptian cotton is subordinated to the American varieties, we have still the great obstacle to overcome, observed by Kearney,[1] that varieties are instantaneously produced by mutation: "Two of the best types (the Yuma and Somerton varieties) are so distinct from the Mit Afifi variety from which they have been derived as to warrant the belief that they are mutations and have originated in the same manner as Abbasi, Jannovitch, and other superior types which have been developed in Egypt from the Mit Afifi variety." Even if it should turn out that cotton existed in the West Indies previous to Columbus, it still could have been introduced by earlier colonists, and all the varieties recorded in Peru, Mexico and Brazil are merely mutations of an original plant, which need not be of American origin.

[1] *Ibid.*, Bulletin No. 200, p. 33.

# CHAPTER III.

## Cotton in Mexico.

We can study the introduction of cotton into Mexico from an analysis, in chronological order, of the XVI. century references to it. In 1518 Grijalva saw the Yucatan Indians wearing *cotton* cloth about the middle of the body.[1] As the usual cloth of the Indians from all reliable accounts was made from the maguey plant, "cotton" is merely a generic name for cloth not made from wool, linen or hemp. This is corroborated by the fact that Grijalva, according to Oviedo's account, referred the word "cotton" both to a delicate and a coarse material.[2] We have, however, an older account of Grijalva's expedition, which was published in Italian in 1522.[3] Here we find the costly mantles referred to as of silk.[4] Just as this anonymous author uses "silk" for hare's wool, so his term *bambagia* "cotton" must,

---

[1] "Por medio de los cuerpos trayan muchas vueltas de vendas ó listones de algodon tan anchos, como una mano," G. F. de Oviedo, *Historia general y natural de las Indias*, Madrid 1851, vol. I, p. 512.

[2] "Truxeron algunas mantillas de algodon teñido," *ibid.*, p. 523; "y dió el caçique junto con esto al capitan Grijalva una india moça con una vestidura delgada de algodon," *ibid.*, p. 528; "çiertas mantas gruesas de algodon de poco valor," *ibid.*, p. 530.

[3] J. García Icazbalceta, *Colección de documentos para la historia de México*, México 1858, vol. I, p. 281 ff.

[4] "La seta con che lavorano, è che pigliano i peli della pancia del lepre & conigli, & gli tengono in lana di quel colore che vogliono, & glielo danno in tanta perfettione che non si puo dimandare meglio, dopo lo filano & con esso lavorano, & fanno si gentili lavori quasi come con la nostra seta, & ancora che si lavi, mai perde il suo colore, et il lavoro che si fa con essi dura gran tempo," *ibid.*, p. 377 f.

to say the least, include the maguey and henequen, from which most Indian cloth was made.[1]

The same looseness of expression is found in Cortes' letters: "The clothing which they wear is like long veils, very curiously worked. The men wear breechcloths about their bodies, and large mantles, very thin, and painted in the style of Moorish draperies. The women of the ordinary people wear, from their waists to their feet, clothes also very much painted, some covering their breasts and leaving the rest of the body uncovered. The superior women, however, wear very thin shirts of *cotton*, worked and made in the style of *rochets.*"[2] Not a word is said here of the maguey cloth, which was the common material from which the Indian cloths were made. Similarly, though cotton cloth is specifically named, there is no mention of maguey or hare's wool cloth in the collection sent by Cortes in 1519 to the King of Spain,[3] nor in the market place of the City of Mexico, where "they also sell skeins of different kinds of spun cotton, in all colours, so that it seems quite like one of the silk markets of Granada, although it is on a greater scale."[4] Yet Sahagun, writing in the second half of the XVI. century, knows only of maguey, nequen and palm cloth, some of which

[1] "I vestimenti loro son certi manti di bambagia come lenzuola, ma non cosi grandi, lavorati di gentili lavori di diverse maniere, & con le lor franze & orletti, & di questi ciascun n'ha duoi ò tre & se gli liga per davanti al petto. . . Le donne portano certe lor camicie di bambagia senza maniche, che assomigliano a quelle che in Spagna chiamano sopra pelize, sono lunghe & larghe, lavorate di bellissimi, & molto gentili lavori sparsi per esse, con le loro frangie, ò orletti ben lavorati che compariscono benissimo: et di queste portano due, tre & quattro di diverse maniere, & una è piu lungha dell'altre, perche si vedano come sottane: portano poi dalla cintura à basso una altra sorte di vestire di bambagia pura, che gli arriba al collo del piede, similmente galante & molto ben lavorate," *ibid.*, p. 376 f.

[2] F. A. MacNutt, *Letters of Cortes*, New York, London 1908, vol. I, p. 162.

[3] P. de Gayangos, *Cartas y relaciones de Hernan Cortés al Emperador Carlos V*, Paris 1866, p. 33.

[4] F. A. MacNutt, *op. cit.*, p. 258.

was of a delicate texture.[1]  Sahagun refers to those who sell raw cotton, which in his day was apparently raised in a few isolated places,[2] but there is no reference whatsoever to cotton cloth, although we have several references to European articles.

The same confusion is observed in the references to paper.  In a grant of Cortes to the caciques of Axapusco, written probably in 1526, we read: "On the [twenty] second of April of this year (1519), at eleven o'clock P. M. there came said Tlamapanatzin and Atonaletzin with many of their Indians, loaded with presents and provisions, and paintings on cloths such as they use, which are called *nequene*, and books of

---

[1] "El que vende mantas delgadas de maguey suele tener lo siguiente: conviene á saber tostar las ojas y rasparlas muy bien, echar maza de maíz en ellas, y lavar bien la pita, é limpiar y sacudirla en el agua, y las mantas que vende son blancas, adobadas con maza, bruñidas, bien labradas, y de piernas anchas, angostas, largas ó luengas, gordas ó gruesas, tiesas ó fornidas, al fin todas las mantas de maguey que tienen labores; algunas vende que son muy ralas que no parecen sino toca, como son las mantas muy delgadas, tejidas en hebras de nequen, y las hechas en hebra torcida; y por el contrario algunas que son gordas, tupidas, y otras labradas, ó bastas y gruesas, ya sean de pita, ya de hilo de maguey," B. de Sahagun, *Historia general de las cosas de Nueva España*, in *Biblioteca Mexicana*, Mexico 1896, lib. X, cap. 20.  "El que hace y vende las mantas que se hacen de palmas que se llaman 'iczotl' de la tierra, llévalas fuera á vender y véndelas á mas de lo que valen.  Las mantas que vende son de dos brazas, y las que son sin costura y bien proporcionadas al cuerpo, y las que tienen las bandas como arcos de pipas, y las que son como arpilleras para envolver cosas estas mantas son muchas maneras como en la letra parece," *ibid*.

[2] "El que vende algodon suele tener sementeras de él y síembralo; es regaton el que lo marca de otros para tornarlos á vender: los capullos de algodon que vende son buenos, gordos, redondos, y llenos de algodon.  El mejor algodon y muy estimado, es el que se dá en las tierras de riego, y en segundo lugar el algodon que se hace hácia oriente: tambien es de segundo lugar el que se dá hácia el poniente.  Tiene tercer lugar el que viene del pueblo que se llama 'Veytlalpan', y el que se dá hácia el septentrion; y el de postrer lugar el que se dice 'quauhichcatl', y cada uno de estos géneros de algodon, se vende por sí segun su valor sin engañar á nadie: tambien por sí se vende el algodon amarillo, y por sí los capullos quebrados.  El mal tratante de esto, de cada esquina quita un poco de algodon, y los capullos ó cascos, vacíalos é hinche tupiéndolos de otro algodon, ó espeluzándolos con agujas sutilmente, para que parezcan llenos," *ibid*.

maguey paper, such as are in use among them."[1]  This is in keeping with what Toribio de Motolinia has to say of the Mexican paper. "Of the maguéy good paper is made in Tlaxcallan, which is in use over a great part of New Spain.  There are other trees in the hot lands, from which a great quantity of paper was made and sold. The tree and paper are called *amatl*, and by this name, *amatl*, the Spaniards call the letters and paper and books."[2]  It is not possible to ascertain the tree which he here calls *amatl*, as no other source mentions it, but since Hernández has a tree *amacoztic* or *texcalamatl*, literally "stone paper,"[3] there must have been a tree *amatl*, as given in Motolinia, from which paper was made. Zorita,[4] who quotes Motolinia, adds that the paper made from maguey was not as good as the one from *amatl*. Orozco y Berra[5] quotes from an article on *anacahuite*, to show that Hernández described the "paper tree," *amacuahuitl*, from which paper was made at Tepoxtlan. I am unable to find the passage in Hernández, while the dictionaries give only *amacapulquauitl*, literally "paper plum tree," that is, "mulberry tree."  No doubt,

[1] "En dos dias del mes de Abril 21 de dicho año, á las once de la noche llegaron los dichos Tlamapanatzin y Atonaletzin con muchos indios de los suyos cargados de presentes y bastimentos, y las pinturas en unos lienzos que acostumbraban, que se llama *nequene*, y libros del papel de maguey que se usa entre ellos; todo se manda por pinturas, estatuas (sic) y figuras imperfectas, y todo género de la tierra, árboles, cerros é rios, calles y todo, sin faltar cosa, en ellas, pintadas y figuradas, y con ellos un buen escribano de los que entienden y estudian para sus efectos; y traien unas varitas delgadas y sutiles con que iban señalando y llamando por sus tenores y órdenes," J. García Icazbalceta, *op. cit.*, vol. II, p. 8 f.

[2] "Hácese del *metl* buen papel: el pliego es tan grande como dos pliegos del nuestro, y desto se hace mucho en *Tlaxcallan*, que corre por gran parte de la Nueva España.  Otros árboles hay de que se hace en tierra caliente, y desto se solia hacer y gastar gran cantidad; el árbol y el papel se llama *amatl*, y este nombre llaman á las cartas y al papel y á los libros los españoles *amatl*: el libro su nombre se tiene," J. García Icazbalceta, *Memoriales de Fray Toribio de Motolinia*, Méjico 1903, p. 318 f.

[3] N. León, *Cuatro libros de la naturaleza, Extracto de las obras del Dr. Francisco Hernández*, Morelia 1888, p. 52.

[4] A. de Zorita, *Historia de la Nueva España*, Madrid 1909, vol. I, p. 130.

[5] M. Orozco y Berra, *Historia antigua y de la conquista de México*, México 1880, vol. I, p. 337.

paper could be made from various barks, even as it is manufactured today from pulp, but there is no evidence that it was manufactured of anything but maguey. At least Orozco y Berra shows that in 1580, at which time Hernández wrote, there was a maguey paper mill at Culhuacan.

The large Goupil collection of Mexican manuscripts[1] records only paper from the *agave americana*, that is, maguey, or European paper.[2]   The same is true of the Humboldt collection,[3] with one exception.   Number XVI, according to Seler, "looks as though it were European ragpaper, but the microscopic investigation showed a fiber, which in appearance, strength, and luminosity, etc., seemed  to be identical with the fiber of which the coarse agave paper of pages III and IV is made.   Only there are among it slender, spirally twisted fibers, which seemed to stretch themselves a little and to untwist in the water under the cover glass."[4] The stretching and unrolling of the fiber points at once to *ceiba* cotton.   This material was also used in the *Lienzo de Tucutacato:* "the fiber of the cloth is brilliant and very smooth, much resembling that of cotton (*Gossypium herbaceum*), and identical with that of *Eriodendron anfractuosum*.   As it is not possible to subject the latter to permanent spinning, we must suppose either that it is not of the material, or that the 'Tarascos' understood some peculiar method, now lost, of preparing it so as to use it to advantage."[5]   The preparation is described by Motolinia.   "The *amanteca*, who work in

[1] E. Boban, *Documents pour servir à l'histoire du Mexique, Catalogue raisonné de la collection E. Eugène Goupil*, Paris 1891.

[2] "In Sahagun's time Spanish paper was sold in the Mexican market," *op. cit.*, lib. X, cap. 21.

[3] E. Seler, *Die mexikanischen Bilderhandschriften Alexander von Humboldt's in der Königlichen Bibliothek zu Berlin*, in *Gesammelte Abhandlungen zur amerikanischen Sprach- und Alterthumskunde*, Berlin 1902, vol. I, p. 162 ff.

[4] *Ibid.*, p. 289.

[5] N. León, *Studies on the Archaeology of Michoacan (Mexico)*, in *Smithsonian Report, 1886*, Washington 1889, p. 307.

feathers and gold, make much use of the shredded maguey leaves: over these leaves they make a paper of pasty cotton, which is as fine as a thin veil, and on this paper and over the leaves they paint their pictures, and the paper is the principal instrument of their office."[1] There can be little doubt that the "cotton" here mentioned was *ceiba* cotton, which needed a paste in order to make the fiber stay twisted. Of real cotton paper not a trace has been found in ancient Mexico.

In 1532 the Indians were compelled to plant those things which they had to render as a tribute, and mayordomos or *calpixques* were placed over them, to see that the work was done.[2] These *calpixques* were chiefly Negroes, who immediately after the conquest treated the Indians with great severity.[3] In 1533 some

[1] "De estas pencas hechas pedazos se sirven mucho los maestros, que llaman *amanteca*, que labran de pluma y oro: encima de estas pencas hacen un papel de algodon engrudado, tan delgado como una delgada toca, y sobre aquel papel y encima de la penca labran todos sus debujos, y es de los principales instrumentos de su oficio," *op. cit.*, p. 317.

[2] "Al presente para les sacar el tributo es menester que un mayordomo ó calpixque esté en cada pueblo para les hacer sembrar lo que son obligados, y para que den el tributo que le está señalado, y con todo esto no se les saca ni lo dan enteramente," J. García Icazbalceta, *Parecer del Sr. Fuenleal*, in *Colección de documentos para la historia de México*, México 1866, vol. II, p. 177.

[3] "La cuarta plaga fué los *calpixques* ó estancieros y negros; que luego que la tierra se repartió, los conquistadores pusieron en sus repartimientos y pueblos á ellos encomendados criados ó negros para cobrar los tributos y para entender en granjerias, y estos residian y residen en los pueblos, y aunque por la mayor parte son labradores de España, acá en esta Nueva España se enseñorean y mandan á los señores y principales naturales; y porque no querria escribir sus defectos, digo que me parece á los opresores egipcianos que afligian al pueblo de Israel, porque en todo les semeja en las obras y en el hacer de los ladrillos. Tambien son como las moscas gravísimas de la cuarta plaga de Egipto que agraviaba la casa de Faraon y de sus siervos: y de esta plaga fué corrompida la tierra: bien asi estos *calpixques* que digo agravian á los señores naturales y á todo el pueblo, y ansi se hacen servir y temer más que si fuesen señores naturales, y nunca otra cosa hacen sino demandar, y nunca están contentos a do están y allegan: todo lo enconan y corrompen, hediondos como carne dañada de moscas por sus malos ejemplos; moscas en ser perezosos y no saber hacer nada sino mandar; zánganos que comen la miel que labran las abejas, esto es, que no les basta cuanto los pobres indios pueden dar, sino que siempre son importunos, como moscas gravísimos. En los años primeros eran (tan) absolutos estos

Indians of the province of Guanavaquez came before Pedro Garcia, interpreter of the Real Audiencia, with eight paintings of the tribute they were paying to Cortes, and complained that the latter treated them not as vassals of the King of Spain, but as slaves, who were maltreated by his servants and were obliged to pay excessive tributes and do excessive services. The province of Guanavaquez paid to Cortes every eighty days 4800 four-ply sheets of two ells broad and two ells long, besides twenty richly worked petticoats and shirts, ten damask bed sheets, ten other Indian damask sheets, and four cotton quilts, and had to furnish the food, the planting, and the house service. They had to plant each year twenty units of cotton and eight of maize, and to reap and house it all. Among the long list of other contributions they made, are mentioned Spanish chickens, which shows that we are not dealing with lists of Aztec tributes in the paintings, but with those of Spanish origin. Indeed, Pedro Garcia testifies that the paintings contained lists of tribute, food, and services, and of extortions, that is, that they were dealing with contemporary, not pre-Spanish conditions.[1]

We have a contemporary reference to the extraordinary rapidity with which the Indians accommodated themselves to the new conditions, and raised and manufactured European articles or, to be more correct, Indian articles with European improvements. In 1541 the Christian Indians of Tlaxcalla offered on Easter day a large number of mantles, "woven of cotton and hare's wool, and those are of many kinds: most of them have a cross in the middle, and these crosses differ much among themselves; other cloths have in the middle a

calpixques en maltratar los indios y en enviarlos cargados lejos tierra, y poniéndolos en otros trabajos, de los cuales hartos murieron," J. García Icazbalceta, *Memoriales de Fray Toribio*, p. 22 f.

[1] *Colección de documentos inéditos relativos al descubrimiento, conquista y organización de las antiguas posesiones españolas de América y Oceanía*, Madrid 1870, vol. XIV, p. 142 ff.

TOCULPOTZIN, from Boban's *Documents pour servir à l'histoire du Mexique.*

QUAUHTLAZACUILOTZIN, from Boban's *Documents pour servir à l'histoire du Mexique.*

striped colored shield; others have the name of Jesus
or Mary, with their tassels and embroidery all around
them; others have flowers and roses beautifully woven
into them, and this year a woman offered on one such
cloth the crucifix woven on both sides, although one
seemed to be the face of it, and this was so well done
that all those who saw it, both churchmen and lay
Spaniards, admired it greatly, and said that she could
do even better and should produce tapestry."[1]   The
Indians of Tlaxcalla built two chapels in Spanish fashion
soon after 1525, and produced all kinds of cloth on
Spanish looms, and in a little more than twenty days
learned to construct a loom and work in wool, estab-
lishing a factory for wool cloth at Quauhquechulla.[2]

[1] "Lo que ofrecen es algunas mantas de las con que andan cubiertos:
otros pobres traen mantillas de cuatro ó cinco palmos en largo, ó poco menos
de ancho, que valerán un maravedí: otros paupérrimos ofrecen otras aun
menores: otras mujeres ofrecen unos paños como de portapaz, é de eso
sirven despues, que son de obra de tres ó cuatro palmos, tejidos de labores
de algodon é de pelo de conejo, y estos son muchos é de muchas maneras:
los mas tienen una cruz en el medio, y estas cruces muy diferentes unas de
otras: otros de aquellos paños traen en medio un escudo de plagas tejido
de colores: otros el nombre de Jesus ó de Maria, con sus caireles ó labores
alrededor: otros son de flores y rosas tejidas y bien asentadas, y aun en
este año ofreció una mujer en un paño de estos un Crucifijo tejido á dos
haces, aunque la una parte se parecia ser mas la haz que la otra, harto bien
hecho, que todos los que lo vieron, ansí frailes como seglares españoles, lo
tovieron en mucho, diciendo que quien aquel hizo, mejor haria y tejeria
tapiceria.   Estas mantas y paños tráenlas cogidas, y allegados cerca las
gradas del altar, hincan las rodillas, y hecho su acatamiento, sacan y descogen
su manta ó paño, y tómanlas por los cabos con ambas las manos, tendida, y
levántanla hácia la frente una ó dos ó tres veces é luego asiéntanla en las
gradas, y retráense un poco, tornando á hincar las rodillas, oran un poco,
y muchos de ellos traen consigo niños, por quien tambien traen ofrenda, y
dánselas en las manos, y avézanlos allí á ofrecer y hincar las rodillas, que
ver con el recogimiento y devocion que lo hacen, es para poner espíritu á los
muertos," J. García Icazbalceta, *Memoriales de Fray Toribio*, p. 96 f.

[2] "Tejen estos naturales con telares de Castilla sayal y mantas frazadas,
paños y reposteros: en solo *Tezcuco* hay tantas y muchos telares de paños,
que es una hacienda gruesa.   Téjense muchas maneras de paños hasta
resimos, y de esto los maestros son españoles, pero en todo entienden é ayudan
los indios, y luego ponen la mano en cualquier oficio, y en pocos dias salen
maestros; ya este oficio de paños está en otras partes.
   "Un señor de un pueblo llamado *Aquauhquechula*, en los años primeros que
comenzaron los telares, como él toviese ovejas y lana, deseaba tejerla en
telares de Castilla y hacer sayal para vestir á los frailes que en su pueblo
tiene, é mandó á dos indios suyos que fuesen á México, á una casa que habia

The complaint of the Indians that they had to plant cotton, as something out of the ordinary, is justified by a letter of the same year from the vicar, Fray Francisco de Mayorga, who pitied the Indians and tried to have their lot alleviated. He wrote: "He now oppresses these poor souls still more and sends them to plant some of Montezuma's fallow lands in cotton and other things, in order to pay for a certain part of the house they are making for him in Mexico, as if they were not doing their part, and more than any other vassals."[1]   We have only one reference to cotton being raised in the time of Montezuma, but this is from a loose sheet written by an unknown man after 1539: "The King placed mayordomos and taxcollectors over those whom he took captive in war, and, although they were governed by their masters, they were under control of the King of Mexico, and these ordered them to plant every kind of seed and tree for the people of the cities, and *cotton*, over and above the tribute."[2]   But this is mere hearsay

telares, para que buscasen si pudiesen hallar algun indio de los ya enseñados, para que asentase en su pueblo un telar y enseñase á otros, y si no, que mirasen si ellos podian deprenderlo por alguna via; y como no hallaron quien con ellos quisiese venir, ni tampoco cómo se enseñar poniendo la mano en la obra, ca de otra manera muy mal se deprenden los oficios, sino metiendo las manos en ellos: estos indios estuvieron mirando en aquella casa todo cuanto es menester, desde que la lana se lava hasta que sale labrada y tejida en el telar, y cuando los otros indios maestros iban á comer y en las fiestas, los dos tomaban las medidas de todos los instrumentos y herramientas, ansí de peynes, tornos, urdidero, como del telar, peines y todo lo demás, que hasta sacar el paño son muchos oficios, y en veinte y tantos dias, que no llegaron a treinta dias, llevaron los oficios en el entendimiento, y sacadas las medidas y vueltos á su señor, asentaron en *Quauhquechulla* y pusieron los oficios, hicieron y asentaron los telaron (telares), y tejieron su sayal. Lo que más dificultoso se les hizo fué el urdir," *ibid.*, p. 184 f.

[1] "Lo que les añaden agora nuevamente a estos pobres es que los manda sembrar unas tierras baldías que eran de Munteçuma, de algodón y otras cosas, para pagar cierta parte de la casa que le hacen en México, como si estos no hiciesen su parte, y más que los otros sus vasallos," P. M. Cuevas, *Documentos inéditos del siglo XVI, para la historia de México*, México 1914, p. 47.

[2] "Los que tomaba de guerra decian *tequitin tlacotl e*, que quiere decir, tributan como esclavos. En estos ponia mayordomos y recogedores y recaudadores; y aunque los señores mandaban su gente, eran debajo de la mano destos de México; y estos mandaban sembrar toda semilla y todo

to justify precisely the same procedure by the Spaniards who tried to make their clauses legal, by referring to Aztec customs. The very phrase "*cotton, over and above the tribute*" shows that that was not the usual custom.

This same authority tells of the origin of wheat culture in Mexico, which was similarly imposed upon the natives, and here we know positively that wheat was only introduced by the Spaniards. "When the marquis had conquered Mexico and while he was at Cuyoacan they brought him from the port a little rice. In it three grains of wheat were found. He asked a free Negro to plant them. Only one came up, and upon investigation it was found that the other two had rotted. The one which came up produced forty-seven ears of wheat. From this there was such an abundance that in 1539 I sold good wheat, indeed, especially good wheat, at less than a real per hanega. Although the marquis later received some wheat, it all spoiled and did not grow. From this one grain comes all the wheat with all its varieties in the lands where it has been sowed and it seems to be different in every province, although coming all from one seed."[1]

This account may be apocryphal, since Gómara tells a variant of it: "A Negro of Cortes, whose name, I believe, was Juan Garrido, planted in a garden three grains of wheat which he had found in a bag of rice. Two of them sprouted, and one of these produced one hundred and eighty grains. They planted these, and soon a mass of wheat came from it: one grain produces one hundred and even three hundred, and even more if properly attended to and irrigated. While some is being planted, other wheat is garnered, and other

árbol para granjería á los vecinos, y algodón, demas de los tributos; y tenian casas grandes do hacian llegar la gente mujeres de cada pueblo ó barrio á hilar, tejer, labrar; y demas de todo, en sabiendo que alguno tenia algo de cudicia tomábanselo," J. García Icazbalceta, *Colección de documentos*, vol. II, p. 592.

[1] *Ibid.*, p. 592 f.

is still green, and all at one time, and thus there are several crops a year. All this is due to a Negro and slave."[1]

A number of Mexican picture writings, dealing with the tribute, may now be examined. We begin with a dated one, of Otlazpan and Tepexic,[2] of the year 1549. In this *Códice Mariano Jiménez* little trace is left of pre-Spanish taxes, as we have not only payments in Spanish gold, but contributions on Christian holidays and planting of wheat, as well as maize. Here we also find a provision that two thousand women were to weave each a piece of a mantle of cotton, altogether 325 mantles. The Indians were also to provide *tochimitl* mantles for the chiefs and *tequitlatos* of the place. We have no means of ascertaining the period at which cotton was actually employed, since before Spanish times the common Indians wore mantles of maguey and henequen, if not exclusively, certainly more often than any other material, and those are not mentioned here.

Far more interesting is the very elaborate *Codex Kingsborough*,[3] of the British Museum, which deals with the history of the pueblo of Tepetlauztuc from Aztec times up to about 1549. Here we can study, not only the changes brought about by the Spanish conquest, but also the extraordinary rapidity with which Spanish ideas and words became incorporated in Aztec thought and language.

The first civilized cacique of Tepetlauztuc was Cocopin, who possessed several villages. From Magaguacan, with one hundred households, he received every eighty days four feather mantles and one load of rich

---

[1] F. López de Gómara, *Conquista de Méjico*, Barcelona 1888, vol. II, p. 268.

[2] N. León, *Códice Mariano Jiménez, Nómina de tributos de los pueblos Otlazpan y Tepexic en geroglífico Azteca y lenguas Castellana y Nahuatl, 1549*, Mexico [1904].

[3] The Peabody Museum at Harvard University has both a fine colored copy and a photographic reproduction of this *Codex*.

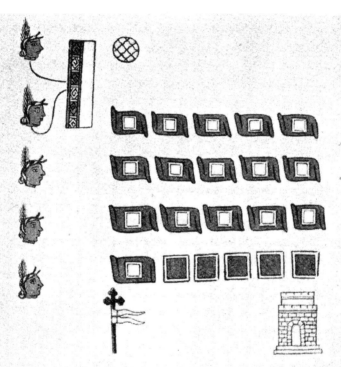

lan sy mismo. dexo hordenado el Sõr Juez q̃ el Sõr p̃u se hiziese cada año açerta
cantidad de ropa de mantas labradas con tochimitl p̃a dar alos principales
y tequitlatos del pueblo. dela manera sig.ᵗᵉ / a cada uno dos mantas en un año
y para saber la cantidad delas mugeres q̃ay el Sõr pueblo las conto y hallo
dos mill mugeres de trabajo. y dexo y h... i dio q̃ cada año hiziesen de mugeres una pieça de manta delas susodichas de algodon. q̃ suman y montan
por todas las mantas q̃ sean de hazer trezientas y veynte y una. an se de
entregar alos mayordomos dla casa publica y ellos dan q̃ estan ...

CHRISTIAN ELEMENT in *Codice Mariano Jimenez.*

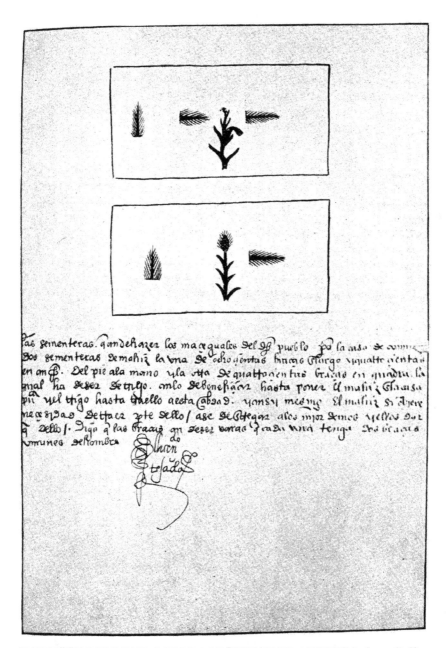

EARLIEST REPRESENTATION OF WHEAT IN AMERICA, from *Codice Mariano Jimenez.*

petticoats, one of shirts, and two of *maguey* shirts, one load of fine mantles, four of mats, eighty burdens of *ocote*, and had one sowing of maize of 400 bracas. From Caltecoya, with forty households, he received as tribute every eighty days twenty fine large mantles and twenty shirts, and sowed 400 square tragas of maize. Hiecazinco, with forty households, gave the same; from Tlapechuacan he got two sowings of maize; Hazahuac, with twenty households, gave only building material, and so forth. After him came his wife, and then his nephew Tlilpotonqui, who, as a Christian, was called Don Diego and had left to him by Cortes only a part of Cocopin's possessions, namely 265 houses, from which he received tribute. There were in all, in Cortes' time, twenty chiefs, who received tribute from their tenants, which apparently was transferred to Cortes. In the three years that Cortes owned the villages, he received forty squares of fine gold, each of which weighed 30 pesos of gold, one gold buckle and rich plumes. Besides, he received four loads of fine mantles and eleven richly wrought mantles, and still another load of rich mantles, and 3000 hanegas of maize.

After three years, Cortes turned this pueblo over to Diego de Ocampo, who received in one year forty squares of gold, ten loads of richly wrought mantles, and eleven loads of more richly wrought mantles of *tochomitl*, "which is the silk of the country." This tribute is obviously of the same character as that given to Cortes, and we learn from this that the richly wrought mantles were made from hare's wool. The following year the *encomienda* was held by Miguel Diaz, who received as tribute forty squares of gold, twelve loads of rich cloth, 80,000 grains of axi, 200 salt loaves, 800 loads of beans, 800 loads of maize flour, 800 loads of differently ground maize, 20 loads of native bread, and a large quantity of pots, pigs and dishes, 300 crates of fowls, 60 loads of ground cocoa, 200 load carriers, 33,600 loads of maize, 10 millers per day, and all this although the excessive taxes had already greatly reduced the population.    The terrible extortion in articles not produced on the land was an intolerable burden to the Indians: "This first year the Indians gave to the factor fruit, axi, salt, honey, pitchers, pots, coal, *ocote*, which they bought in the market at the price of 7300 loads of *enequen* mantles, each load containing 20 mantles of *enequen*."    It is not necessary to pursue further the exactions of the factor, and the toll in Indian lives.    We have so far gleaned a number of important points for our purpose.

By this time we find the gold weighed on Spanish scales, which are represented in the Mexican hieroglyphics.    The Spanish word *peso* "weight" was at once adopted by the Aztec and other languages, and we find in the earliest Aztec dictionary *pexouia* "to weigh," and similarly, Kiche *pis-oc*, Pokonchi *paj-am*, Kakchiquel, Uspanteca *paj*, Maya *ppiz* "to weigh, measure," hence Maya *ppiz-ah* "to weigh, compare, arrange, mix mortar," *ppiz-bo* "to try oneself, understand, fight, war," *ppiz-ib* "rule," *ppiz-kin* "week," *ppiz-muk* "to try, attempt."    Without a careful study of the whole group of the Maya words, one would hardly have suspected that they are of Spanish origin, and that in the twenties of the XVI. century many of these words were already current in Mexico and the neighboring countries.    It was this extraordinary rapidity of the dissemination of borrowed words, which immediately undergo phonetic changes, that set me to investigate the archaeological data, which deal with centuries and aeons, instead of years, where documentary evidence may be found.

Another such word is the Spanish *Castilla* "Spain." In the *Codex Kingsborough* we have a few references to a tribute in chickens, as "gallinas de *Castilla*."    Hence

the earliest Aztec dictionary gives *caxtil* "chicken."
In Kekchi *caxlan* is not only "chicken," but also
"Spanish," hence *caxlan lem* "Spanish mirror," that
is, "eyeglasses," *caxlan oua* "Spanish bread," that is,
"wheat bread." In Maya the word has reduced itself
to *cax* "chicken."

But what is of greater importance to us is the fact
that we have no reference to "cotton" mantles. We
hear only of those of *tochomitl, maguey*, and *enequen*.
The first refers to wool cloth, the second to common
mantles, and the last, obviously to the "mantas delgadas," or "ricas," the delicately wrought mantles of
the text. The statement that the Indians exchanged
their *enequen* mantles for articles in the markets is made
in order to show that it was not common *maguey* mantles that the Indians paid for them. but the better kind.
*Enequen* of the text is the same as *pita* of the Spaniards.
Of this Hernández[1] says: "*Pati*, or *metl*, from which the
finest threads are made, resembles *metl*, but has nar-
rower, smaller, and thinner leaves, which are inclined
to be purple and form a thick fibrous root. It is the
kind which is called *pita* and from it are spun very fine
threads, which are held in high esteem and are adapted
for the weaving of costly linen cloth." "*Quetzalychtli*,
which some call *metl pitae*, seems to belong to the *metl*.
It grows as high as a tree and has a large fibrous root,
which by degrees grows slender. Its leaves are spinous
and resemble those of the *metl*. From them anything
can be made that is made from the *metl*, and from its
threads very delicate and costly garments are made. It
grows in hot places."

In the third year of the *encomienda*, which is about the
year 1527, the factor asked for Don Diego's wife and,
not getting her, sent Don Diego to pasture his sheep,

[1] F. Hernández, *Nova plantarum, animalium et mineralium mexicanorum historia*, Romae 1651, p. 275.

and here we get a very good representation of two sheep. A year later the Indians raised wheat for the mayordomo, and gathered two thousand hanegas of wheat. Here we get, I believe, for the first time, a Mexican picture of an ear of wheat. The following year we once more hear of mantles of *tochomitl* "which is the silk of the country." A few years later the Indians were obliged at their own expense to paint the factor's house, for which they spent 800 loads of mantles of *enequen*, each of twenty mantles. From this nightmare of tributes the Indians were freed only after four years of the *encomienda*, approximately in 1548, by Doctor Quezada, who examined the case and compelled the factor to pay back to the Indians 1600 pesos.

We can now approach the great Book of Tributes in the *Codex Mendoza*[1] and the *Libro de los tributos*.[2] The latter is, probably, an older copy than the first, but as so many deductions have been based on the Spanish interpretation in the *Codex Mendoza*, we shall examine this one more closely. Kingsborough says that "the M. S. containing this collection of paintings is not original; the outline of figures is done with a pen, and they are drawn on European paper." This copy was, according to Orozco y Berra, executed about the year 1549, just before Viceroy Mendoza's reign came to an end. The contemporary editor of the *Codex* craved the excuse of the reader for the faulty interpretation of the Mexican figure writing, which was frequently a matter of guesswork. The Spanish translation was made a few days before the departure of the fleet, and the reader should keep in view only the subject matter.[3]

---

[1] E. Kingsborough, *Antiquities in Mexico*, London 1830.

[2] A. Peñafiel, *Monumentos del arte mexicano antiguo*, Berlin 1890.

[3] "El estilo grosero é interpretacion de lo figurado en esta ystoria supla el Lector, porque no se dió lugar al ynterpretador, y como cosa no acordada ni pensada, se interpretó a uso de proceso . . . Diez dias antes de la partida de la flota se dió al ynterpretador esta ystoria para que la ynterpretase, el cual descuido fué de los Yndias que acordaron tarde, y como cosa corrida

The list of tributes paid by the subjected cities to Montezuma is found on plates XIX–LVII. Whatever reliance there may be placed on the Mexican writing, the Spanish interpretation of it is of extremely doubtful value. The tribute begins with the city of Tlatelulco, which later became a part of the city of Mexico, and the Spanish translation says that the tribute began in the time of Quauhtlatoa and Moquihuix, masters of Tlatelulco. The masters of Mexico who started those of Tlatelulco and made them pay tribute recognizing the vassalage were Yzçoaçi and Axayacaçi.[1] In the Mexican text there are merely pictures and hieroglyphics of Yzçoaçi, Axayacaçi, Quauhtlatoa, Moquihuix, and Tlatelulco. The Spanish interpretation is absurd, since Tlatelulco began to pay tribute after Moquihuix's suicide, and more than thirty years after Quauhtlatoa's reign, which was about the same time as that of Yzçoaçi of Mexico. Indeed the same Spanish interpreter says in the history, which precedes the Book of Tributes, that Moquihuix committed suicide, "when the Mexicans were victorious, and since then the city of Tlatelulco was a vassal of the masters of Mexico, until the Spaniards came, paying them tribute and recognizing the vassalage."[2]

In the *Codex* there is given a very large number of mantles, from pure white to very elaborate colored designs, of which the material is not specified, neither in the Mexican text, nor in the Spanish interpretation. In plates XXXII, XXXV, XXXXI they are specifi-

no se tuvo punto en el estilo que convenia ynterpretarse, ni se dió lugar para que se sacase en limpio limando los vocablos y orden que convenia, y aunque las interpretaciones van toscas, no se a de tener nota si no á substancia de las aclaraciones, lo que significan las figuras, las cuales van bien declaradas por ser como es el ynterpretador buena lengua Mexicana."

[1] "Tuvo principio el dicho tributo desde el tiempo de Quauhtlatoa y Moquihuix, señores que fueron de Tlatilula. Los señores de Mexico que dieron principio a los de Tlatilula, y a que le tributasen reconociendo vasallage, fueron Yzçoaçi, y Axayacaçi," *ibid.*, vol. V, p. 54.

[2] *Ibid.*, plate X.

cally mentioned as of *henequen* (*eneguen*), although the Mexican text has no corresponding hieroglyphics. In plates XXXI, XXXVII, XXXVIII some of the mantles are crossed by a thorn, and the translator mentions them as of *henequen*. But he is mistaken. The town of Çoçolan is marked by the same kind of maguey needle, and it is clear that here *çoço* stands for the needle and means "worked with a needle, peculiar kind of weaving or embroidery." The Aztec dictionary gives "*çoço* ensartar cuentas, axi, flores," *çoçoa* "tender ó desplegar mantas ó abrir libros," and there is no reference to material; hence the thorn mantles have some reference to workmanship, not material. In plate XXXVI the fairly elaborate and the white mantles are given as of *eneguen*, the very elaborate mantle is not mentioned as to material, but in the preceding résumé is given as of *cotton*. In plate XXXV the more elaborate and the white mantles are given as of *eneguen*, while the one with a single blue and white border is of *cotton*. In plate XXXVIII only the very elaborate mantle is given as of *cotton*. Peñafiel, in the *Libro de los tributos*, wisely abstained from mentioning any material in connection with these mantles.

We have unmistakable references to *cotton* in plates XXXIX, L, LVII, where an enormous mass of raw cotton is represented by mat-covered loads topped by an open cotton boll. If the tribute is correctly rendered in the paintings, there is no escape from the conclusion that at least raw cotton was in use among the Aztecs. But it can be shown, chiefly from linguistic considerations, that the reference is to the cotton of the *Eriodendron anfractuosum*, that is, the *ceiba* tree, which was used for stuffing protective garments of war and pillows. Of this *ceiba* Oviedo says: "The fruit of this tree is a pad of the size of the middle finger and as thick as two fingers, round, and full of fine wool, which opens up

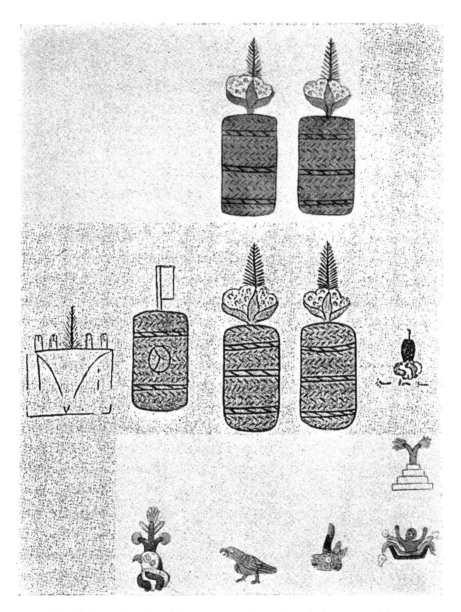

TRIBUTE OF COTTON, from Kingsborough's *Antiquities in Mexico.*

COTTON MANTLES, from Kingsborough's *Antiquities in Mexico*

when ripe by the action of the sun; and then the wind carries this wool, among which there are the seeds, just as there are in cotton. This wool seems to be wonderful, and the fruit of the *ceiba* is like the wild cucumber of Castille, except that it is larger and thicker, but the largest is not bigger than the hand. When it is ripe, it opens up lengthwise in four parts, and with the first wind the wool is carried away, and it looks as though it had snowed, since the wool covers the whole earth. This wool is very short, and, it seems to me, it cannot be spun; but for pillows and cushions (when it does not get wet) it is very fine, both through its whiteness and lightness, and for gentlemen's beds it is the most precious of wools: it is like silk, and finer than the finest silk fiber, so that no down, cotton or wool can equal it; but if it gets wet, it is all ruined."[1]

The Aztec name for cotton is *ychca*, and this word is found in a number of townnames in the Book of Tributes, such as *Ychcatlopan*, *Ychcatlan*, hence must be older than the Conquest of Mexico, but did *ychca* originally mean "cotton" or "ceiba wool?" This can be determined only from a philological study of the word. In Maya *ix* means "woman, female," hence *ix-cax* "hen," *ix-nuc* "old woman," *ix-tux* "turkey hen." But *ix* is also used to express that which is not genuine, not good, hence *ix-kanabal* "bitter cherry," *ix-nabatun* "tinsel gold," *ix-tun* "chalk," that is, "false stone." Similarly we have Kiche *x-cab* "wax," from *cab* "honey."

The same evolution has taken place in Nahuatl with the related *ich*. Its original meaning is "female," hence *tel-pocatl* "lad," *ich-pocatl* "lass." No doubt *ich-teco*, *ich-taca* "secretly," *ich-tequi* "thief," *ich-tectli* "a stolen thing" are pejoratives in which *ich* refers to the wrong in the doing, *teca* "to put away."

[1] *Historia general y natural de las Indias*, vol. I, p. 342 ff.

A similar pejorative is found in Maya *x-mulis* "curliness," and this idea of curliness, as something unworthy, is found in several languages of Mexico. Thus we have Nahuatl *ich-tli* "anything fluffy," *ix-pochina* "to fluff, card." In Tarascan we have, side by side, *ura-pe-ni* "white," *ura-pi* "maguey," *ura* "strong, healthy," and *x-ura-ni* "to unravel," *x-uri* "worthless," *x-ura* "cotton." Nahuatl *tla-ch-pan-tli* "broom," *och-pana* "to card," by the side of Tarascan *pan-qua* "broom," shows that *ch*, *och* has here the same meaning of "fluffy," and the same is true of *tla-ch-ayotl* "fine parrot feathers." Nahuatl *me-ca-tl* "rope" is obviously composed from *me-tl* "maguey," and a word which is found in Pokonchi *c'aj-am*, *caj-am*, Kekchi *c'am*, *c'am-al*, Maya *kaan* "rope, anything rope-like," so that in Nahuatl we have the specific reference to maguey rope. Hence *ych-ca-tl* can only refer to anything rope-like, but of a fluffy character. Whenever real cotton was introduced, whether before or after the Conquest, the old name, which may have referred to *ceiba*, or anything else of little value as a textile, was transferred to cotton, and similarly to sheep's wool, and the sheep itself, which are all given in Nahuatl as *ych-ca-tl*. Just as *ych-ca-tl*, from the very beginning of the Conquest, meant "sheep's wool" and "sheep," both of which were unknown before, so the reference to "cotton" under the name of *ych-ca-tl* is no proof whatsoever that cotton was known before the appearance of the Spaniards.

The complaints of the Indians that they were obliged to buy things in the market by means of loads of mantles are borne out by Motolinia himself, who in 1550 testified to this in a letter to the King of Spain. He also testified to the fact that the Indians had only the cheapest of clothes to wear.[1]   In 1554 Nicholas de

---

[1] "Lo que traen vestido, es tan poco y tan vil, que apenas sabrán qué precio le poner," P. M. Cuevas, *op. cit.*, p. 163.

Witte answered in full the questions put by the government as to how the Indian tribute was to be distributed.[1] As to the inquiry whether the Indians could not have been taxed according to their ancient pictures, he said that there was no order, no time, no precise measure as to what they were to give, and that they contributed only upon special occasions, as they still did secretly among themselves. In reply to the question whether the Spaniards were paying any attention to the ancient tribute, he said: "They did not pay the slightest attention to what they paid anciently, but only to gold and silver and their farmwork, for formerly they did not pay such large quantities of mantles, *nor did they know what beds were, nor cotton cloth*, nor a thousand other things, such as covers and blankets, and shirts, and *hueypilles*, but they only used to do their planting and fix their temples, and serve in their masters' houses, and gave only what grew upon their lands, whenever the master asked for it, and no attention was paid to what they used to pay in Aztec times."[2]

From the examination of all the accessible documents it appears that, at whatever time cotton may have been introduced into Mexico, whether before or after the Conquest, it had not formed a part of the tribute to the Mexican Emperor, and that only ceiba wool was furnished for the purpose of stuffing the protective

---

[1] *Ibid.*, p. 221 ff.

[2] "Acerca de la 9ª, si subieron respecto a lo que los indios daban antiguamente, cuando echaron los tributos: No tuvieron respecto ninguno a lo que antes daban, sino a oro y plata y sus granjerías, que antes no daban cargas de mantas tan grandes, ni sabían qué eran camas, ni cotonías, ni cera, ni otras mil sacalinias, como sábanas y manteles, y camisas y hueypilles, sino hacían sus sementeras y reparaban sus cues de los demonios, y hacían las casas de sus señores y daban de lo que nacía en sus tierras cuando el señor lo pidía, y ningún respecto hubo en si pagaban más o menos en su infidelidad," *ibid.*, p. 225.

military garments with it.    Immediately after the Conquest, cotton became as familiar to the Indians as maguey, even as they at once began to raise wheat, and chickens and sheep, but the evidence up to the year 1554 is conclusive that the cotton cloth paid as a tribute was an innovation by the Spaniards and did not have the sanction of the Aztec tribute.

# CHAPTER IV.

## Cotton in Peru.

When Pizarro conquered Peru, he, according to his secretary's account, found there a large quantity of cotton garments,[1] and thus it would seem that cotton was known in Peru before the discovery of America, and that the archaeologists may be right in assuming a very old date, as far back as 200 A. D., for the cotton cloth found in Peruvian sepulchers. We must, therefore, first become acquainted with Peruvian chronology, as established by the archaeologists, and for this purpose we shall examine the interesting work of Ph. A. Means, *A Survey of Ancient Peruvian Art*,[2] where all the conclusions are discussed in full.

Mr. Means attempts in chapter IV. to establish a chronology and dates for early Peruvian art, but admits that "the dates hereto presented are only approximate. In the nature of things, we must be prepared to allow for an error of a century or more in the remoter epochs."[3] After showing the insufficiency in the historical data, as deduced from the Peruvian lists of kings, Mr. Means proceeds to base his chronology on the one approximately certain criterion derived from the *guano* de-

[1] "Los hombres visten camisetas sin mangas y unas mantas cubiertas. Todas en su casa, tejen lana y algodón, y hacen la ropa que es menester, y calzado para los hombres, de lana y algodón, hecho como zapatos," F. de Jerez y Pedro Sancho, *Las relaciones de la conquista del Perú*, in *Colección de libros y documentos referentes á la historia del Perú*, Lima 1917, vol. V, p. 49; "La ropa es la mejor que en las Indias se ha visto; la mayor parte della es de lana muy delgada y prima, y otra de algodón de diversas colores y bien matizadas," *ibid.*, p. 63.

[2] In *Transactions of the Connecticut Academy of Arts and Sciences*, vol. XXI, p. 315 ff.

[3] *Ibid.*, p. 383.

posits: "The islands off the coast of Peru have long been famous for their deposits of *guano*. These lie in masses of enormous thickness. Markham says that two and one-half feet a century is approximately the rate of accumulation. The rate no doubt fluctuated slightly, but the careful investigations made by Markham have led him to accept the above rate as a fair average. According to González de la Rosa, antiquities occur in the guano at depths varying from nine feet to forty or more. This means that in 1870 (at which date the investigations were made) the antiquities presumably varied in age from about four centuries (i. e. 9 feet gives a date of about 1450) to about sixteen centuries (i. e. 40 feet gives a date roughly equal to 200 A. D.). Perhaps future work will yield more detailed information as to which cultures are found at various depths in the guano. At all events, it seems possible that for want of a better criterion we must bear the evidence of the guano deposits in mind."[1]

Mr. Means has apparently not verified Markham's "careful investigations," for Markham did not take them seriously. Speaking of the *guano* islands he says: "The Islands off the coast, called Guanape and Macabi, were looked upon as sacred cemeteries, and had been so used for more than a thousand years. Besides pottery and other works of art, numerous mummies have been found at various depths, all females, and all headless."[2] To this he adds the footnote: "The height of the mass of guano deposit on these islands was 730 feet in many places, and the antiquities have been found at a depth of 100 feet. The accumulation of guano is *calculated* at ten feet in four centuries, 100 feet in 4000 years. Articles found at 40 feet must, on this estimate of the time taken for the deposits, have been there for

[1] *Ibid.*, p. 387 f.
[2] C. Markham, *The Incas of Peru*, New York 1910, p. 218.

1600 years. It is now doubted whether the deposits can possibly be due entirely to the excreta of birds. The deposits are regularly stratified. But no other explanation has been forthcoming." It will be observed that Markham does not speak of careful investigation, but only of somebody's calculation. In fact, ten pages further on he distinctly admits that there is no cogency in the calculation: "The depth at which ancient relics have been found in the deposits of guano on the Chincha Islands has been considered as another proof of the very remote period when there were inhabitants in these coast valleys. *There is, however, some reason to doubt the cogency of this argument.*"[1] Here again we have a footnote, in which the calculation is completely negatived: "Mr. Squier argues that articles may have been buried in the guano at considerable depths, also that they may have been placed on the surface and have fallen down to an apparent great depth with the disintegration of the material in course of removal, and thus appear to have been deposited there." But the case is much worse. As early as 1854 the Peruvian government made a careful survey of the Chincha Islands[2] and gave plans of the guano deposits from which it results that the guano is found in irregular heaps which bear little relation to the physical condition of the islands. Sometimes the level of the guano follows that of the earth, sometimes it seems to be entirely the reverse, and again the guano sometimes rises abruptly without any accountable reason. The thickness of the guano varies from a few feet to a few hundred feet. An object deposited at the bottom of the guano would not be any older in one place than in another, yet there would be hundreds of feet difference in the thickness of

[1] *Ibid.*, p. 228.
[2] *Informes sobre la existencia de huano en las Islas de Chincha presentados por la comision nombrada por el Gobierno peruano, con los planos levantados por la misma comision*, Lima 1854.

the layers above them.    Similarly, an object deposited
one hundred feet below the surface would in one place
be hundreds of feet above the earth, in another fifty or
more feet below the earth.    It is evident that no conclusions whatsoever can be drawn from this, since it
appears that the guano was not deposited in horizontal
layers, but arbitrarily in spots, and no calculation is
equally applicable to the various parts of the islands.
Thus Mr. Means' only criterion for the determination
of the age of objects found in the guano deposits
vanishes completely.

In 1873 an inquiry was sent to García, governor of
the guano island of Guanape,[1] in regard to the mummies
and artifacts disinterred from the guano.    He says that,
among other things, a vast number of pieces of some
kind of *cotton* (piezas de genero de algodon) in a rotten
condition had been found there, but that the idols came
from a depth of three to four meters.    To this González de la Rosa remarks:    "If the finds come from the
sacrifices found only at a depth of from three to four
meters under the guano, according to García, then it is
to be assumed that they are of a relatively modern
period, but, in any case, anterior to 1532, when the
Spaniards came, and most likely, before the Incas ruled
at the coast and suppressed the sacrifices."[2]    All this is
mere supposition, but González de la Rosa is certainly
nearer the truth than Means.

Unfortunately it is impossible to ascertain from the
Spanish documents how and when cotton was intro-
duced into Peru, because from the very beginning of the
Conquest a number of European or other foreign articles
were constantly and persistently demanded of the
Indians.    In the cedula of 1537 it was determined that

---

[1] González de la Rosa, *Estudio de las antiguedades peruanas halladas bajo
el huano*, in *Revista Histórica, órgano del Instituto Histórico del Perú*, Lima
1908, vol. III, p. 39 ff.
[2] *Ibid.*, p. 44.

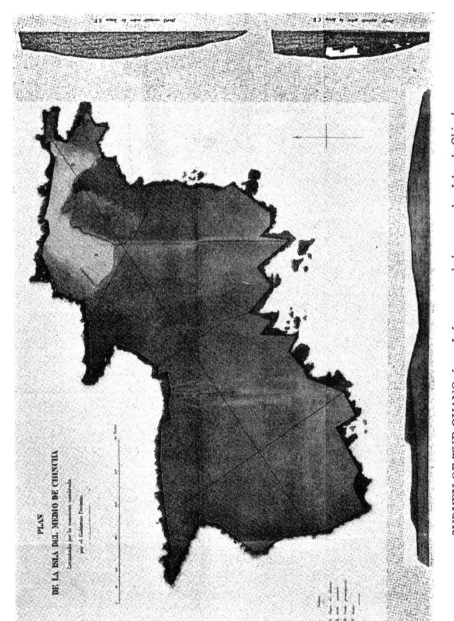

SURVEY OF THE GUANO, from *Informes....de huano en las Islas de Chincha.*

the Indians should pay tribute in kind, of what they raised or possessed in their own lands,[1] but in the *Reform of the "encomiendas,"* published by Governor Pedro de la Gasca in 1549,[2] we have a definite proof that the tribute was practically identical with that in existence in Mexico, and was based on the Spanish needs, and not on the ancient Peruvian custom. The Indians had to pay a certain amount of gold, and a given quantity of cotton mantles, maize, wheat, fowls, fish, eggs, salt, and charcoal, besides planting maize and wheat for the encomenderos. The same articles were demanded in the Governor's *Reform* of 1552.[3] As the wheat was an innovation, in comparison with the Inca times, so is cotton here an innovation, since at Lima, with its moderate climate, it is not likely that cotton was raised, and since the ancient tribute of the Incas refers only to cloth made of llama and vicuña wool, and not to cotton.

In 1571 and 1577 extensive inquiries were sent out by the Spanish government as regards the Indians of Peru, and from the answers one sees how greatly at that time, and unquestionably much earlier, the European methods had been forced upon the natives. Cotton mantles formed an important part of the tribute, not only in the hot coast region, where cotton prospered,[4] but also in the temperate regions, where they had to buy it from the hot yungas.[5] Furthermore it is distinctly mentioned

[1] E. Torres Saldamando, *Libro primero de cabildos de Lima, segunda parte*, Paris 1900, p. 98.

[2] *Ibid.*, p. 152 ff.

[3] *Ibid.*, p. 155 ff.

[4] M. Jiménez de la Espada, *Relaciones geográficas de Indias*, Madrid 1881-97, vol. I, pp. CXI, CXII, 34, 102, vol. III, p. 116, vol. IV, pp. XLVII, XLIX, 135.

[5] "A los treinta y tres capítulos se dice que sus tributos lo pagan en dineros de oro y reales y ganados de la tierra que tienen, y en maíz y trigo, que en la tasa que tienen señalada (así); y que sus granjerías son de los ganados de la tierra que tienen y ropa de *cumbi* y *abasca* que hacen y las venden á españoles y á indios que vienen á sus pueblos á buscallos, y ellos los llevan á las ciudades; y que tambien van ellos á valles callentes á comprar

that the cloth industry among the Indians was further-
ed by the Spanish industry,[1] and that Spanish cloth was
equally manufactured by the Indians.[2]

It is only natural that cotton should have at a very
early time been cultivated by the Indians, since they
were soon after the Conquest put in charge of Negroes.
In 1535 a complaint was entered in the Cabildo of Lima
that the Negroes brought from Panama to Jauja were
prejudicial to the Indians and caciques by taking their
food and doing them other harm.[3]   The early legisla-

axi y camarones y algodón y otras cosas y lo tornan á revender," *ibid.*,
vol. II, p. 20.  "Benefician y hacen lienzo de algodón, aunque no se coge
en él por demasiada f escura y fertilidad."  "Vístense todos por la orden
que los del Pirú, de algodón y lana que sus encomenderos les dan," *ibid.*,
vol. II, p. 149.

[1] "Criaban avestruces mansas en sus casas, gallinas y patos, y así lo hacen
ahora, aunque, despues que los xpianos entraron en aquella tierra, se visten
todos en general, á fuer de los del *Pirú*, de lana y de algodón.  Es gente
bien partida; tenian tratos unos con otros con las cosas que habia en la
tierra, que son las dos declaradas, no para grangerías, sino para suplir sus
necesidades.  Hoy tienen algunas granjerías los que son ladinos que tratan
con los españoles."  "Dan de tasa el servicio de sus personas con mucha
moderacion, para beneficio de *chácaras* y heredades y algodonales de que
ellos se visten, como dicho es, y despues benefician en telares este algodon y
lanas de ganados de Castilla que tienen los xpianos y naturales, de que se
hace, mediante el industria de los españoles, sobre-camas, vestidos de indios,
lienzos y telillas y otras cosas de que se aprovechan los encomenderos y lo
envian al *Pirú* y dello sacan dineros con que se proveen de cosas de Castilla,
así medicinales como necesarias al sustento de la vida," *ibid.*, vol. II, p. 144.

[2] "Cógese abundancia de miel y cera y cochinilla, pastel y anill (*así*), y
hay mucha raíz con que tiñen gualda y otros colores que se crian y dan en
la tierra, y mucha abundancia de pez y *cabuya*, que sirve de cáñamo, y otra
resina que llaman incienso, olorífera y saludable," *ibid.*, vol. II, p. 145.
"Hay dos obrajes de jerga é sayal," *ibid.*, vol. I, p. 89.

[3] "Dixeron q.e porquanto enla cibdad de xauxa se fizieron ciertas hor-
denanzas sobre los negros q.e enesta governacion seme tian etrayan dela
cibdad de panama segund q.e mas largamente porellas parecia eagora parece
yes publico q.e los dichos negros fazen mucho daño eperjuizio en los casiques
e yndios desta cibdad tomandoles sus comydas e haziendas e haziendoles
otros malos tratamyentos los no seles devia de hazer equebrantando las
dichas ordenanzas q.e sobre ello estan fechas mandaron q.e qualquier
español q.e pillare negro eaziendo daño lo pueda traer preso ala justicia q.e
lo castigue mandaron q.e qualquier negro o esclavo q.e fuere por yerva
otraxere hoja de mayz q.e lesean dados cient azotes por la primera vez
eporla segunda q.e pague su amo veynte pesos eporla tercera vez q.e tal
negro oesclavo sea echado dela tierra."  E. Torres Saldamando, *op. cit.*,
vol. I, p. 27.

tion against the Negroes[1] shows that their influence
upon the Indians was at least as great as that of the
white overseers, hence the introduction of African
methods of agriculture is only natural, and such methods would not be specifically mentioned in the documents, that is, while we have specific references to the
introduction of wheat, bananas, sheep, horses, we never
hear of the similar importations from Africa, which
were indirect, from one Negro colony of slaves to
another, as in this case from Panama, without any mention whatsoever of the fact.

The oldest literary source for conditions in Peru is
Pedro Cieza de Leon's account of his travels in Peru
from 1532 to 1550, which was first published in 1553.[2]
Authorities agree to Markham's judgment that this
work, "bearing evident marks of honesty of purpose,
and skill in the selection of materials, on the part of its
author, is at the same time written by one who examined
almost every part of the empire of the Yncas, within a
few years of the conquest. It is, therefore, a work of
the greatest possible value to the student of early South
American history, and has always stood very high as an
authority, in the estimation of modern historians."[3]
We shall therefore examine this account closely as to
the presence of cotton in Peru. Cieza de Leon frequently refers to the custom or the Indians of burying
their dead in deep holes. "In the other provinces,
when a chief dies, they make a very deep sepulchre in
the lofty parts of the mountains, and, after much lamen-
tation, they put the body in it, wrapped in many rich
cloths, with arms on one side and plenty of food on the
other, great jars of wine, plumes and gold ornaments.
At his feet they bury some of his most beloved and

[1] *Ibid.*, p. 73.
[2] C. R. Markham, *The Travels of Pedro de Cieza de Leon* (The Hakluyt
Society), London 1864.
[3] *Ibid.*, p. XVI.

beautiful women alive; holding it for certain that he
will come to life, and make use of what they have placed
round him."[1]   "Thus, when the chiefs die, their bodies
are placed in large and deep tombs, accompanied by
many live women, and adorned by all they possessed of
most value when living, according to the general custom
of the other Indians of these parts."[2]   "When their
chiefs die, they make large and deep tombs inside their
houses, into which they put a good supply of food, arms,
and gold, with the bodies."[3]   "In many other provinces,
through which I have passed, they bury their dead in
very deep holes, while in others, as those within the
jurisdiction of the city of Antioquia, they pile up such
masses of earth in making their tombs, that they look
like small hills."[4]

This custom of burying the dead deep below the
ground once more emphasizes the correctness of Squier's
view that the distance below the surface of the guano
where burial objects have been found is no criterion
whatsoever as to the age of these deposits.   But the
case is much worse still, for we have the information
from so excellent an authority as Ondegardo, in 1571,
that artificial layers of sand were created in the Peruvian
sepulchers, at least in the cities of Cuzco and Quito:
"These natives had another kind of tribute, which,
though not common, was heavy and troublesome and
arose from their strange whims, engendered by their
Incas, who wished to impress one with the greatness of
the City of Cuzco.......... They say that from the
whole square of Cuzco the earth had been removed and
had been taken to other parts as of great esteem, and
that it had been filled in with sand from the sea-shore,
two palms and a half in thickness and in some places

[1] *Ibid.*, p. 65.
[2] *Ibid.*, p. 81.
[3] *Ibid.*, p. 102.
[4] *Ibid.*, p. 227 f.

more.  In it they placed many gold and silver vessels, small sheep and manikins of the same, of which we have seen removed a great quantity.  The whole square was filled with that sand, when I went to govern the city, and if it is true that this sand was brought as is affirmed and contained in their accounts, it seems to me that the whole earth thereabout must be understood by it, for the square is large and there is no counting the loads that entered unto it, and the nearest coast is more than ninety leagues, so far as I know, and I am satisfied, as all say, that there is no such sand any nearer than the coast;  for I made all possible inquiry, both among Indians and Spaniards, asking for the cause of its transportation, and found that they did so out of respect for Tizibiracocha, to whom they principally direct their sacrifices . . . . . . . . . . . When the ground was broken for the great Church at Cuzco, the sand there being of poor quality and far away, the architects said that if the sand from the square were not used, the cost would be great, for that which was found was poor and hard to transport, and so I had it all taken from there, and there was a great quantity of it, and we leveled it up with other dirt, which the Indians out of their superstition took very hard, but would not think ill if we restored the square to its old condition, and when I understood this, I gave it so much more the readily to the church, and there is no doubt that it was worth more than four thousand castellanos, for it would have cost a great deal more to transport it and would not be profitable, and with it I made four stone bridges over the river of this city, by which much labor and cost was saved, for there was a great quantity of it, and other useful works were produced with it, but above all it helped to destroy the reverence which they had thus had for this square. The old people say that they brought it by tambos and provinces, the whole people assembling on the highway, and every province brought it to its boundaries, which they did in times of leisure, and thus this square was held in great veneration not only in Cuzco, but also in the whole realm . . . . They also affirm that the Inca did the same when a wife of his to whom he was attached died in Cuzco, the earth for her sepulcher being brought from her place of birth.    I satisfied myself that this was so, because they averred that there was a sepulcher in the houses of Captain Diego Maldonado worked in masonry under the ground, where a wife of the Inca, a native of the Yungas, was buried.    We found it very deep and built of very fine masonry, three stories high and about twelve feet square, and they affirmed that the sand was from the sea-shore, and when the sand was brought out there was found but one body in a certain hollow in the tomb and to one side, which seemed to be a proof of it.    There is also no doubt that in Quito there is a house which the Incas had built, from the stoneworks of Cuzco, from which, although not large in itself, it was a big job to bring, considering the distance on the road, which is five hundred leagues."[1]

I have given this long extract in as readable a form as the bad Spanish of the original permits, in order to show the faulty method of the archaeologist who applies the Egyptian stratification of the sand to the Peruvian necropolis, where we have the emphatic statement that enormous stratifications were produced by hand and suddenly.    This also confirms the conviction otherwise obtained that the depth at which bodies are found in the guano deposits is no criterion whatsoever as to the age of the respective interment.    But the cotton which is found in such artificial sepulchers, or in any other sepulchers in Peru, is frequently not even as old as the

[1] *Colección de libros y documentos referentes á la historia del Perú*, Lima 1916, vol. III, p. 109 ff.

original burial. Cieza de Leon tells the following of the burial customs in the coast valleys: "The Indians of many of these coast valleys have great walls made, where the rocks and barren mountains commence, in the way from the valleys to the Sierra. In these places each family has its established place for burying its dead, where they dig great holes and excavations, with closed doors before them. It is certainly a marvellous thing to see the great quantity of dead bodies that there are in these sandy and barren mountains, with their clothes now worn out and mouldering away with time. They call these places, which they hold to be sacred, *Huaca*, a mournful name. Many have been opened, and the Spaniards, when they conquered the country, found a great quantity of gold and silver in them. In these valleys the custom is very general of burying precious things with the dead, as well as many women and the most confidential servants possessed by the chief when alive. *In former times they used to open the tombs, and renew the clothes and food which were placed in them;* and when a chief died the principal people of the valley assembled, and made great lamentations. Many women cut off their hair until none was left, and came forth with drums and flutes, making mournful sounds, and singing in those places where the dead chief used to make merry, so as to make the hearers weep. Having made their lamentations, they offered up more sacrifices, and had superstitious communion with the devil. Having done this, and killed some of the women, they put them in the tomb, with the treasure and no small quantity of food; holding it for certain that they would go to that country concerning which the devil had told them. They had, and still have, the custom of mourning for the dead before the body is placed in the tomb, during four, five, or six days, or ten, according to the importance of the deceased, for the greater the lord the more honour do they show him, lamenting with much sighing and groaning, and playing sad music. They also repeat all that the dead man had done while living, in their songs; and if he was valiant they recount his deeds in the midst of their lamentations. When they put the body into the tomb, they burn some ornaments and cloths near it, and put others with the body.

"Many of these ceremonies are now given up, because God no longer permits it, and because by degrees these people are finding out the errors of their fathers, and how little these vain pomps and honours serve them. They are learning that it suffices to inter the bodies in common graves, as Christians are interred, without taking anything with them other than good works. In truth, all other things but serve to please the devil, and to send the soul down to hell more heavily weighted. *Nevertheless, most of the old chiefs order that their bodies are to be buried in the manner above described, in secret and hidden places, that they may not be seen by the Christians;* and that they do this is known to us from the talk of the younger men."[1]

Cieza de Leon's statement is emphatic. The cloth and the food in the graves were frequently changed, and the custom was still in use in his day. But we have also the positive assertion of Ondegardo that in 1571 the practice was still common: "It is common for the Indians secretly to disinter the dead from the churches or cemeteries, in order to bury them in the *huacas*, or hills, or prairies, or ancient sepulchers, or in their houses, or the house of the deceased, in order to give them food and drink in proper time. And then they drink and dance and sing in company with their relatives and friends. . . . When the Indians bury their dead, they place silver in their mouths and hands, in their bosoms, or elsewhere, and dress them in new

[1] *Op. cit.*, p. 228 ff.

clothes, and place other clothes folded inside the tombs, even woolen bags and foot gear and headdresses, to serve them in the other life, and in the dirges which they recite they tell of their past heathen times. They eat and drink a lot during these funerals and give drinks to the deceased while reciting a mournful song, wasting in this and other ceremonies the time of the funeral, which lasts in some parts eight days, in others less, and they celebrate their anniversaries from month to month, or from year to year, with feasting, chicha, silver, clothes and other things, in order to sacrifice them and do other ancient ceremonies in all possible secrecy. They believe that the souls of the deceased wander about alone in this world, suffering hunger, thirst, cold, heat and fatigue, and that the heads of their deceased or phantasms visit their relatives or other persons, to indicate to them that they are about to die or suffer some evil. Because of their belief that the souls suffer hunger, thirst, or other inconveniences, they offer in the sepulchers chicha and food, silver, clothes, wool, and other things which may be useful to the deceased, and that is why they are so particular in celebrating their anniversaries. And the very offerings which many Indians bring in the churches for the sake of the Christians they make for the very purpose for which their ancestors used to make them."[1]

Bernabé Cobo, nearly one hundred years later, tells the same story about the renewal of the clothes and food.[2] Ondegardo says that at the death of Guayanacapa, the last Inca, one thousand persons of all ages were killed, and that the same immolation took place with a number of lords in Spanish times.[3] The body of a

[1] *Op. cit.*, p. 194 f.
[2] "Celebraban sus aniversarios acudiendo á ciertos tiempos a las sepulturas, y abriéndolas, renovaban la ropa y comida que en ellas habían puesto, y ofrecían algunos sacrificios," P. Bernabé Cobo, *Historia del Nuevo Mundo*, Sevilla 1893, vol. IV, p. 238.
[3] *Op. cit.*, p. 118 f.

deceased Inca was taken out every day to the square, where a mass of woolen mantles were burned over a quantity of cotton. The women, who attended to the deceased Inca, never returned home, but were kept "to cleanse and wash the corpse and to renew the clothes and the cotton."[1]   Nothing is said about cotton clothes, which do not seem to have been common, because under the chapter of *De la ropa*[2] we have long accounts of woolen clothes, but not a word is said of cotton clothes. Cobo says that the Indians wove both woolen and cotton cloth, but only the Yungas and the inhabitants of the coast valleys dressed in cotton clothes, and that "the people of the mountains, which is the greater part of the realm and where the ancient nobility of the Incas and Orejones lived, made only woolen clothes."[3]

That a large number of the Peruvian mummies found in museums are no longer encased in their original cloth wrappings, but in later textiles, is proved by the archaeologists themselves. Reiss and Stübel[4]

[1] "No era pequeña pesadumbre aunque se hacía pocas vezes el serviçio que estos davan al Ynga quando susçedía por Señor en el rreyno porque como está dicho, el serviçio de su anteçesor ny en la rropa que en el discurso de su vida se hallaba en los depósitos del Cuzco, ny en su vaxilla de oro e plata, que era muy notable lo que se hacía para cada Ynga quando susçedía en el rreyno, ny en otra cosa quel tuviera por propia, sino que todo esto e la gente de su serviçio que dava para el cuerpo para el qual e para el serviçio se le haçían chácaras e tenyan gran gasto porque cada día se sacavan los cuerpos todos de los yngas a la plaça, e allí se les haçía su fuego, muy cuviertos e embueltos en muncha suma de mantas rricas sobre cantidad de algodón, y estavan devajo sentados en sus sillas, e allí delante se les haçía su fuego como al propio Ynga bivo, e su gente y mugeres con sus cántaros de chicha ques el vino de que ellos usan, hecho de mayz; y esta gente nunca bolbia a su tierra, sino siempre estavan allí acompañando al cuerpo, e antes quando faltava se les proveya de más para aquel serviçio, e tenya siempre el cuerpo un capitán a cuyo cargo quedava toda aquella gente dende que fallesçía, y solo éste y las mugeres a cuyo cargo estava *el linpiarle y lavarle de hordinario e rrenovarle la rropa y algodón*, le podían ver el gesto, aunque dizen que çiertas vezes le veya el hijo mayor que susçedía en el rreyno; e ansí lo hallé yo en diferentes con toda esta custodia," *ibid.*, p. 123 f.

[2] *Ibid.*, p. 94 f.; 2a parte, 84 ff.

[3] *Op. cit.*, p. 204.

[4] *The Necropolis of Ancon*, Berlin 1880-1887, vol. I, plate 17.

MUMMY PACK, from Baessler's *Peruanische Mumien*.

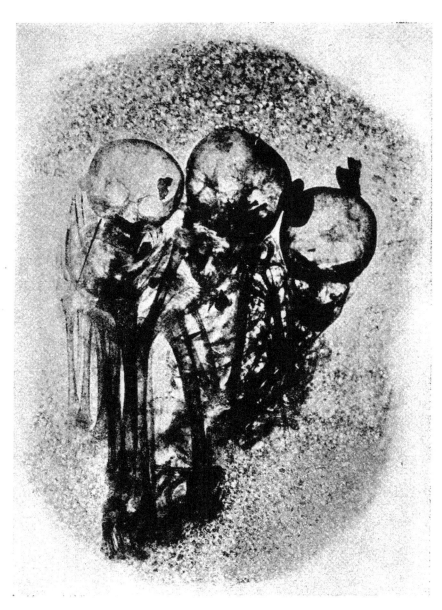

X-RAY PICTURE OF MUMMY PACK, from Baessler's *Peruanische Mumien.*

write: "In the present case the bundle contains the bones of a human skeleton no longer connected together, but packed up in a small space. It would therefore appear as if some older body, which had already fallen to pieces, had been dug out and again consigned to the grave in a fresh and carefully prepared equipment. Many peculiarities of the Ancon graves point at such opening and re-burial of those who had long departed this life, and the practice is confirmed and explained by the religious customs of the inhabitants of this coast, as handed down by tradition." Baessler[1] investigated eleven mummy packs consigned to the Royal Museum for Anthropology at Berlin, some of them with the aid of X-rays, and came to the same conclusion. In one pack "there were bones of four separate individuals, but of none were there enough to construct even distantly one complete skeleton. Besides, there were some animal bones present. Hence these must have been older, broken-up bodies, which were exhumed and then buried together." Baessler refers to a mummy pack from Trujillo which contained two incomplete skeletons of adults and one of a child, "hence it seems to have happened frequently that the bones of several broken-up bodies were disinterred and buried anew in a common pack." These were the cases that were obvious at a glance, but several other packs of the collection contain two and three mummies, which would indicate later re-burials, since it is not likely that so many packs taken at random should represent original multiple interments.

In a paper read before the Second Pan-American Congress,[2] Tello tells of his investigations of four types,

[1] Arthur Baessler, *Peruanische Mumien, Untersuchungen mit X-Strahlen*, Berlin 1906.

[2] J. C. Tello, *Los antiguos cementerios del Valle de Nasca*, in *Proceedings of the Second Pan-American Scientific Congress*, Washington 1917, vol. I, p. 283 ff.

supposedly very ancient, of cemeteries in the Nasca Valley. In the Inca cemetery bodies were found only one or two feet underground, generally wrapped in cotton, but these burial places are of late origin, mostly post-Columbian, although no objects of Spanish origin are found in them.[1] In a Tiahuanaco cemetery proof was found that the tombs were periodically opened and the mummies removed or the space filled up with new mummies.[2] Since objects of the Inca period, though rare, are found here,[3] and the native offerings of mummies are the same as at Ancon,[4] the great antiquity of the cotton, which may have been found there, though not specifically mentioned, is negatived. In the Nasca cemetery so well preserved corpses were found that Tello doubted their antiquity.[5] It is true he assumes that below that stratum the Nasca burials are older, and here cotton is recorded. Here again we have no criterion whatsoever as to the age of the mummies, for if they were disinterred like the other bodies the presence of cotton by the side of wool may be of very late origin.

[1] "El aspecto de todas estas tumbas es de data muy reciente; algunas son seguramente post-colombinas aunque no se encuentra en ellas objeto alguno de origen español," *ibid.*, p. 284.

[2] "La pared occidental está protegida por una hilera de estacas bien apiñadas que dejan a un lado una abertura destinada probablemente a servir de entrada a la cámara. Ésta se abría quizás periódicamente sea para incrementar el contenido o para sacar a las momias y hacerlas partícipes de las festividades u otras ceremonias del ayllu o tribu, si es que aquí existió también esta curiosa costumbre consignada como es sabido por alguno de los cronistas españoles," *ibid.*

[3] "Tampoco son infrecuentes los objetos de estilo incásico y no pocas momias llevan cubierta la cabeza con largas hondas de color rojo predominante las que se hallan también en las momias provenientes de las tumbas de esta clase," *ibid.*, p. 286.

[4] "El *unku* o comisión de tapestría, y armas, utensilios diversos y ofrendas votivas como las de las momias encontradas en Ancón y otros lugares de la Costa," *ibid.*, p. 285.

[5] "Enterradas casi en la superficie se encuentran también en estos cementerios unas ollas grandes conteniendo cadáveres de criaturas, algunas tan bien conservadas que hace dudar sobre si dichas ollas funerarias son realmente de la misma época o si son de origen más moderno," *ibid.*, p. 287.

ANCON GRAVES, from Reiss and Stuebel's *The Necropolis of Ancon.*

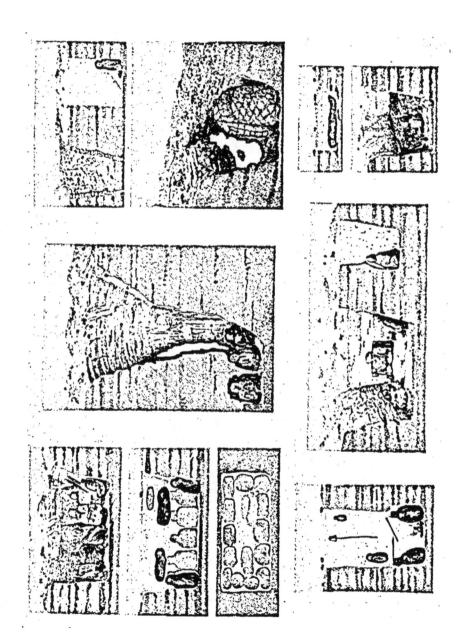

ANCON GRAVES, from Reiss and Stuebel's *The Necropolis of Ancon.*

By far the most extensive excavations were made at Ancon by Cessac and Savatier and later by Reiss and Stübel. Opinions vary as to the antiquity of the mummies at Ancon, but Hamy[1] is certainly not far from the mark when he says that the graves at Ancon do not go beyond the first half of the XVI. century. The proof of this, at least for some of the graves, is given in Rochebrune's list of plants found in the Cessac and Savatier collections,[2] where, among other plants, we find the *musa paradisiaca*, that is, the banana. We have already seen that the banana was introduced from the Canaries into America in 1516.[3] Cobo[4] tells the same story and adds that another variety was introduced from Guinea to Panama and in 1605 from Panama to Peru. Llano y Zapata,[5] writing in 1761, mentions a third native variety, named *coyllo*, which Cuyus-Mancu had transplanted from the Andes, and that Pedro Antonio de Llano y Zapata at the end of the XVII. century extended its cultivation in Lima. No dictionary, no other work records such a banana, and it is impossible for any banana to have been transplanted from the Andes, where it cannot exist. De Candolle's conclusion[6] must stand that there was no native banana in America. But there is a blunder in de Candolle which makes his argument appear inconclusive, and which shall be corrected here. De Candolle refers to Garcilasso de la Vega, who lived between 1530 and 1568 and who spoke of the banana as cultivated in the days of the Incas. In reality Garcilasso de la Vega was born in 1539 and wrote his *History* at the end of the sixteenth century. He nowhere says that the banana was known to the Incas and only mentions Acosta and Blas Valera whose

[1] *Botanisches Centralblatt*, Cassel 1880, vol. III, p. 1634.
[2] *Ibid.*, p. 1633 f.
[3] *Africa and the Discovery of America*, vol. I, p. 129.
[4] *Op. cit.*, vol. II, p. 444 ff.
[5] *Ibid.*, p. 448 n.
[6] A. de Candolle, *Origine des plantes cultivées*, Paris 1883, p. 242 ff.

opinion he gives in regard to the banana.[1] Acosta[2] says
that "there are small bananas, white and delicate,
which in Hispaniola are called *dominicos,* while the
others are larger and red in color.    They do not grow
in Peru.    They are brought from the Andes, as in
Mexico from Cuernavaca and other valleys."[3]    Garcilasso de la Vega simply mentions the two varieties, but
Llano y Zapata misunderstood Acosta's "de los Andes,"
which refers to the eastern province of Peru and not to
the mountains, and translated "blancos" by the current Aymara word *coyllu* "white," and created a new,
non-existing variety which his ancestor popularized in
Lima.    It is quite possible that *dominico* was by him
misread *Cuyus Mancu,* and a Chimu chief was thus
made the originator of the species.    With this correc-
tion the very last trace of a native variety of banana
in America disappears completely, and the antiquity
of the Ancon graves is permanently destroyed.

If bananas are found in Ancon graves, why not peanuts?    Hence the large amount of peanuts (*Arachis
hypogaea*) actually deposited in Peruvian tombs is no
criterion whatsoever as to their age.    The sophisticated
question may be asked, "But why are there no European
objects, no distinctly European fruits in the graves?"
Tello, who had no doubt of the post-Columbian origin of
some of the graves, none the less had to admit that no
Spanish articles were found in them.    The fact is that
burial customs persevere as nearly as possible according
to the ancient rites, and new objects make their appearance in them but sparingly.    And yet, Rochebrune
reports beans in the Ancon graves, and their American

[1] VIII. 14.
[2] IV. 20.
[3] "Hay unos plátanos pequeños, y mas delicados y blancos, que en la
Española llaman *dominicos:* hay otros mas gruesos, recios y colorados.
En la tierra del Perú no se dan: traense de los Andes, como á Méjico de
Cuernavaca y otros valles," J. de Acosta, *Historia natural y moral de las
Indias,* Madrid 1894, vol. I, p. 377.

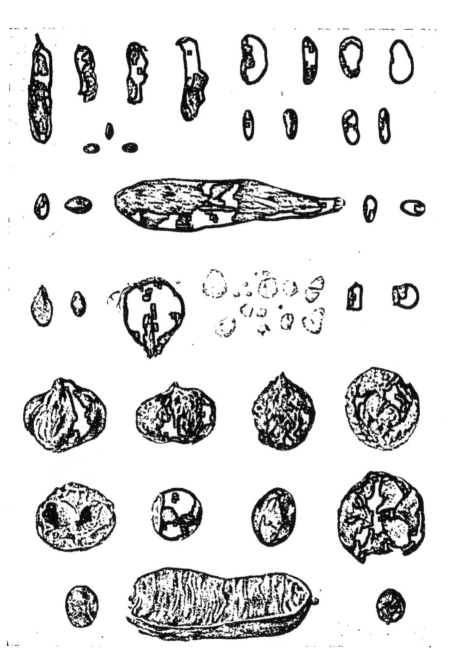

PEANUTS IN PERU, from Reiss and Stuebel's *The Necropolis of Ancon.*

origin seems doubtful.[1] We have chiefly African plants, sweet potatoes, yams, manioc in the mummy packs, because the food for the common people was chiefly due to Negro influence, and, besides, as Reiss and Stübel have remarked, the vast majority of the vegetables found are those of a starchy nature.

We have the emphatic and detailed proof that the bodies were disinterred at least as late as 1621. In the *Extirpación de la idolatria del Pirú*, by Pablo Joseph de Arriaga, printed at Lima in that year, we are told of the continued adoration of the *huacas*, in spite of their wholesale destruction by the Spaniards. "Since February 1617 up to July 1618, 5694 persons came to confession, 679 ministers of idolatry were discovered, and did penance as such, 603 principal *huacas* were taken from them, 3418 *conopas*, 45 *mamazaras*, and as many *compas*, 189 *huancas* (which are different from the *huacas*), 667 *malquis*, and 63 wizards were chastized in the plains, 357 cradles were burned, and 477 bodies were stolen from the church, without counting many bodies of *chacpas* and *chuchas*, which they also reverence and keep in their houses, nor the *pactos, axomamas, micsazara, huantayzara, hayriguazara,* or other things, with which a thousand superstitions are connected, which all were burned, as we shall explain in the following chapters. The villages where all these were found were to the number of 31, some of them very small, four of which were visited three years before by Doctor Don Placido Antolinez, who was their curate by especial commission of the Archbishop and who had taken away and burned many *huacas* and *conopas*, and yet not a few escaped him."[2] The only objects we are interested in here are the *malquis* "which are the bones or whole bodies of their gentile progenitors,

[1] *Op. cit.*, p. 1634.
[2] *Op. cit.*, p. 9.

who, they say, are the children of the *huacas*, which
they have in the fields or secluded places, in the *machays*, which are their ancient sepulchers, and sometimes they adorn them with very costly shirts or many
colored feathers or *cumbi;* these *malquis* have their especial priests or ministers, and they offer them the same
sacrifices and celebrate for them the same feasts as for
their *huacas*.    And they have with them the same tools
which they used in life, the women spindles and tufts of
spun cotton, and the men *tacllas* or *lampas* with which
they fought.    And in one of these *machays* of the *malquis* there was a lance with its iron and shoe, which,
they say, one of the first conquistadores of this realm
had given for a church banner, and in another there
was another handsome lance, which they call *quilcasca
choque* 'painted, or sculptured lance,' which was taken
to the Viceroy.    In these *malquis*, as in the *huacas*, they
have some dishes, in order to give them to eat and drink,
which are gourds or vases, some of clay, others of wood
and sometimes of silver, and seashells.''[1]    Similarly
"the bodies *chuchos*, otherwise called *curi*, when two
are born of one womb, if they die young, are placed in
a vessel and are kept in the house like a sacred thing,
and they say that one of them is the child of a ray  . . .
In the same way they keep the *chacpas* if they die
young, which are those that are born by their feet, in
regard to which they also have great superstitions, and
if they live, they call them *chacpas*, and their male child
they call *masco*, their female *chachi*.    The greatest
abuse in regard to them is that they do not baptize their
*chuchus* and *chacpas*, if they can hide  them from the
curates.    Of these *chuchus* and *chacpas*, which they had
kept in their houses, a great number had been burned
in the exhibitions.''[2]

[1] *Ibid.*, p. 14.
[2] *Ibid.*, p. 16 f.

As regards the disinterment from churches, Arriaga says: "But the greatest abuse consists in disinterring and carrying off the dead from the churches and taking them to the *machays*, which are the cemeteries they have in the fields for their ancestors, and in some places they call them *zamay*, which means resting places, and the dead they equally call *zamarcam* 'requievit.' And when they are asked why they do so, they say it is *cuyaspa*, for the love of them, because they say that the dead are in the church much oppressed by the earth and that in the field they are in the air and rest better disinterred. And a few days before we came to a village there was a chief Indian with his wife who had carried away from the church their two children, and in order to do this more easily they had buried them about two months one before the other in a kind of vault made of slabs, and they took them home and kept them there two days and had a great celebration for them and put new clothes on them and took them in a procession through the village and invited all the relatives to the feast and then took them back to the church. We had them disinterred a second time and broke up the vault and filled it with dirt. And thus it must be understood as of importance that by no means should consent be given to their being buried in vaults."[1]

We also have a complete explanation for the presence of bodies in the guano islands: "In the village of Huacho, whenever they went for guano to the islands which are the steep rocks of Huaura, they made offerings of chicha upon the shore, that their rafts should not be wrecked, after two days of fasting, and when they came to the island they worshipped the *huaca* Huamancantac as the lord of the guano, and offered sacrifices to him that he might allow them to take the guano, and

[1] *Ibid.*, p. 35.

upon returning to the harbor they fasted two days and then they danced, sang, and drank."[1]

From Arriaga's account it becomes clear that a vast number of the interments in ancient cemeteries were made as late as the year 1621, and that the presence of multiple burials of imperfect skeletons, of a child's skeleton without the lower parts, found in the mummy packs by Baessler, is due to the burial of corpses long after their death.    Moreover, the constant occurrence of bodies buried upside down is not, as Baessler thinks, the result of mere carelessness, but may be an attempt at burying persons born with their feet foremost, the so-called *chacpas*, whose very children bore special designations.[2]    Similarly the burials in the guano islands took place there where excavations were made for guano, and the depths at which sacrificial objects were found are no indication whatsoever of the age of the burial.    Thus we once more have upset the chronology derived from mummy-packs and cemeteries, and the whole question must be settled in a different way.

The first apparently authentic account of cotton cloth is found in an anonymous account of Pizarro's and Almagro's discoveries in 1525, previous to their conquest of Peru.[3]    They departed from Panama in 1525.    Their pilot, Bartolomeo Ruiz, who went down the coast, saw an Indian boat with twenty men, which he captured.    The boat was of about thirty tons, had henequen tackle and cotton sails.    The Indians were carrying a great variety of objects for trade, among them woolen and cotton mantles, which they intended to exchange for wampum, with which their boat was filled.    There would seem to be no escape from the fact that cotton was already in use in Columbia in 1525, nor

[1] *Ibid.*, p. 31.
[2] *Jbid.*, p. 17.
[3] *Colección de documentos inéditos para la historia de España*, vol. V, p. 193 ff.

is there any need for denying the fact. But toward the end of the report we read: "There is an island in the sea near the villages where there is a meeting-house in the form of a tent, made of very rich mantles, where they have an image of a woman with a child in her arms, by the name of María Meseia. If any one has any infirmity in a limb, he makes a limb of silver or gold and offers it to her, and at a given time sacrifices before the image some sheep."[1] The reporter was not shrewd enough to recognize the Virgin Mary and the Catholic adoration of the Virgin by idolatrous Indians, or he purposely omitted to make the obvious deduction. But, if the Catholic faith had already made its entrance among a distant Indian tribe, there must have been there white men or Christianized Negroes before that time, and the cotton mantles and cotton sails are a matter of course. Again the proof of native cotton vanishes, and we are once more in the dark.

Holmes[2] quite correctly remarks: "But little is known chronologically of the various groups of art products obtained from the burial places of the coast belt of Peru, but most of them belong in all probability to what may be called the Incarial epoch . . . In the Sierra and upland regions, where the conditions of burial were not so favorable, but slight traces of the more perishable articles appear to have been preserved." This being the case, the very oldest cotton objects could not go beyond the XIII. century, and such representations of peanuts as are found in Chimu vessels cannot be any older.

So far we have only established the absence of all criteria of chronology for Peruvian cotton, and now we shall by the linguistic criterion show that if cotton was

[1] *Ibid.*, p. 200.
[2] W. H. Holmes, *Textile Fabrics of Ancient Peru*, in *Smithsonian Institution, Bureau of Ethnology*, Washington 1889, p. 5 ff.

present before Columbus, it must have been introduced into Peru directly or indirectly by Mandingo Negroes.

We have Bambara *kotondo, korandi, kori, kuori,* Malinke *kotondin,* Mandingo *korandē, kutando, koyondyi, kodondi,* Soninke *kotollin* "cotton," Dyula *korho* "cotton plant," which are all derived from the Arabic word for "cotton."

In South America the Mandingo *kotondo* words are found southwards from Venezuela to Peru, and Central Brazil. In Venezuela the Mandingo word is best preserved in some Carib languages. Here we find Cumanagota *otocuare,* Chayma *otoquat,* while Makusi (south-west of Guiana) *kotoka* shows that an initial *k* has been lost in the other languages. Bakairi in Central Brazil, near the Xingu River, has *atakxera, atakxira, tatakxera,* which in Nahuqua is corrupted in *torokire.* Still farther south, on the Rio Tocantins, we find the non-Carib Apinages *kathodnie* and Guaycurus *cottamo.* Other languages, apparently related to Carib, have similar words: Yabarana (on the Bentuari) *quetejuate,* Mapoyo (between the Paruaza and Suapure) *quetate.* From these forms it would appear that the languages of Venezuela and to the south began with a form like Malinke *kotondin* or Soninke *kotollin,* which is still preserved in Apinages *kathodnie,* Guaycurus *cottamo,* and that Makusi *kotoka,* Cumanagota *otocuare* are corruptions of it. But it is more likely that we have here the Soninke *kotollin-khare,* and similar forms in the other Mandingo languages, literally "cotton plant." In the extreme south-west the latter Indian forms are abbreviated to Moxa *cohore,* but these forms abound throughout the whole region, where we have Mandauaca *cauarli,* Caruzana *jariderli,* Piapoco *sawari,* Puinabe *saurlot,* Uarao (in the delta of the Orinoco) *ahuaramuto,* Baniba *auarli, aualri.* Some of these languages seem to have Carib affinities, but Baniba is classed as Nu-Arawak.

In the Kechua of Peru we have an abbreviated *otocuare*, namely *utku*, while Aymara *qhuea* is another abbreviation of an original (*ata*) *kæera* of the Bakairi or a similar form, while Chibcha *quihisa* is another transformation of the same word.

All these words apparently proceed from the shores of Venezuela, in any case from the north. But there is another series of words which began at the eastern shores of South America, from somewhere in Brazil, and from there proceeded northward and westward. We have in the Tupi languages Brazilian *amaniu*, *amaju*, *amanyju*, *amydu*, Apiaca *amuijo*, Emerillon *muiniju*, Cocama *amano*, *hamaniu*, Auetö *amatsitu*, Kamayura *amuniju*, Guarani *amandyju*, Oyampi *amoniu*, and in the Carib languages these become Galibi *amulu*, *manhulu*, *mauru*, in the islands *manholu*. Von den Steinen[1] also records Trumai *moneyu*, Mehinaku Kustenaa *ayupe*, Yaulapiti *aliupö*, *ayupö*. That these are corruptions of the same original word becomes clear from Anti *ampe*, *ampegi* in the western part of Peru, where the latter is obviously a development of Apiaco *amuijo*, etc. But this Anti *ampe* explains Chimu *jam*, the furthest corruption of the word. Chimu (Mushika) has the tendency to turn words as much as possible into monosyllables, and Spanish *caballo* "horse" here becomes *col* and *coj*. Even thus *jam* represents the Tupi word for cotton. But the Brazilian words are all obviously derived from Kimbundu *mujinha* "cotton." Kimbundu is the language of Angola, whence therefore the Portuguese brought the cotton to Brazil, whence it spread westward as far as Peru and northward to Guiana and the West Indies. But another path of distribution very likely preceded it from the West Indies or Venezuela toward Peru. "Welwitsch in *Apontamentos*,

---

[1] K. von den Steinen, *Unter den Naturvölkern Zentral-Brasiliens*, Berlin 1894.

p. 558, states that three distinct kinds of cotton are cultivated in Angola with greater or less frequency. He calls them *G. vitifolium*, *G. barbadense*, and *G. herbaceum*, the two first being also met with wild in the neighborhood of villages."[1]   According to Welwitsch, *Gossypium peruvianum* grows wild at Golungo Alto.[2] It is, therefore, not at all unlikely that the cotton in Peru was introduced from Brazil, and, since Angola was discovered only in 1482, this introduction must be of a more recent date.   As the banana in Peru originates from the province of the Antis, that is, on the eastern side of the Andes, precisely where the Antis are domiciled, where it still was the source of the Peruvian banana in 1555, and this banana has been discovered in the Ancon necropolis, it follows that we have no proof of any cotton in Peru before that which was brought to Brazil from Angola, unless another variety came down earlier from Venezuela or Darien, and this could have come only from a Mandingo pre-Columbian colony in America.   We are not yet in a position to determine the date for such a colony from the data so far obtained.

[1] W. P. Hiern, *Catalogue of the African Plants collected by Dr. Friedrich Welwitsch in 1853-61*, London 1896, vol. I, p. 78.
[2] *Ibid.*

# PART II:   THE SOVEREIGN REMEDY.

# CHAPTER I.

## SMOKING IN ANTIQUITY.

Galen has the following remedy for a toothache: "A toothache is soon relieved by alcyonium smoke; another smoke of henbane seed relieves pain."[1] "Alcyonium," says Galen,[2] "wears down and dissolves everything, having an acrid quality and hot power, but there are different degrees of such acridity and pungency, according to the consistency of their whole nature, for one is dense and heavy and of a bad odor, smelling of rotten fish, and resembling a sponge in form; another is rather long in shape, light and thin, having the odor of seaweed; the third resembles a worm in shape, is of a purple color and of soft consistency, and is called *milesium;* there is a fourth, soft and thin like the second, resembling unwashed wool; at last, a fifth has a light outside, but is rough within, of no odor, apparently acrid in taste, and is the hottest of all the alcyonia, so that it will burn off the hair. While the first two are good for the scurvy, vitiligo, mange, and leprosy, and, besides, possess the power of making the skin more shining, the last cannot do that, for it does not purify the skin, but excoriates it, penetrating into the depth and causing sores. The third is by far the most delicate, hence, when burned, it cures foxbaldness, when dissolved in wine, and is of a yellow color and soft sub-

[1] ‹Ὑποθυμίαμα τοῖς ἀλγοῦσιν ὀδοῦσιν . Ἀλκυόνιον ὑποθυμία καὶ εὐθέως ἄπονος ἔσται . ἄλλο . ὑοσκυάμου σπέρμα ὑποθυμασθὲν ἄπονον ποιεῖ,› Περὶ εὐπορίστων, ΙΙ. 8.4.

[2] Περὶ τῆς τῶν ἁπλῶν φαρμάκων κράσεως καὶ δυνάμεως, XI. 2.3.

stance. The fourth shares its powers with it, but is not a little weaker." Dioscorides[1] tells nearly the same about the *alcyonium*, but with some important additions: "The third is good for those who suffer from urinary trouble or bladder stones, also for those who suffer from the kidneys, the dropsy, or the spleen. Burnt and dissolved in wine it restores the hair. The last will whiten the teeth. Mixed with salt it is also used for other perfumes or hair removers. If one should want to burn it, let him add salt and throw it into an unglazed vessel, and close the aperture with clay, and put it into the furnace. When the clay is baked, let him take it out and keep it for use. It is distilled like cadmia." Pliny[2] gives nearly the same information about *alcyonium:* "There is a sea production called 'halcyoneum,' composed, as some think, of the nests of the birds known as the 'halcyon' and 'ceyx,' or, according to others, of the concretion of sea-foam, or of some slime of the sea, or a certain lanuginous inflorescence thrown up by it. Of this halcyoneum there are four different kinds; the first, of an ashy colour, of a compact substance, and possessed of a pungent odour; the second, soft, of a milder nature, and with a smell almost identical with that of sea-weed; the third, whiter, and with a variegated surface; the fourth, more like pumice in appearance, and closely resembling rotten sponge. The best of all is that which nearly borders on a purple hue, and is known as the 'Milesian' kind; the whiter it is, the less highly it is esteemed.

"The properties of halcyoneum are ulcerative and detergent: when required for use, it is parched and applied without oil. It is quite marvellous how efficiently it removes leprous sores, lichens, and freckles, used in combination with lupines and two oboli of sul-

[1] Περὶ ὕλης ἰατρικῆς, V. 118.
[2] XXXII. 86 f.

phur. It is employed, also, for the removal of marks upon the eyes."[1]

In spite of the definite references to *alcyonium* in the ancient medical writers and in Avicenna, there is no reference to this *sea-foam* in mediaeval literature as a medium for the toothache, no doubt because this zoophyte was hard to obtain. It is certainly no accident that in the XVIII. century the mineral *meerschaum* was being used as a material for pipeheads. The best *alcyonium* was of a purple color, and the necessity for a substitute, which by the purple or brown discoloration of the pipehead would prove itself to be an equal of the traditional *sea-foam*, led to the adoption of the universal *meerschaum*, which was also found floating in the sea near the region from which the *alcyonium* is recorded. Thus a trade device has preserved for us the fact that *meerschaum*, that is, *alcyonium*, was at one time used for the fumigation of the mouth, which is the initial step toward smoking, as the idea is understood now. That other products of the sea were used for fumigation appears from the fact that *aphronitrum*, that is, an efflorescence of saltpeter, according to Dioscorides and others, is mentioned in this connection: "some place *aphronitrum* on burning coal, putting it first in a new vessel, until it ignites."[2]

In the mediaeval medical literature, *henbane* became the "smoke" medicine *par excellence*, especially in the Salerno school. The *Catolica Magistri Salerni* says:[3] "Henbane seed wrapped in a little wax may be put on hot coal and the smoke should be drawn into the tooth, and the worms will soon be killed." There is a poem on the toothache which is repeated in all the textbooks

[1] See also *Avicennae Liber Canonis*, Venetiis 1582, fol. 164 (No. 605).
[2] *Op. cit.*, V. 130.
[3] "Semen iusquiami cum pauco cere involutum seu calido superponatur et fumus inde respiret in dente et statim vermes pernecabuntur," P. Giacosa, *Magistri Salernitani*, Torino 1901, p. 106.

of the Salerno school.   In the *Flos Medicinae*[1] we read:
"This is the way to treat the teeth:   Collect the grains
of leek and burn them with henbane, and catch the
smoke through an *embotus* into the tooth."[2]

This is found in a variety of versions, from which it
follows that incense was mixed with henbane:

> "Dentes sic sana:  porrorum collige grana
> Nec careas thure cum iusquiamo simul ure;
> Hinc ex *amboto* fumum cape dente remoto."[3]

In the *De cirurgia* we have a longer account, from
which it follows that henbane, with other ingredients,
was put on hot coals, and the smoke was inhaled through
an *embotus*.   Or the ingredients could at first be made
into troches and then smoked.

> "Aut sic:  jusquiami, portulace quoque semen
> Et porri;  super ardentes apponito prunas,
> Inde per *embotum* fumum quem sumat in ore
> Egrotum supra dentem, qui fumus honeste
> Lenit et educit quem fecit reuma dolorem;
> De quorum foliis tritis formato trociscos
> Quosque super prunas ardentes ponito, fumum
> *Emboto* capiat patiens in dentibus ipsum.—"[4]

The prose accounts are not less interesting.   In the
*De adventu medici ad aegrotum*[5] we are told that the henbane was smoked through a reed:   "Semen jusquiami
et porri igniti cum aliquantulum cere et thuris impone."
In the *Chirurgia Willehelmi de Congenis*, of the end of
the XII. century, we similarly have:   "Ad idem accipe
semen iusquiami et porri et ceram et pone super car-
bones ardentes et per *embotum* paciens fumum inde reso-

---

[1] S. de Renzi, *Collectio Salernitana*, Napoli 1852, vol. I, p. 509 f.
[2] "Sic dentes serva:  porrorum collige grana, Ne careas jure, cum jus-
quiamo, quoque ure, Sicque per *embotum* fumum cape dente remotum."
[3] *Ibid.*, vol. II, p. 678, vol. V, p. 94.
[4] *Ibid.*, vol. IV, p. 69.
[5] *Ibid.*, vol. II, p. 178.

lutum recipiat."[1]    We are more fully informed of the
efficacy of the henbane in the *Chirurgia* of Roger Fru-
gardi: "Accipe semen casillaginis (id est iusquiami)
et porri equaliter et super prunas ardentes pone, super
prunas etiam *embotum* ponas et per canellum *emboti*
patiens super dentem patientem recipiat; hic enim
fumus qui inde progreditur, reuma, quod dolorem facit,
mirabiliter dissoluit et educit et ipsum mitigat."[2]

We must first ascertain the manner in which the henbane was smoked.   The *embotus, embocus* would seem
to be some kind of funnel, and, indeed, Provençal
*embutz* is distinctly mentioned as the implement by
which wine or water is poured into a vessel,[3] and here
also it is a surgical implement for introducing smoke
into the anus.[4]   Only in the XVI. century is *embut*
recorded in French as a funnel, and the famous Paré in
1573 gave the shape of an implement for producing
smoke with which to cure the toothache as a vessel topped by an inverted funnel.   His concoction is more
violent:   "Take ginger, pepper, pyretrum, half a dram
of each, crush it, let it all boil in a pot, in wine and vinegar, and take the smoke to the tooth through a well-
attached funnel, just like this figure."[5]

Obviously the Middle Ages no longer followed the
precepts of the ancients, or had forgotten the precise
method, which must have prevailed among the laymen.
Dioscorides tells us precisely how fumes were transferred from a vessel by distillation:   "An iron vessel

[1] Karl Sudhoff, *Beitrage zur Geschichte der Chirurgie im Mittelalter*, in
*Studien zur Geschichte der Medizin*, Leipzig 1918, vol. II, p. 339.
[2] *Ibid.*, p. 181.
[3] Emil Levy, *Provenzalisches Supplement-Worterbuch*, Leipzig 1892-1915.
[4] "El fendement dels pos  . . .  pren grana de camilhada e met sobre las
brasas ardens: pueis met I.I. *embut* desobre las brasas, el malautes recepia
aquel fum el fendement," *ibid.*
[5] J.-F. Malgaigne, *Oeuvres complètes d'Ambroise Paré*, Paris 1840, vol. II,
p. 446.   But he has still more violent smokes, that must have cured or
killed the patient: "Faites fumigation de graines de coloquintes, et de
moutarde, et d'ails, receuè par entonnoir," *ibid.*, p. 447 f.

containing cinnabar is placed in a clay retort, over
which an *ambix* (ἄμβιξ) is fastened by means of clay,
and then the coals are ignited."[1]    Here we have the top
of a still through which the fumes pass.    Caelius Aure-
lianus calls *ambix* a kind of cupping glass, made of glass
or clay,[2] and Athenaeus similarly mentions the word as a
designation of a cup ending in a sharp point.[3]

From the writings of the alchemists it follows that
the distilling glass, into which the fumes were condensed,
was called βίκος, βίκιον, while the *ambix* was the cup
of the still or the whole distilling apparatus.    Zosimus,
in the IV. century, described the process of distillation.
"Take a male-female (ἀρσενόθηλυ) glass vessel called
*ambix*," he says, in a discussion of the Divine Water,[4]
"and close the *ambix* and the top (μαστάριον) with the
receiving cup (ῥόγιον)," etc.    Here the *ambix* refers to
the lower containing bottle, but usually it refers to the
upper part which here is called *mastarion*, "the teat,"
as, indeed, the implement resembles a teat with a long
nipple.    We have a large number of illustrations of
alchemists' alembics in Berthelot.[5]    The oldest of these
is from a manuscript of Zosimus, of the IV. century
after Christ.[6]    Here the *mastarion* is of a typical form.
The same is reproduced in manuscripts up to the XVII.
century,[7] though in some of these the nipple is barely
indicated by a small knob.    It is clear from these illustrations that the process of distillation was conceived
as a union of the male and the female, the large bowl
of the *mastarion* being the uterus in which the ascending

---

[1] *Op. cit.*, V. 110, also in *Der Leidener und Stockholmer Papyrus*, in
*Entstehung und Ausbreitung der Alchemie*, by E. von Lippmann, Berlin
1919, p. 10.
[2] A. de Haller, *Artis medicae principes*, Lausannae 1774, vol. XI, p. 328.
[3] XI. 61.
[4] M. Berthelot, *Collection des anciens alchimistes grecs*, Paris 1888,
vol. II, p. 141, French translation, p. 143.
[5] *Ibid.*, vol. I, p. 127 ff.
[6] *Ibid.*, p. 164.
[7] *Ibid.*, pp. 136, 161.

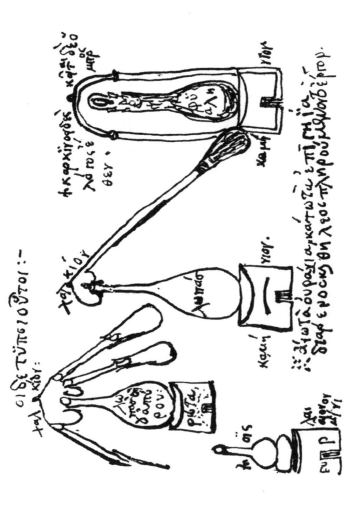

THE ALCHEMIST'S DISTILLING CAP, from Berthelot's *Collection des anciens alchimistes grecs.*

fumes, the male sperm, is transformed into the new chemical combination, which is deposited in the glass vessel at the end of the tube of the *mastarion*.

A vast number of pipes have been found in Roman graves. The excellent series of articles by B. Reber on such pipes from Swiss burial places[1] make it possible to dispense with other sources, and to discuss their use from the illustrations given by him. We shall also refer to the résumé of all the latest articles on smoking by H. Lamer, *Das Rauchen im Altertume*.[2]

Gustave Lejeal describes a pipe found by him in Rome: "This Roman pipe was found in Rome in 1845. It is now part of the collection Campana at the Louvre. It is a vessel of which the pipe is arranged in such a way as to receive the pipestem, which Pliny has clearly indicated. But, they will say, one testimony does not count. Excuse me, the testimony is not unique, for some fifty similar pipes were found and thrown into the Tiber as useless articles, probably without value in the eyes of the official archaeologists. One or two specimens were saved, to which ours belongs. The fact is attested by Count de l'Escalopier, as great a smoker as fervent archaeologist, who visited Rome just as the act of vandalism was accomplished."[3] Reber reproduces this and a similar pipe. A glance at them shows that they are *mastaria*, if they are turned upside down. The large bowl ends in a nipple, and the stem which comes out of it at an angle of 45° is obviously intended to be set into a distilling glass, as may be seen from the rim at the end of the stem.

All the other pipes described by Reber, to the number of 93, are of a totally different character. Whether they are ancient or belong to the Middle Ages, they are

[1] *Les pipes antiques de la Suisse*, in *Anzeiger für schweizerische Altertumskunde*, N.F., vol. XVI, pp. 195, 287, vol. XVII, pp. 33, 241 ff.
[2] In *Jahresberichte des philologischen Vereins*, vol. XLIV, p. 47 ff.
[3] Reber, *op. cit.*, vol. XVI, p. 198.

distinctly smoking pipes in the modern sense of the
word. The bowl is much smaller and at an angle of
135° from the stem. Whether of metal or of red or
white clay, they are all of nearly the same size. Some
of them have heads molded upon the bowl, and from
their position it is evident that the bowl was kept with
the orifice up as in modern pipes because the heads were
then standing up. This is still further proved by the
metal caps attached to many of the pipes, just as in
certain modern pipes. Nearly all the pipes still have
visible a protruding knob where the nipple is in the
*mastarion*, which shows that the pipes from which substances were smoked are a direct development of the
distilling cap of the alchemists.

We can now show the tremendous influence which the
alchemists have exerted upon the European nations by
means of the distilling apparatus, especially the distilling cap. In the alchemist's vocabulary the word
κνούφιον is, according to Ducange, used for the *mastarion*. This word is not recorded anywhere else. A
guess has been made[1] that this word is derived from the
Egyptian God *Knuph*, whose headgear the lid resembles.
But as Knuph is represented with a ram's head and a
headgear totally different from the *mastarion*, the case
is impossible. The Greek κνούφιον is, indeed, taken
from the Egyptian, but, in all probability indirectly,
through the Arabic. We have Egyptian *qenu, qená*
"embrace, hug, breastbone, bosom, breast, body, belly,"
and *qená* "sheaf, bundle of grain," the latter obviously
from the idea "to embrace, hug," hence *qenb* "to tie, bind"
and "corner of a building" are, no doubt, of the same
origin. The Coptic *koun* "breast, embrace" and *knaau,
knau, ḥnau*, that is, *knaaw, knaw, ḥnaw* "sheaf, bundle
of grain" are from the corresponding Egyptian words.

This leads to Arabic قنب *qunb*, pl. *qunub*, "the calyx of

[1] Lippmann, *op. cit.*, pp. 305, 344.

ANCIENT PIPES, from Reber's *Les pipes antiques de la Suisse.*

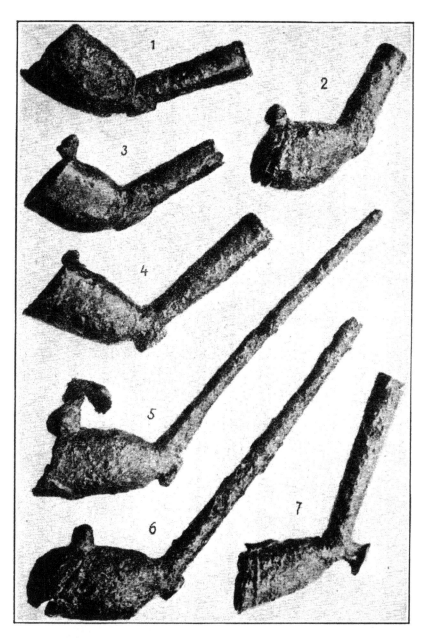

ANCIENT PIPES, from Reber's *Les pipes antiques de la Suisse.*

the flower of a plant, sheath of the penis of a beast, pre-
puce of the clitoris, part of the forepaw of the lion into
which the claws enter," hence قنب *qnaba* "he entered
into it, withdrew his claw, cut off from the grapevine
what would be injurious, the flowers, or blossoms, came
forth from their calyxes." This word is rare in the
Semitic languages, only the Talmud recording קְנַב
*qĕnab* "to nip off, pluck," קְנוּבָה *qĕnubah* "what is
plucked off."

Neither Greek nor Latin records any borrowing from
this Egyptian stem, except the alchemist κνούφιον, but
the Germanic and Romance languages have borrowed
extensively from the Arabic. German *knoph, knopf*
"button, bunch" is recorded early, and from this comes
English *knob* and a large number of words. The very
phonetic irregularity indicates a borrowing from without. ONorse *knappr* "knob, stud, button, scanty" at
once indicates how German *knapp* "scanty," *Knabe*
"boy," and English *knave, knap* are related to it as
meaning originally "bunchy, small." The relation to
the Arabic is indicated by a large number of Germanic
words with the underlying meaning of "to pinch off,"
hence German *kneifen* "to pinch," English *nip, nibble,*
etc., ONorse *kneif* "nippers, pincers," hence Gothic
*dishniupan* "to tear to pieces," where the phonetic
irregularities once more indicate borrowings. OIcelandic *knifr,* modern *hnifr,* English *knife,* LLatin *knivus,*[1]
OFrench *canivet, ganivet* are all derived from the same
word, since the statement frequently made in the
mediaeval glosses that it is a small pointed dagger
places it, with AS. *cnafa* "parvulus," in the same family
with Arabic قنب *qanaba,* but here we have a much closer
relation still, since already in Arabic there developed

---

[1] "Cultellum cum cuspide, qui vulgo *knivus* dicitur," (1231), Ducange.

the meaning "he cut off from its upper part what would not bear and what would perhaps injure its produce," that is, "to prune."

From Greek ἄμβιξ the word ἀμβικισμός, ἀμβυκισμός "distilling"[1] is formed, and we have also ἀμβυκίζω "to distil."[2] Just as Greek *ambix* has produced Latin *embocus, embotus*, so to Greek ἀμβυκίζω corresponds Latin *imbotare*, Catalan *embotar*, Spanish *embudar* "to pour through a funnel into a cask." But the Latin *buttis* "cask" is already recorded in the year 562 A. D., and from this come Latin *buta, butta* "vat" and the very large Romance family of "bottle "words. But *embotus* is also the equivalent of Greek κνούφιον hence we should expect the meaning "knob" to develop from it. Indeed, an enormous mass of Romance and Germanic words is derived from the simpler *botus, bocus*, meaning "bud, boss," such as French *bout* "end," *bouton* "bud," *bosse* "boss," etc. All these may be found in Körting's *Lateinisch-Romanisches Wörterbuch*, though their origin is not understood. The two groups of words illustrate how wrong philology may be if it does not invoke the historical sciences. Without a study of the Graeco-Arabic alchemy an enormous mass of words would forever remain a mystery. Similarly anthropology suffers from a neglect of the historical method. Only by overlooking the mediaeval alchemy could the origin of tobacco smoking have been placed in America. We shall soon see how the tobacco pipes and the tobacco-smoking develop from the alchemist's distilling cap.

Smoking was also resorted to in troubles of the chest, especially in coughing. According to one treatise of Salerno, "the smoke of orpiment and of colt's foot taken through an *embotus* into the mouth would cure a

[1] Berthelot, *op. cit.*, vol. III, p. 273.
[2] *Ibid.*, p. 411.

cough."[1] According to the same authority, the same
with arsenic and ammonia was good for asthma.[2] Long
before that Pliny wrote: "The smoke of this plant
(bechion, colt's foot) in a dry state, inhaled by the aid
of a reed and swallowed, is curative, they say, of chronic
cough; it is necessary, however, at each inhalation to
take a draught of raisin wine,"[3] and also: "They say,
too, that the smoke of dried cow-dung—that of the
animal when grazing, I mean—is remarkably good for
phthisis, inhaled through a reed."[4] For *bechion* or *tus-
silago* Pliny also uses *chamaeleuce*, which Linné identified with colt's foot: "The Chamaeleuce is known
among us as the 'farfarum' or 'farfugium;' it grows
on the banks of rivers, and has a leaf like that of the
poplar, only larger. The root of it is burnt upon cy-
press charcoal, and, by the aid of a funnel, the smoke
inhaled, in cases of inveterate cough."[5] Similarly Dioscorides prescribed smoking of colt's foot for a cough,[6]
and it is right here that we have a good description of
this pipe. "Fumigation is good for an old cough.
Through a reed and an *ambix* perforated at the bottom
the smoke is taken into the mouth, the *ambix* being

---

[1] "Fumus auripigmenti, radicis ungule caballine per embotum ad divi-
sionem ore suscipiatur et tussis ad expulsionem provocetur," P. Giacosa,
*op. cit.*, p. 205.

[2] "Fumus auri pigmenti, arsenici, amoniaci puri, radicis ungule caballine
per embotum ore suscipiatur," *ibid.*, p. 215. See also *De aegritudinum
curatione*, in *Collectio Salernitana*, vol. II, p. 208.

[3] "Huius aridae cum radice fumus per harundinem haustus et devoratus
veterem sanare dicitur tussim, sed in singulos haustus passum gustandum
est," XXVI. 30.

[4] "Fimi quoque aridi, sed pabulo viridi pasto bove, fumum harundine
haustum prodesse tradunt," XXVIII. 230.

[5] "Chamaeleucen apud nos farfarum sive farfugium vocant. nascitur
secundum fluvids, folio populi, sed ampliore. radix eius inponitur carbonibus
cupressi, atque is nidor per infundibulum bibitur inveteratae tussi,"
XXIV. 135.

[6] «'Υποθυμιώμενα δὲ ξηρὰ εἰς ὑποκαπνισμὸν τοὺς ὑπὸ ξηρᾶς βη-
χὸς καὶ ὀρθαπνοίας ἐνοχλουμένους θεραπεύει, ὅταν χανόντες τὸν καπνὸν
δέξωνται τῷ στόματι καὶ καταπίωσι.» Περὶ ὕλης ἰατρικῆς,
III. 112.

placed on the fire."[1]   The same bechion is smoked for
cough according to Galen,[2] but the best description of
the pipe is given by Marcellus Empiricus:   "An efficacious medicine for the cough.   The herb, called in Gallic
*calliomarcus*, in Latin *horse's hoof* (apparently colt's
foot), gathered in the old moon, dried on Thursday, is
at first put in a new vessel with burning coals, which are
put into the vessel;  the top is closed carefully with clay
and a reed is inserted, and through it the humor or hot
smoke is drawn into the mouth, until it penetrates all
the arteries and the stomach."[3]

A large number of other substances were smoked.[4]
The best summary of smoking in mediaeval times was
made by Paré, and this we give in the English translation.   "Suffitus or fumigation is an evaporation of
medicines having some viscous and fatty moisture: of
fumigations some are dry, othersome moist, the dry have
the form of trochisces or pills:  their matter ought to be
fatty and viscous, so that it may send forth a smoake by
being burnt:  such are ladanum, myrrhe, masticke,
pitch, waxe, rosine, turpentine, castoreum, styrax,
frankincense, olibanum, and other gummes, which may
bee mixed with convenient powders:  for they yeeld

---

[1] ̔'Υποθυμιώμενα δὲ ὠφελεῖ χρονίας βῆχας, καὶ διὰ καλαμίνου
σίφωνος καὶ ἄμβικος τετρημένου κατὰ τὸν πυθμένα, δι' οὗ καὶ ὁ σίφων
καθιέμενος ἀναπέμπει εἰς τὸ στόμα τὸν ἀτμόν· ἀρσενικόν, σανδαράχη
λεία, βραχέντα ὕδατι καὶ πλασθέντα τῷ τετρημένῳ ἄμβικι, περιτιθεμένου
τῷ πυρὶ τοῦ ἄμβικος· βηχίου φύλλα θυμιώμενα, θεῖον ἄπυρον, κάλαμος,
ἀρωματίτης καθ' ἑαυτὸν καὶ σὺν ῥητίνῃ τερμινθίνῃ, πρόπολις, σανδαράχη σὺν ῥητίνῃ τερμινθίνῃ, ἄσφαλτος, λιβανωτὸς σὺν ῥητίνῃ, σκίλλα
ξηρά, ἐρύσιμον, ἔλαιον κέδρινον, κενταυρίου ῥίζα, μαράθρου καρπός,›
Π ε ρ ὶ   ε ὐ π ο ρ ί σ τ ω ν,   II. 33.

[2] VI. 7.

[3] "Ad tussem remedium efficax: Herba, quae Gallice calliomarcus, Latine
equi ungula vocatur, collecta luna vetere liduna die Iovis siccata prius in
ollam novam mittitur cum prunis ardentibus, quae intra ollam mitti debent;
superficies sane eius argilla diligenter claudi debet et calamus inseri, per
quem umor vel fumus caloris hauriatur intra os, donec arteria omnia et
stomachum penetret," II. 101.

[4] Lamer, *op. cit.*, p. 56.

them a body and firme consistence; the fumigations that are made of powders only, yeeld neither so strong nor long a fume.

"The quantity of the powders must bee from ℨβ. to ℨi.β. but the gummes to ℥ii. as, ℞ sandarachae, mastiches, rosar. an. ℥ i. benioini, galang. an. ℥ iii. terebinthina excipiantur, & fiant trochisci, quibus incensis suffumigentur tegumenta capitis. 4. marcasitae, ℥ ii. bdellii, myrrhae, styracis, an. ℥ i β. cerae flavae, & terebinth. quod sufficit, fiant formulae pro suffumigio. 4. cinnabaris, ℥ ii. styracis & benzoini, an. ℥ ii. cumterebinth. fiant trochisci pro suffumigio per embotum.

"Wee use fumigations in great obstructions of the braine, ulcers of the lungs, the *asthma*, an old cough, paines of the sides, wombe, and the diseases of some other parts; sometimes the whole body is fumigated, as in the cure of the *Lues venerea* to procure sweat; sometimely onely some one part whereto some reliques of the *Lues* adheres; such fumigations are made of *cinnabaris*, wherein there is much *hydragyrum*. The fume must be received by a funnell, that so it may not bee dispersed, but may all be carried unto the part affected, as is usually done in the affects of the womb and eares.

"In fumigations for the braine and chest, the vapour would be received with open mouth; which thence may passe by the weazon into the chest, by the palate and nostrils into the braine: but in the interim let the head bee vailed, that none of the vapour may flye away. Moist fumigations are made somewhiles of the decoction of herbes, otherwhiles of some one simple medicine boiled in oile, sometimes a hot fire-stone is quencht in vinegar, wine, aqua vitae, or the like liquor, so to raise a humide vapour. We oft time use this kinde of fumigation in overcoming scirrhous affects, when as we would cut, discusse, penetrate deep, and dry: take this as an example thereof.

"℞. *laterem unum satis crassum, aut marchasitam ponderis* ℔ i. heat it red hot, and then let it bee quencht in sharpe vinegar, powring thereon in the meane while a little *aqua vitae*, make a fumigation for the grieved part.

"Fumes of the decoction of herbes doe very little differ from fomentations properly so called; for they differ not in the manner of their composure, but onely in the application to the affected parts: therefore let this be an example of a humide fumigation.

"℞. *absinth, salv. rut. origan. an.* p. i. *rad. bryon. & asar. an.* ℥β. *sem. sinap. & cumin. an.* ℥ ii. *decoquantur in duabus partibus aquae, & una vini pro suffitu auris cum emboto.*"[1]    It will be observed that the substance smoked must be fatty or viscous, such as pitch.    This at once leads to Lat. *bitumen* and Arabic *dibq* or (dialectically) *tibq*, hence *tubbaq*, as the designation for the substance smoked.    Before doing so, we shall show that smoking was popularized in the Spanish peninsula by the Arabs, who left many proofs of the fact in the languages of Europe.

[1] Th. Johnson, *The Workes of that famous Chirurgion Ambrose Parey*, London 1634, p. 1072 f.

# CHAPTER II.

## THE SMOKE VENDER.

In Portuguese we have *bufarinha* "a peddler's tray, trifles, cosmetics," *bufarinheiro, bofarinheiro* "peddler." This is unquestionably from Arabic بوخارى *būḫāriy* "seller of incense, cosmetics," from بوخار *būḫār,* باخور *bāḫūr* "fumigation, smoke, incense." Indeed, in the Spanish-Arabic dictionary[1] we get for "sahumar," that is, "to use incense or smoke," the Arabic *baḳár,* for "sahumaduras" *boḳór.* This *bufarinheiro* was early corrupted into *bufo,* as which it appears in the thirteenth century Portuguese documents as the designation for a small trader. A *bofon* paid the lowest tax in the Foro of Ericeira of 1229.[2] The same is recorded at Ega (1231)[3] and at Midões (1257),[4] while at Coja (1260) a *bufonus* is mentioned as crying his wares (*preconizare*).[5] By a Spanish law of 1562[6] the *buhoneros* were not permitted to walk the streets or enter the houses in order to sell their *buhonerias,* even though these could legitimately be sold. These vagabond hawkers had obviously never been in favor, and their wares were considered as trifles. No wonder, then, that in the XIV. century a *bufo* should have been classed with jugglers and should have received the designation of a buffoon. The *bufonerus* originally sold cosmetics, just like the

---

[1] P. de Lagarde, *Petri Hispani de lingua arabica libri duo,* Gottingae 1883.
[2] *Portugaliae monumenta historica,* Olisipone 1856, vol. I, p. 621.
[3] *Ibid.,* p. 622.
[4] *Ibid.,* p. 674.
[5] *Ibid.,* p. 696.
[6] *Novisima recopilacion,* IX. 6. 10.

Portuguese *bufarinheiro*, and the Span. *albafor*, Port. *albafar* "incense, perfume" still bear witness to the Arabic origin of the trade. But we have also the abbreviated Span., Port. *bafo*, *baho* "breath, exhalation," Port. *baforada* "breath, bad odor." The latter word also means "cheating, boasting" and the relation to *bufo* "buffoon" is at once obvious. Hence we have Port. *bafejar*, *bofar* "to boast, blabber, breathe," hence Span., Port. *bofe* "lung," *bufar* "to boast, to snort." The other Romance words related to these need not be adduced here.

We shall now treat of the particular kind of *bufarinheiro* which was developed in Africa and America, as this will bear upon the distribution of African plants in America. In the pharmacy of the XVI. century, and unquestionably much earlier, *pulpa* was the technical term for a jamlike extract from exotic fruits, such as *pulpa cassiae, colocynthidis*. This was readily confused with *pulmentum*, which may itself be a derivative of *pulpa*, but which, in any case, was early understood, like *pulpa*, to refer to sweetmeats or delicacies, hence Joannes Janua wrote: "*pulmentum* is said of delicate and sweet food, from *pulpa*, similarly *pulmentum* or *pulmentarium* is said of any food other than bread."[1] We, therefore, read in the Italian "*polpa di fichi secchi*," and "si adulterano i tamarindi colla *polpa delle susine*." Similarly the Portuguese dictionary records "a *polpa do figo* fartum" and "*polpa de canafistula* concretum casiae stramentum." But the Portuguese has also "*polme*, the denser part of a liquor" and translates it similarly by "crassamentum." There is also here a corrupted *pombinha*, the fleshy part of the thigh of an ox, "bubulis cruris pulpa intima," which is obviously related to the Latin *pulpa*.

[1] Ducange, sub *pulmentum*.

In the Bantu countries of Africa there is made a liquor known as *pombe*. André Fernandes, writing from Mozambique, in 1560, said: "As the millet is the best and chief part of their provisions and they use what would feed them for thirty days to make a drink called *empombe* for one occasion, it is said that they often die of hunger."[1] A fuller description of the preparation of *pombe* was given by João dos Santos, in 1605: "The wine usually drunk by these Kaffirs is made of millet, and is called *pombe*. It is made in the following manner: first they soak about three gallons of millet in water, where it remains for two days, in the course of which it sprouts; the water is then drained off, and it is left to dry for two or three hours, and when it is well dried, they pound it thoroughly to a pulp. This is done in a large wooden mortar which reaches to a man's waist, which the Kaffirs call *cuni*, and the Portuguese *pilão*, as has been said. This being done, they place a large cauldron half full of water on the fire, and when it boils they gradually mix in about a gallon and a half of millet flour, as if making a broth, and when it has boiled a little they take the cauldron off the fire and throw into it the pulp made of the ground millet, mixing it until it dissolves. The cauldron is then left for two days, during which the liquor cooks and boils without fire, like the must of grapes, and after these two days they drink it. They make it in this manner every day. This *pombe* is as intoxicating as wine if much of it is drunk; it is so sustaining that many Kaffirs eat and drink nothing else, but live on *pombe* alone. If they leave it in the cauldron for four or five days it becomes very sour, and the more sour it is the more intoxicating

[1] G. McC. Theal, *Records of South-Eastern Africa,* [London] 1898, vol. II, p. 64.

it becomes, and the Kaffirs esteem it greatly so, because they say it gives them more strength."[1]

It is clear that in *pombe* we have a Portuguese word, related to *pombinho* and meaning "fruit, pulp." A word for wine and wine itself could not have been fostered by the Arabs, who are opposed to it. At the same time the word *pombe* is not universal in the Bantu languages but only coincides with the Portuguese trade, hence it is found also in non-Bantu languages. In Angola, *mbombo* is fermented manioc from which *fuba* is made. In the Kongo we have "a fermented liquor made from maize and cassava or manioc. The maize is malted by placing it on the ground, sprinkling with water, and covering with leaves until it sprouts; when the grain has run out roots about an inch long it is dried by exposure to strong sunshine for a day or two, when it becomes menia. It is sweet, and is proper malted grain. Cassava is peeled and dried in the sun, when it is called kela. The menia and kela are then pounded together in a mortar until fairly crushed. It is then mixed with a due proportion of water, and the mash thus made is boiled for 12 hours, strained and left to cool. It is then a sweet, not intoxicating beverage called mulu. After two or three days it ferments and becomes intoxicating, sour, and more or less acid, and is called *mbamvu*."[2] In Swahili we have "*pombe* native beer, an intoxicant made from many kinds of grains and some fruits, e. g. bananas, by fermentation." In Hausa we get *bumbo, bam, bummi* "palmwine," which is "obtained by direct incision into the stems of the palm-tree, it begins to ferment on the second or third day."

[1] *Ibid.*, vol. VII, p. 210. See also vols. II, pp. 293, 329, VII, pp. 190, 196, 307, VIII, p. 110.

[2] W. H. Bentley, *Dictionary and Grammar of the Kongo Language*, London 1887, p. 19.

Having fostered the habit of intoxication among the natives, the Portuguese early employed native traders to corrupt the Negroes by the sale of *pombe*. Such traders were known as *pombeiros*. We have a good description of such *pombeiros* in the Congo region by Dapper, who unfortunately tried to derive the word from that of a mythical country, *Pombo*, in the interior of Africa. "The country properly called *Pombo*, lies more than one hundred leagues landwards from the seacoast, or from the city of Lovango and, as some say, towards Abyssinia. Some think that what the Portuguese call *Pombo*, is a collection of kingdoms and lands near a certain large sea (I think the sea of Zambre which lies in the interior between both the seas). But it is quite uncertain where that place is, since no Christian has ever been there; but it is said that a certain Kaffir of Mozambique who traveled over land from Sofala to Angola has come to it, as the Portuguese report. All the blacks who dwell at the sea-coast, receive their laws, rights and privileges from *Pombo*.

"Both the Portuguese who live in Lovango, Congo, and Lovango Saint Paul, have a great trade with this *Pombo*, through their trusted slaves, whom they bring up in their houses and send thither with merchandise, who for slaves, elephants' teeth (but these are not as large as those which come from Bukkameale), and *panos limpos*, barter Canary, Spanish, or Madeira wine, large *simbos* from the island of Lovando, beads, and other wares. The masters let these their slaves, generally called *pomberos* after the emporium *Pombo*, if they show any aptitude, be instructed in reading, writing, and arithmetic, as much as is necessary for the trade. These *pomberos* have yet other slaves under them, some times as many as one hundred or one hundred and fifty, who carry the goods upon their heads up in the country, such as wine in pots called *pereleros*, which are

covered with esparto or a certain Spanish grass of which
frails are made.

"Sometimes these *pomberos* stay out a year, sometimes eighteen months and two years, and then bring
back with them four, five, and six hundred slaves.
Some of the most trusted remain up in the country and
send the slaves they have bought to their masters, who
return to them other commodities.   Occasionally dis-
honest *pomberos* deceive their masters and run away
with the slaves and commodities.

"The whites or Portuguese are obliged to carry on
the trade through these their Negroes or *pomberos*, because, according to their statement, it is impossible for
white men to carry on the trade, because of the difficulty of the journey, the hunger and trouble they have
to undergo, and especially on account of the unwhole-
someness of the country and the like.   The country is
said to be so unwholesome that the heat of the sun
makes the head swell to double its size.

"The journey from the seacoast, from Lovango and
Lovango Saint Paul to *Pombo*, is slow, on account of the
difficulty of the road, and because of the rocky mountains and many ravines which sometimes, after a rain,
hold up the travelers for ten or fourteen days."[1]

Diogo de Couto long before that pointed out the fact
that the Portuguese from Tete carried on their trade far
inland by means of natives:   "Those who wish to do so
go themselves, others send their Kaffirs, as some of these
merchants have one or two hundred Kaffir slaves whom
they employ in this trade, and they are so faithful that
up to the present no one was ever known to be guilty of
any dishonesty, or to remain there with his master's
property."[2]   It is clear that *pombeiro* originally meant

[1] O. Dapper, *Naukeurige Beschrijvinge der Afrikaensche Gewesten van
Egypten, Barbaryen, Lybien, Biledulgerid, Negroslant, Guinea, Ethiopiën,
Abyssinie:* Amsterdam 1676, p. 219 f.
[2] Theal, *op. cit.,* vol. VI, p. 368.

"a wine dealer," and that the mythical *Pombo* is merely the interior where the *pombeiros* carried on business in the name of their Portuguese masters. Just as the *bufarinheiro* was a peddler who began by corrupting the people's manners with illicit fumigations, that is, smoking, so the *pombeiro* began his career as a liquor dealer. The Kimbundu dictionary[1] gives *púmbêla* as a native word and translates it by "a kind of *bufarinheiro*, merchants' agent for the retail trade." Without these *pombeiros* the trade with the interior of Africa would have been well nigh impossible, and Dapper tells of their traveling two hundred leagues inland.[2] History does not record the deeds of the lowly, and these vanguards of European civilization have passed away unnoticed.

In 1603 "the king of Congo now reigning is a tyrant and shows the same bad will as the previous kings in everything he can, because every time that he wants to close the roads to the *pombeiros* who in his country trade cloth, he does so."[3] A description of the *pombeiros* was given by Vieira in his *Arte de furtar:* "The Portuguese go to Guinea, Angola, Cafraria, and Mozambique, filling ships with Negroes . . . For these purposes they have instructed people, whom they call *pombeiros* and the Negroes call *tangomaos:* these carry cloths, iron articles, and trifles which they give for slaves, and these they fetch naked and in chains."[4] From all this it follows that the *pombeiros* were active before the XVII. century, in fact, must have had their beginning with the first Portuguese settlement in Guinea, in the middle of the fifteenth century.

[1] J. Cordeiro da Matta, *Ensaio de diccionario kimbúndu-portuguez,* Lisboa 1893, p. 128.
[2] *Op. cit.,* p. 234.
[3] L. Cordeiro, *Da Mina ao Cabo Negro,* in *Memorias do Ultramar. Viagens, explorações e conquistas dos Portuguezes,* part 2 (of 1574-1620), Lisboa 1881, p. 8.
[4] A. Vieira, *Arte de furtar,* in *Historia do futuro,* Lisboa 1855, cap. XLVI.

Vieira's *tangomao* throws a light upon the Portuguese trade in Africa. A law of the year 1565[1] provides "that when the heir of a *tangomão*, deceased in some part of Guinea, asks the Hospital of all the Saints of the City of Lisbon to restitute to him the property left after such a *tangomão* he has to go through certain formalities in order to ascertain the death of the *tangomão*." In 1607 a large number of *tangos maos* congregated at Cape Verde, to trade with the Negroes in ivory, gold, wax, and slaves,[2] to which the editor quotes from Father Fernão Guerreiro's *Relação annua*, 1605: "The *tangos maos* or *lançados* with the Negroes and who are slave traders in the interior; who are a sort of people who by nativity are Portuguese and by religion or baptism Christians, but who live in such a fashion as if they were neither, for many of them walk about naked, and who accomodate themselves to the native customs of the country where they trade. They mark their bodies with an iron, drawing blood and tattooing them, by anointing them with the juice of certain herbs, making various figures appear, such as locusts, snakes, or whatever they like, and in this way they march through this Guinea trading and buying slaves." Guerreiro tells of a number of Europeans who settled in Africa and became thoroughly Negroized.[3]

[1] *Boletim do conselho ultramarino, Legislação antiga,* Lisboa 1867, vol. I, p. 85 f.

[2] L. Cordeiro, *op. cit.,* part V (of 1607), *Estabelecimentos e resgates portuguezes na costa occidental de Africa,* Lisboa 1881, p. 8 f.

[3] "Neste reino achei hum Christam crioulo da ilhade Sanctiago que auia muytos annos viuia como gentio sem mais differença que enxergarse nelle ainda algum lume da Fè. Estranheilhe quanto era rezam o estado em que estaua, & o nam se ter ido confessar comigo despois que vim a estas partes podendoo fazer, conheceose & humilhouse, & prometeo que viria comprir com esta obrigaçam, & traria consigo hum filho que tinha de dezasete. ou dezoito annos pera eu o bautizar, & instruir nas cousas de sua saluaçam oqual comprio dahi a algum tempo, & o filho depois de bautizado ficou encarregado a hum Portugues casado que o cria, & ensina com muyto charidade, & elle se foy a buscar isso que tinha pera se vir morar entre os Christãos. Tambem achei hum Alemam que tomaram com certos cossarios nas ilhas que chamam dos idolos pertencentes ao mesmo Fatema, & por

Somewhat earlier Alvares d'Almada wrote: "Among these Negroes there are many who can talk our Portuguese language, and are dressed like ourselves. And there are also many Portuguese (ladinas) Negresses called *Tangomas*, because they serve the *lançados*. And these Negresses and Negroes go with them from one river to another and to the Island of Santiago and elsewhere."[1] Among the Balolas "there are many *lançados*, because the country is pacified and quiet, and many congregate there for the sake of barter, both of slaves (who are very cheap here), and of produce, because these Negroes are more addicted to work."[2]

Alvares d'Almada gives us a detailed account of these *lançados* or "outcasts:" "This kingdom of Budumel has many parts, besides those of the Senegal River, and beginning there and running down the coast as far as Sereno, the two principal ones being Angra and Biziguiche, which is a very beautiful bay, constant refuge of the English and French, where a large number of ships can stay without peril from the weather, since they are protected from the winds. And in this very Angra there is an island which is in the lee of the winds, and between it and the mainland there is a large channel where the ships can stay; and between this island and the land the French have several times escaped our galleys. In this island a very good port could be built,

ser grande tangedor de trombeta bastarda lho mandaram. Fallaua ja bem a lingoa da terra, & viuia como os outros gentios tam contente, que nem consentimento quis dar peraque eu o pedisse disse ao Rey, & tambem fora difficultoso tirarlho das mãos porque hia ensinando a tanger a alguns moços da terra. He lastima ver como andam estes homens entre gentios, sem se lembrar que sam Christãos, & sem se quererem apartar delles polla largueza, & liberdade de consciencia em que viuem. Em Bena achei tres, ou quatro tam arreigados na terra, que por mais que fiz pollos tirar della com nenhum delles o pude acabar." F. Guerreiro, *Relaçam annal das cousas que fizeram os padres da Companhia de Jesus, nas partes da India Oriental*, Lisboa 1611, fol. 234.

[1] A Alvares d'Almada, *Tratado breve dos rios de Guiné do Cabo-Verde*, ed. by D. Kopke, Porto 1841, p 60.

[2] *Ibid.*, p. 66.

and with little cost, because from the land shore the
island is protected by a rock built by nature itself, and
on the ocean side it can be fortified at little cost, and
being fortified would keep the enemy from making port,
and with brigantines (which are vessels of little cost)
one could keep the *lançados* from giving aid and solace
to the enemies, as they now do.   This island serves the
English and French as a refuge, where they congregate
their ships and boats; and is the narrows through which
most of the hostile ships pass, those that make for
Sierra Leone, as well as for the Pepper Coast, for Brazil,
or for the Spanish Indies.   All of them stop at Angra,
and here overhaul and repair their ships, and live on it,
and consider it their own, as if it were one of the English
or French ports; so much so that the Negroes of these
ports speak very good French, and many times travel
to France, and now, since they are friendly with the
English, travel to England, to learn English and see the
country, by order of the Alcaide of the Port of Ale, who
serves as a commercial agent of the king.   This Angra
is almost at the point of Cape Verde, between it and
Cape Mastros, but nearer to Cape Verde.  Anciently the
greatest business done by the inhabitants of the Island
of Santiago was with this land of Budumel, in the days
when in it ruled a king named Nhogor, a great friend of
our nation, in the days when the locusts had caused
such a famine on the coast that slaves were sold for a
half a bushel of corn or beans, and the mothers drew
among their children and sold them for food, saying
that it was better to live, even as slaves, than to die of
mere hunger.   And from the Cape Verde Isle each year
went loads of horses and other wares for this trade.

"There succeeded in this reign the king called Budumel Bixirin, who drank no wine and ate no pork.   He
lived constantly in his court at Lambaya, along the sea,
and treated our people badly and gathered at his ports

the French, whom he liked, and for this cause the inhabitants of the island lost the business, which is now more in the hands of the English than of the French, to both of them succor is given by many Portugese and some strangers, who live at the port of Joala, in the land of the Barbacins, in the kingdom of Ale-Embicone. And these Portuguese are those who aid the English and the French, despatching their business from river to river and many leagues inland. And every year the English and French export a large quantity of hides of oxen, buffaloes, gazelles, and other animals called *dacoy* at the Gambia River, which they say is the true *anta*, and also much ivory, wax, gum, amber, musk, and gold, and other things, bartering these for iron and other wares brought from England and France, and these our Portuguese *lançados* are much fondled by these our enemies. And on the days when they receive their pay and hand in their goods the English give them banquets on land, with much music of fiddles and other instruments, and thus the whole trade from Cape Verde to the Gambia River is lost. And nobody does business there except these *lançados* with the enemies, who at S. Domingos River and Grande River do business with those who live there, whither they send their iron and whatever else they have, and they send their wares to our enemies; and if it were not for these Portuguese *lançados*, these two nations would not have such business or commerce in Guinea as they have nowadays, because the pagans have not the ability to give them such business, since they do not navigate and do not carry the goods inland except at a great loss. Now these Portuguese *lançados* roam all the rivers and lands of the Negroes, acquiring everything they find there for the ships of their friends, so much so that there is a Portuguese who went inland as far as the Kingdom of the Great Fulo, which is many leagues away, and from there he sent

much ivory to the Senegal River, whence the ships at
Angra fetch it in their boats.   This Portuguese *lançado*
went to the kingdom of the Great Fulo by order of Duke
Casão, who is a powerful Negro living in a port in the
Gambia River above sixty marine leagues.   He sent
him with his people, and at the court of the Great Fulo
he married a daughter of his, with whom he had a
daughter, and wishing to return to the seaport, his father-
in-law permitted him to take her along, and his name is
João Ferreira, native of Crato, and called by the Negroes
Ganagoga, which in the language of the Beafares means
'man who talks all the languages,' as, indeed, he speaks
the Negro languages, and this man can traverse all the
hinterland of our Guinea, of whatever Negro tribe.   And
with the aid of these *lançados* the trade of our enemies
is growing in Guinea, and ours is disappearing."[1]

Jobson describes these *lançados* under the name of
*Portingales:* "I must breake of a while from them,
and acquainte you first, of another sort of people we
finde dwelling, or rather lurking, amongst these Mandingos, onely some certaine way up the Riuer.

"And these are, as they call themselves, *Portingales*,
and some few of them seeme the same; others of them
are *Molatoes*, betweene blacke and white, but the most
part as blacke, as the naturall inhabitants: they are
scattered, some two or three dwellers in a place, and
are all married, or rather keepe with them the countrey
blacke women, of whom they beget children, howbeit
they haue amongest them, neither Church, nor Frier,
nor any other religious order.   It doth manifestly appeare, that they are such, as haue beene banished, or
fled away, from forth either of *Portingall*, or the Iles
belonging vnto that gouernement, they doe generally
imploy themselues in buying such commodities the
countrey affords, wherein especially they couet the

[1] *Ibid.*, p. 13 ff.

country people, who are sold vnto them, when they commit offences, as you shall reade where I write of the generall gouernement: all which things they are ready to vent, vnto such as come into the riuer, but the blacke people are bought away by their owne nation, and by them either carried, or solde vnto the Spaniard, for him to carry into the West *Indies*, to remaine as slaues, either in their Mines, or in any other seruile vses, they in those countries put them to: Some few of these sorting themselues together, in one time of the yeare, haue vsed to go vp this Riuer, in a boate or small barke, as farre as *Setico*, and there to remaine in trade, from whence it is certainely knowne they haue returned much gold, aboue which place they neuer attempted, which is not halfe the way, we haue already gone vp, since our trading there. With these, in their places of dwelling, wee are very conuersant, notwithstanding, we receiued such a horrible treachery from them, as is set downe in my beginning, in regarde they tell vs, those that were the Actors thereof, are banished from amongst them, as being hated and detested for the fact. Howsoeuer, wee hope, and desire it may stand, for all our Nations warning, neuer to let them haue the like occasion, but beleeue, euer they will doe as they say, in telling vs they do loue and wish vs wel, prouided they may neuer haue vs vnder their power, to be able to doe vs ill, which it behooueth vs to take especiall care of.

"The conditions they liue subiect vnto, vnder the the black Kings, makes it appeare, they haue little comfort in any Christian countrey, or else themselues are very carelesse what becommeth of their posteritie; for whensoeuer the husband, father, or maister of the familie dies, if hee be of any worth, the King seizeth vpon what hee hath, without respect, either to wife, children, or seruant, except they haue warning to prouide before, or are capable of themselues, to looke out for the future time; whereby we finde in some those few places we trade with them, poore distressed children left, who as it were exposed to the charitie of the country, become in a manner naturalized, and as they grow up, apply themselves to buy and sell one thing for another as the whole country doth, still reseruing carefully, the vse of the *Portingall* tongue, and with a kinde of an affectionate zeale, the name of Christians, taking it in a great disdaine, be they neuer so blacke, to be called a *Negro*: and these, for the most part, are the *Portingalls*, which liue within this Riuer.''[1]

A *tangomao, tangomão* was, accordingly, a European naturalized in Africa or a Negro speaking Portuguese, who traveled through the country for barter, that is, a *pombeiro*. Obviously the word is supposed to be a Guinea word, and we can identify it and pursue its history. We have the word in many of the Mandingo dialects, but generally in that fragmentary form which causes the despair of the philologist. In Dyula we have *tarhama* "to march, travel," hence *tarha* "to walk, go away." This is in Bambara contracted to *tama* "march, travel," *tamaba* "traveler," but also "lance," which shows that the latter was formed under Portuguese influence, on account of the meaning of *lançado* "trader," that is, "traveler." In Malinke the Bambara "lance" word *tama* (or *tamba*) remains, but otherwise we have *tokhoma* "march, travel," while *takha* is "to walk." In Vei we have *tamba* "lance," but *ta* "to walk," while Mandingo has *tama* "to walk."

The Dyula *tarhama* is clearly Arabic طرجمان *tarǧamān* "interpreter," which leads to Eng. *dragoman*, etc., precisely as *tangomão* is "one who speaks two languages," hence "trader," and that this is unquestionably the case is proved by the use of the corresponding word in French

[1] R. Jobson, *The Golden Trade: or, A Discouery of the Riuer Gambra, and the Golden Trade of the Aethiopians*, London 1623, p. 28 ff.

for the Indianized French trader in Brazil in the XVI. century. Nicholas Barré tells of a Norman *truchement*, who had been given to Villegaignon and who had been married to an Indian woman and lived in a truly Indian fashion.[1] This was about the year 1550. About the same time Hans von Staden found in Brazil a number of "mammelucks" of a Portuguese father and Indian mother, who were as savage as any Indian,[2] while a little later, in 1587, Soares de Sousa described the large number of descendants of French fathers and Indian women, who had turned Indian in their habits: "When the French returned home with their ships filled with brazil wood, cotton, and pepper, they left among the natives a few lads to learn the language and to help them in the country, when they would return to France, to carry on their barter. These became naturalized in the country where they lived and did not wish to return to France and lived like the natives, with many wives, from whom and from those who every year came from France to Bahia and the Segeripe River, the land was filled with mammelucks, who were born, lived and died as Indians; of these there are now many descendants, who are blonde, white-skinned and freckled, but are considered to be Tupinamba Indians, and are more savage than they."[3]

[1] "Nous auons sceu que ce auoit esté conduict par vn truchement, lequel auoit, esté donné audict seigneur par vn gentilhomme Normand, qui auoit accompagné ledict seigneur iusques en ce lieu. Ce truchemēt estoit marié auec vne femme Sauuage, laquelle il ne voulait ny laisser ne la tenir pour femme. Or ledict seigneur de Villegaignon, en son commencement regla la maison en hōme de bien, & craignant Dieu: deffendāt que nul hōme n'eust affaire à ces chiēnes Sauuages, & sur peine de la mort. Ce truchement auoit vescu (comme tous les autres viuent) en la plus grande abomination & vie Epicurienne, qu'il est impossible la raconter: sans Dieu, sans foy, ne loy, l'espace de sept ans." N. Barré, *Copie de quelques letres sur la navigation du chevallier de Villegaignon es terres de l'Amérique oultre l'Aequinoctial, iusques soulz le tropique de Capricorne*, Paris 1558, second letter.

[2] A. Tootal, *The Captivity of Hans Stade of Hesse in A. D. 1547-1555, among the Wild Tribes of Eastern Brazil* (The Hakluyt Society), London 1874, p. 44 f.

[3] G. Soares de Sousa, *Tratado descriptivo do Brasil em 1587*, Rio de Janeiro 1879, p. 309 (cap. CLXXVII).

That the same Negro *pombeiros* were active in America is shown by a large number of documents. The Spanish did not develop the word *pombe*, but stuck closer to the Latin *pulpa*, as a base of a word for native liquor, hence *pulpería* is, according to the Spanish dictionary of the Academy, "in America, a shop where all kinds of products are sold, wine, brandy, liquor, and things referring to drugs, *buhonería*, market wares, but not cloth or any other textile." But the word varies in meaning in the different Spanish countries of America.[1] Simon[2] says that "a *pulpero* is he who sells in public Spanish and native fruit, but not cloth, especially uncooked eatables" and gives an atrocious etymology for the word. Garcilasso de la Vega[3] says that in Peru a *pulpero* was the humblest kind of vender, and gives the same etymology, while Escalona more specifically says[4] that wine, bread, honey, cheese, butter, oil, bananas, sails and other trifles were sold there, although a law of the year 1623[5] prohibited the manufacture of sails by a *pulpero*, and as early as 1586 a *pulpero* could not sell any "vino cocido," that is, distilled wine. Solorzano[6] says that such a shop was in the Indies called *pulpería* or *pulquería*, from *pulque*, the intoxicating drink used by the Indians of New Spain.

There can be little doubt that Span. *pulpa* entered into the American languages, whither it was carried as *pulque*, even as the corresponding Arabic term حشيش *ḥašiš* has survived in Spanish and Portuguese *chicha*

---

[1] D. Granada, *Vocabulario rioplatense razonado*, Montevideo 1890, p. 329 ff., and L. Wiener, *Pseudo-Karaibisches*, in *Zeitschrift für Romanische Philologie*, vol. XXXIII, p. 526 ff.

[2] *Primera parte de las noticias historiales de las conquistas de Tierra Firme en las Indias*, [Cuence 1627], in the vocabulary.

[3] *Historia general del Peru*, Cordova 1617, parte II, lib. VI, cap. XX.

[4] G. de Escalona y Aguero, *Gazophilativm regivm pervbicvm*, Matriti 1675, parte II, lib. II, cap. XXIV.

[5] *Recopilaciones*, IV. 18. 14.

[6] J. de Solorzano Pereira, *Politica indiana*, Madrid 1647, p. 751.

"meat for children," that is, "soft food," hence intoxicating drink made from "mash." Ramos i Duarte[1] derives *chicha* in the latter sense from Nahuatl *chichilia* "to ferment," while D. Granada[2] says that *chicha* is derived from the Peruvian. This is at once made impossible from the fact that *chicha* is mentioned before either Mexico or Peru was discovered, namely in a document of the year 1516, from Castilla del Oro: "las esposas del dicho cacique me enviaban siempre *chicha*, de su mano fecha."[3] *Chich* is an onomatopoetic sound used for "suck the breast" in a very large number of unconnected languages, and it is a mere coincidence that we have Nahuatl *chicha* "spittle," *chichi* "to suck," *chichina* "to suck, smoke incense through a pipe." The Portuguese dictionary[4] says: "*chicha*, a plebeian word, beef; in general, a certain portion of agreeable food or drink, fried food, cake, pastry, sweets, wine, etc. This is the meaning given to it in the northern provinces of Portugal, food as for children, nursing women, or any food which they enjoy." It is just the kind of word slaves would pick up, and Portuguese *pombinho*, Spanish *pulpa* indicate at once that the *pulpería, pulquería* was an establishment to cater to the sweet tooth of the lowly. The dissemination of *chicha* and *pulque* over America at once shows that the Europeans or the Negro slaves may be responsible for the inebriety of the Indians, so frequently reported by the early writers. The very method of preparing *chicha* by masticating the grain, as reported from Peru and elsewhere, is common in Africa where the fruit of the baobab is masticated and made into a sherbet.[5]

[1] F. Ramos i Duarte, *Diccionario de mejicanismos*, Méjico 1895, p. 165.
[2] *Op. cit.*, p. 190 ff.
[3] *Colección de documentos inéditos del archivo de Indias*, vol. II, p. 485.
[4] A. de Moraes é Silva, *Diccionario da lingua portugueza*, Lisboa 1877, vol. I.
[5] P. A. Benton, *Notes on some Languages of the Western Sudan*, London 1912, p. 190.

The same Portuguese dictionary quotes from a letter
of Vieira to the effect that in the Maranhão in Brazil a
*pombeiro* traded in slaves, and Vieira, in his *Arte de furtar*, says that the same practice as in Africa prevailed
in Brazil in connection with the *pombeiros*, and *pombeiro* has survived in Brazil as the name of a chicken
peddler.  But African *pombeiros* were known in the
West Indies before the so-called discovery of America
by Columbus.  When Columbus started out, in 1498,
on his Third Journey, "he wished to go to the south,
because he intended with the aid of the 'Holy Trinity'
to find islands and lands, that God may be served and
their Highnesses and Christianity may have pleasure,
and that he wishes to prove or test the opinion of King
Don Juan of Portugal, who said that there was conti-
nental land to the south:  and because of this, he says
that he had a contention with the Sovereigns of Castile,
and finally the Admiral says that it was concluded that
the King of Portugal should have 370 leagues to the
west from the islands of the Azores and Cape Verde,
from north to south, from pole to pole.  And the Admiral says further that the said King Don Juan was certain that within those limits famous lands and things
must be found.  Certain principal inhabitants of the
island of Santiago came to see them and they say that
to the south-west of the island of Huego, which is one
of the Cape Verdes distant 12 leagues from this, may
be seen an island, and that the King Don Juan was
greatly inclined to send to make discoveries to the
south-west, and *that canoes had been found which start
from the coast of Guinea and navigate to the west with
merchandise.*"[1]   "He ordered the course laid to the way
of the south-west, which is the route leading from
these islands to the south, in the name, he says, of the
Holy and Individual Trinity, because then he would

[1] J. B. Thacher, *Christopher Columbus*, New York 1903, vol. II, p. 379.

be on a parallel with the lands of the Sierra of Loa and Cape of Sancta Ana in Guinea, which is below the equinoctial line, where he says that below that line of the world are found more gold and things of value: and that after, he would navigate, the Lord pleasing, to the west, and from there would go to this Española, in which route he would prove the theory of the King Juan aforesaid: and *that he thought to investigate the report of the Indians of this Española who said that there had come to Española from the south and south-east, a black people who have the tops of their spears made of a metal which they call 'guanin,' of which he had sent samples to the Sovereigns to have them assayed, when it was found that of 32 parts, 18 were of gold, 6 of silver and 8 of copper."*[1]

There can be no question whatsoever as to the reality of the statement in regard to the presence in America of the African *pombeiros* previous to Columbus, because the *guani* is a Mandingo word,[2] and the very alloy is of African origin. In 1501 a law was passed forbidding persons to sell *guanin* to the Indians of Hispaniola.[3]

---

[1] *Ibid.*, p. 380.

[2] See *Africa and the Discovery of America*, vol. I, p. 32 f.

[3] "Sepades que a nos es fecha Relacion que perteneciendo como pertenecen a nos todos los mineros de metales e otras cosas que ay e se hayan hallado e descubierto fasta aqui e se hallaren e descubrieren de aqui adelante en las dichas yslas e tierra firme del dicho mar oceano algunas personas syn tener para ello nuestra licencia e mandado se han entremetydo a descobrir e sacar mineros de ciertos metales que se disen *gumines* en las yslas de la paria e de quibacoa e otras de las dichas yslas e tierra firme e lo han traydo e traen a vender a los yndios de la dicha ysla española e a otras partes lo qual es en nuestro perjuicio e de nuestras rentas e patrimonio Real de nuestros Reynos e señorios e que nuestra merced e voluntad es que lo suso dicho no se haga de aqui adelante acordamos de mandar dar esta nuestra carta en la dicha razon por lo qual defendemos e hordenamos e mandamos que ningunos ni alguna persona o personas nuestros subditos e naturales vezinos e moradores de nuestros Reynos e señorios e de las dichas islas e tierrafirme ni otras qualesquier personas de Reynos e provincias escrivymos no sean osados de buscar ni descobrir ni llevar a vender á los

But in 1503 *guanines* were still imported secretly.[1]  In
the same year twenty-nine pieces of *guanin* were to be
returned from Spain to Hispaniola, because they were
a base alloy that had more value there than in Spain.[2]
When we turn to Africa we learn that the natives were
given to the adulteration of gold in precisely the manner objected to.  Bosman wrote:  "The Gold which is
brought us by the Dinkirans is very pure, except only
that 'tis too much mixed with Fetiche's, which are a sort
of artificial Gold composed of several Ingredients; among
which some of them are very odly shaped:  These
Fetiche's they cast (in Moulds made of a sort of black
and very heavy Earth) into what Form they please; and
*this artificial Gold is frequently mixed with a third part,
and sometimes with half Silver and Copper*, and consequently less worth, and yet we are pestered with it on
all parts of the Coast;  and if we refuse to receive it,
some Negroes are so unreasonable that they will unde-
niably take back all their pure Gold:  So that we are

yndios de la dicha ysla española ni a otras partes los dichos *guanines* ni otros
metales ni mineros de las dichas yslas de la paria e cuquibacoa ni de otras
algunas de las dichas yslas e tierra firme syn tener para ello nuestra licencia
e mandado so pena quel que lo contrario fiçyere por el mismo fecho sin otra
sentençia ni declaracion alguna aya perdido e pierda los dichos *guanines*
e mineros e metales e todos sus bienes los que desde agora aplicamos a nuestra
camara e fisco e el cargo sea a la nuestra merced," *Colección de documentos
inéditos de Ultramar*, Madrid 1890, series II, vol. V, p. 20 f.

[1] "En quanto a lo que dezis que Rodrigo de la bastida trae muchos
*guaninos* e cosas de algodon que en esa ysla valen mucho mas que aca e
que lo deviamos mandar conpartir para lo tomar e enviar allá, en esto nos lo
mandaremos proveer para que se faga asy," *ibid.*, p. 47.

[2] "Y en lo que dezis de las veynte y nueve piezas de *guanynes* que
recivystes y que vos envie a mandar sy se fundirian para sacar el oro que
tiene ó sy se tornaran a enviar al my governador de la ysla española, pues
que alla valen mas cantidad que aca, en quanto a esto yze por la carta quel
dicho my governador me escrivio abreys visto como por ella dize que los
*guanynes* el los avia fecho dexar alla en la ysla y que enviaba á my ciertas
piezas de cobre rico;  asy que vos debeys ynformar sy estas veynte y nueve
piezas que recivystes son de *guanynes* ó de cobre, e savyda la verdad dello
ynformadme de lo ques. para que yo vos envie á mandar lo que fagays,"
*ibid.*, p. 61.

obliged sometimes to suffer them to shuffle in some of it. There are also Fetiche's cast of unalloyed Mountain Gold; which very seldom come to our Hands, because they keep them to adorn themselves: So that if ever we meet with them, those who part with them are obliged to it by Necessity, or they are filled with the mentioned black heavy Earth."[1] But long before, in 1602, Marees[2] has a long chapter on the deception practised by the Negroes with just such an alloy.

Now, that the presence of *pombeiros* in America before Columbus is made certain, we can at once see why tobacco should have been introduced by them before Columbus, and the passages in all the early writers on America receive a new interpretation. The African slaves, who swarmed in Spain and Portugal ever since the discovery of the Guinea Coast by the Portuguese, that is, since 1440, had become acquainted with the customs and vices of their surroundings and had carried these back to Guinea where they, as *pombeiros*, spread the new ideas into the interior and, simultaneously, into the New World, which their masters, the traders, kept from the knowledge of the authorities, in order to carry on their illicit and profitable trade without molestation from the Portuguese government. Just as they had learned in Portugal and Spain of the use of wine and sweetmeats from children and nurses, so they had become acquainted with the practice of smoking from quacks and *bufarinheiros*, even though the medical property of fumigation had reached them long before through the Arabic medical science.

---

[1] W. Bosman, *A New and Accurate Description of the Coast of Guinea*, London 1721, p. 65.

[2] P. de Marees, *Beschryvinghe ende historische verhael van het gout koninckrijck van Gunea*, 's-Gravenhage 1912, p. 197 ff.

That smoking was already known to them from the Arabs follows from the fact that in the Niger valley *buckoor*, that is, Arabic باخور, *bāḥūr*, is still the name of "incense smoked with tobacco for cold,"[1] even as it was in Spain a name for the medical "sahumerias" of Villalobos and the older physicians. We have in Spain an old reference to smoking in the thirteenth century, though the manuscript is of a later date, in any case long before the discovery of America. Mosen Jaime Febrer composed in 1276 a poem on the *Conquest of Valencia* by Jaime I, in which the following occurs: "They say of the lavender (espigol) that it has the property to withhold sleep and give valor to him who takes it in smoke, because it dries up the humidity of the brain, and the cause being easily removed, it works with great vigor. Peter Espigol, noble Catalan, who came from Gerona, took part in the Conquest and was esteemed by the King, for he contrived to give him great rewards and granted him five stalks of lavender to be placed in his escutcheon over a crimson field, and these look well."[2]

In Spain the Negroes had sufficient opportunity to learn of the sovereign remedy from the quacks. The bane of the average man was the toothache, and there is, as we have already seen, a large number of references to it in the mediaeval medical works. The quack who

[1] P. A. Benton, *op. cit.*, p. 190.

[2] "Dihuen del espígol, que té propietat
de llevar la són é de dar valor
a qui en fum lo pren, perque la humitat
del celebro trau, é ab agilitat
llevada la causa, obra ab gran vigor:
El que Pere Espígol, noble catalá,
Vengut de Gerona, tingué en la Conquista,
Conegué lo Rey, puix que procurá
de darli grans premis, é li senyalá
cinch mates de espígol, que en orles allistá,
sobre camp bermell, que fan bona vista."
*Revista de Archivos, Bibliotecas y Museos*, Madrid 1913, vol.
XXVII, p. 283.

furnished the sufferer with a pipe and henbane[1] was a
deliverer, and other smoking remedies were offered.

[1] The fourteenth century English medical writings are full of such references: "Take þe sed of hennebane and þe sed of lekys and recheles and
do þes iii þynges vp-on an hot glowying tilstoun; and make a pipe þat
haþ a wyd hende and hold hit ouer þe smoke þat may rounse þorwe þe
pipe into þy teyth and hit schal sle þe wormes and do a-wey þe ache,"
G. Henslow, *Medical Works of the Fourteenth Century*, London 1899, p. 8.
"For tothache of wurmes.—Take hennebane-seede and leke-seed and poudre
of encens, of iche Ilike mychil, and ley hem on a tyl-ston hot glowyng and
make a pipe of latoun that the nether ende be wyde that it may ouer-closen
the sedes and the poudre and hald his mouth there ouer the ouerende that
the eyre may in-to the sore tothe and that wil slen the wurmes and do away
the ache," *ibid.*, p. 95. "For wormys þat eten teth.—Take henbane-sede
and leke-sede and stare, and ley þese on a red glowing tile-ston; and make
a pipe with a wyde ende, and hold þi mouth ouyr þe ston, þat þe breth
may come þorw þe pipe to þi teth; and it shal sle þe wormys and don
awey þe akyng," *ibid.*, p. 111 f.

# CHAPTER III.

## Tobacco of the Moors.

Marcellus Empiricus facetiously begins his chapter
on the toothache with the words: "Although very many
say that the best remedy for the toothache is the forceps,
yet I know that many things less forcible have been useful," and he goes on to give two substances which should
be smoked for the toothache, the first thing henbane
seed, the second *bitumen*.[1]   But this remedy is much
older since the recipe is taken word for word from
Scribonius Largus.[2]   We have already seen from Paré's
résumé that *bitumen*, that is, a viscous substance, in
Arabic طبق *tibq*, is the toothache remedy *par excellence*,
even as it may be used for the cough or headache.
Scribonius Largus also recommends chewing of *pyrethrum* for the toothache.[3]   In the mediaeval medical
works *Spanish pyrethrum* is a common substitution for
henbane.   In the XIII. century *pelydr ysbain* was used
for toothache by Welsh pharmacists;[4] in England it is
frequently mentioned as *peletre of Spain*,[5] but it seems
to have been chewed and not smoked.   It is interesting
merely from the fact that a Spanish plant is mentioned
as in use in English medicine.

We have seen from Paré's discussion of fumigations
that any pungent, viscous substance could be used for

---

[1] "Levat dolorem dentium et *bitumen* suffitum," G. Helmreich, *Marcelli
de medicamentis*, Lipsiae 1889, cap. XII, p. 120.

[2] G. Helmreich, *Scribonii Largi compositiones*, Lipsiae 1887, No. LIIII,
(p. 25).

[3] *Ibid.*, Nos. VIIII and LV, (pp. 9 and 25).

[4] G. Henslow, *op. cit.*, p. 234.

[5] *Ibid.*, pp. 47, 80, 95, 111, 130.

them.  In the Arabic practice one of several varieties
of resin could be employed for the purpose: "Steep a
cloth in oil of resin, dry it in the sun, then use it for
fumigations in the case of a cold in the head, and it will
be quickly cured.  These fumigations are equally
efficacious in an old fever.  If you take it in powdered
form a mithkal in two eggs in the shell and before
breakfast, it will help in the case of a cough, asthma,
and lung ulcers.  Take a part of it, add half of rabbits'
dung, red arsenic, and lard, melt it all in a gentle fire,
and make it into tablets, each a mithkal worth, and then
it can be used, when needed, in a cough a tablet at a
time in a fumigation produced by a gentle fire, and
taken through a tube and funnel."[1]  For lung ulcers
*bitumen* could be used instead of resin.[2]  But for our
purposes the most interesting viscous plant is the one
known in Arabic as طبق *tubbāq* or *tabbāq*.  Of this Ibn-
al-Baitār, an Arabic physician of Malaga, in Spain,
wrote: "Al-Gafeki.  In Spain the people call it *tobbāqah* طباقه, while the Berbers call it *tarhelān* or *tarhelā*.
Our physicians used to employ it, thinking that it was
the *Eupatorium*, غافت, before they knew the true *Eupatorium*.  I learn that the Eastern people made the
same use of it, then by mistake applying to it the defi-
nitions of Galen and Dioscorides.  Abu Hanīfa.  The
*tobbāq* is a plant which attains the size of a man.  It
lives in groups, and one never finds one alone.  It has
long, narrow, green, viscous leaves.  Soaked in water
it is applied to fractures where they cause agglutination
and consolidation.  Its flowers are conglomerate and
are visited by the bees."  The same author adds:
"This plant heats in an obvious manner.  It is of ad-

---

[1] L. Leclerc, *Traité des simples par Ibn El-Beithar*, in *Notices et extraits des manuscrits de la Bibliothèque Nationale*, vol. XXV, No. 1581.
[2] *Ibid.*, vol. XXVI, No. 1818.

vantage in cold affections of the liver: it dilates the
obstructions, lowers the inflammation and oedema,
which follow from its weakening, and bring it back to
its functions.  Hence, I think, proceeds the error of the
ancient physicians who have taken the *tobbāq* for the
*Eupatorium*.  Razes says, in regard to the *Eupatorium*,
that it is an emmenagogue, but this is the action of
*tobbāq*, and not of *Eupatorium*.  It is good against
poisoning by animals, especially against scorpion poi-
son, both internally and externally, and against shoot-
ing pains.  It gently evacuates the burnt humors, and
on that account it is good for refractory fevers, the
mange and the itch, taken as a decoction or as an extract.  As to the stinking *tobbāq*, المنتن *almanṭan*, which
in Greek is called *qūnīzā*, قونيزا, it is more active and
hotter, but less efficacious, in the affections of the liver.
It is recognized by the fetidness of its odor.  The *tobbāqah* properly called has an agreeable, though somewhat strong odor.  Its savor is sweet.  As to the *qūnīzā*, it has an acridity and evident bitterness.  Many
physicians use it as a substitute for *tobbāqah* and *Eupatorium*, but they are deceived by the resemblance of the
*qūnīzā*, which the people call 'fleabane.' "[1]

Ibn-al-Baitār confuses two distinct plants.  The *tarhelān* of the Berbers is given in Avicenna as *tarifilon*,[2]
which is the Latin *Trifolium*, and which is, like *Con-
yza*, used against snake bites.  The *tobbāqah* of Spain
is still found in Andalusia as *altabaca*,[3] and is the *Inula
viscosa* of the botanists.  The Spanish and Arabic name
of the plant is due to its viscosity.  Since *Eupatorium* was also used against snake bites, *tobbāq* was occasionally applied to this plant as well.[4]  From all these

---

[1] *Ibid.*, vol. XXV, No. 1448.
[2] *Op. cit.*, II. 688.
[3] Leclerc, *op. cit.*, vol. XXV, No. 1448.
[4] *Ibid.*, vol. XXVI, No. 1618.

botanical names it follows that *tobbāq* was subsequently applied to any viscous plant, which was supposed to be good in fumigations and as a styptic or poison-killer. Ibn-al-Baitār specifically informs us that in Persia, Syria, and Egypt "they employed another plant, of an extreme bitterness, with blue flowers, slightly elongated, with roundish branches, as thin as the stem, with leaves and stems of a yellowish color in all its parts; it is of an extreme bitterness, more bitter than aloe, more active and efficacious in obstructions of the liver and the other organs than the medicine considered by the interpreters to be the gafets of Dioscorides and Galen."[1] The name of the plant is not given, but it apparently is different from Abu Hanifa's *tubbāq* of the IX. century.

From the Arabic sources it follows that *tubbāq* was the name of a number of medicinal plants, not in the Greek pharmacopoeia, which, containing a pungent, aromatic, viscous juice, were eminently fit to the popular mind as a cure-all. We are specifically informed that such a cure-all was in use in Egypt and in Africa, from a plant unknown to the Greek pharmacopoeia. But fumigation spread from the Arabic north to the Negro lands, and there something must have been used which corresponded to the *tubbāq* of the north. The wide distribution of this word for the *Nicotiana tabacum*, which, according to Welwitsch,[2] is found in a wild state, makes it more than plausible that, containing as it does the qualities of a cure-all in a high degree, it must have been in use, since very early time, at least as a medicine.

The anthropologists and historians make much of it that the absence of any reference to tobacco in Africa before the XVII. century is a convincing proof that it was imported there from America. To this it must be remarked that smoking is but once mentioned in the

[1] *Ibid.*
[2] See vol. I, p. 111.

*Belles Lettres* of Europe, namely in Febrer, that pipes are not mentioned at all, and that if it were not for the overwhelming proof from medical works that smoking and pipes have been in use for at least 1700 years, and for the corroborative evidence of the finds of pipes in ancient tombs, one would jump to the conclusion that smoking and pipes never existed. Smoking none the less was so common as a medical practice that it did not attract any attention, anymore than hundreds of medical phenomena which existed but did not find their way into literature. Only when the vice of smoking as a pleasure became common in Europe, and that was only at the end of the XVI. century, did people begin to observe more closely the same phenomenon in Africa, while in America, where the vice spread immediately after the discovery, this observation was being made from the start.

There is no evidence that the tobacco plant was known in Europe before its importation by Thevet in 1556.[1] A few years later the *Nicotiana rustica* was described by Dodoens as *Hyoscamus luteus* and as some kind of henbane by Matthiolus and others. In 1586 it was given as Ital. *Iusquiamo nuovo, Iusquiamo maggiore*, German *Wundt Bilsam, gelb Wundkraut.*[2] Gerarde, in his *Herbal*, in 1597, named it "yellow henbane" or "English tobacco,"[3] and thus it was named by J. Parkinson.[4]

In the second half of the XV. century an Arabic source refers to smoking in Africa: "At Kubacca the tobacco serves also as money. By a singular homo-

---

[1] For the European data on tobacco I use O. Comes' *Histoire, géographie, statistique du tabac*, Naples 1900. Unfortunately this interesting and important work abounds in wrong dates and statements, due to quotations at second hand.

[2] I. Camerarius, *De plantis epytome utilissima*, Francofurti ad Moenum 1586.

[3] II. LXII. 284.

[4] *Paradisi in Sole Paradisus Terrestris*, London 1904, p. 363.

phony with the European name the inhabitants of the Darfur call it in their language *taba*. Moreover, this is the usual name in the Sudan. In Fezzan and at Tripoli in Barbary it is called *tabgha*. I have read a *kasidah*, or a poem, composed by a Bakride or descendant of the Khalif Abu Bakr, to prove that smoking is no sin. These verses, I think, date from the middle of the IX. century of the hegirah. Here are a few of them: 'All powerful God has made a plant to grow in our fields of which the true name is *tabgha*. If any one in his ignorance maintains that this plant is forbidden, ask him to prove his assertion. By what verse in the Koran can he prove it?' "[1]

We have a more definite reference to Negro smoking in 1599: "In the year 1001 (October 8, 1592–September 27, 1593) they brought to Elmansur an elephant from the Sudan. When this animal entered Morocco, it was a great event, for the whole population of the city, men, women, children, and old people, came from their dwellings to see the sight. In the month of Ramadan 1007 (March 28–April 17, 1599) the elephant was taken to Fez. Certain authors pretend that it was as a result of the arrival of this elephant that the use of the dire plant called *tobacco* was introduced into the Magreb, since the Negroes who had brought the elephant also had brought tobacco which they smoked, claiming that the use of it offered great advantages. The habit of smoking which they brought then became general in the Draa, later at Morocco, and at last in the whole Magreb."[2]

These are but late recollections of what has been a custom for centuries. With the XVII. century the references to an inveterate habit of smoking among the Negroes are common. They chiefly come in English

[1] G. Binger, *Du Niger au Golfe de Guinée*, Paris 1892, vol. II, p. 364.
[2] O. Houdas, *Histoire de la dynastie Saadienne au Maroc (1511-1670)*, Paris 1889, p. 264.

sources, since it was the English who by their Virginia
venture were most active in the tobacco trade.   Jobson,[1] who in 1620 and 21 visited Gambia, wrote:
"Another profession we finde, and those are they who
temper the earth, and makes the walles of their houses,
and likewise earthen pots they set to the fire, to boyle
and dresse their food in for all other occasions, they
vse no other mettle, but serue themselues with the
gourd, which .performs it very neatly; onely one principall thing, they canoot misse, and that is their *Tabacco* pipes, whereof there is few or none of them, be
they men or women doth walke or go without, they do
make onely the bowle of earth, with a necke of the
same, about two inches long, very neatly, and artificially
colouring or glasing the earth, very hansomly, all
the bowles being very great, and for the most part will
hold halfe an ounce of *Tabacco;* they put into the necke
a long kane, many times a yard of length, and in that
manner draw their smoake, whereof they are great
takers, and cannot of all other things liue without it."
"They doe likewise obserue their seasons, to set
other plants, as *Tobacco,* which is euer growing about
their houses."[2]   Jobson also tells of some Negroes from
the interior who "had neuer seene white men before;
and the woemen that came with them were very shye,
and fearefull of vs, insomuch as they would runne behind the men, and into the houses to hide from vs; when
we offered to come neare them:   I sent therefore into
the boate for some beades and such things, and went
vnto some of the boldest, giuing them thereof into their
hands, which they were willing to receiue, and with
these curtesies imboldned them, that they soone became
familiar, and in requitall gaue me againe, *Tobacco,* and
fine neate Canes they had to take *Tobacco* with."[3]

[1] R. Jobson, *op. cit.*, p. 122.
[2] *Ibid.*, p. 125.
[3] *Ibid.*, p. 94.

The tobacco habit must have had some time to spread so far, hence it is certain that it was known in Guinea before the XVII. century. We have already seen that tobacco has been found growing wild in Africa.[1] The most emphatic statement to this effect is from the beginning of the XIX. century, when Bowdich[2] saw it growing wild in the Gaboon: "The *tobacco* grows spontaneously, but I do not consider this so strong a proof of its being indigenous to Africa, as that it grows in Inta. The Portuguese have probably introduced it into Gaboon." Bowdich did not wish to be positive on a wild-growing variety in a region reached by the Portuguese. Although the superiority of the imported tobacco caused the Asantes to buy it from the Portuguese, they had recourse to the wild-growing native species, if necessary: "A serious disadvantage opposed to the English trade, is that the Ashantees will purchase no tobacco but the Portuguese, and that eagerly even at 2 oz. of gold the roll. Of this (the Portuguese and Spanish slave ships regularly calling at Elmina), the Dutch Governor-General is enabled to obtain frequent supplies, in exchange for canoes, two of which, though they cost him comparatively nothing, fetch 32 rolls of tobacco; and the General has sometimes received 80 oz. of gold a day from the Ashantees for tobacco only. If they cannot have this tobacco, they will content themselves with that grown in the interior, of which I have brought a sample."[3] But, as he had remarked before, tobacco grew wild in the interior, toward the Mandingo country: "Mr. Park observed the tobacco-plant, which grows luxuriantly in Inta and Dagwumba, and is called *toah*. The visitors from those countries recognized it in a botanical

---

[1] Vol. I, p. 111.
[2] T. E. Bowdich, *Mission from Cape Coast Castle to Ashantee*, London 1819, p. 444.
[3] *Ibid.*, p. 337.

work. They first dry the leaves in the sun, then, having rubbed them well between their hands, mix them with water into oval masses."[1]

Long before Bowdich knew of the wild tobacco in the interior, Labat described the excellent quality of the tobacco in Guinea,[2] although very poorly cultivated by the natives. "The tobacco is here (near Fort St. Louis) excellent. It is a wonder that the heads of the Company have not yet been able to find the means for getting the Negroes to plant a larger quantity. It could be bought from them at a very low price, and a more considerable profit could be obtained from it than from other articles of merchandise which have to be bought for cash from the English and the Dutch. The Island of Jean Barre, which is next to Fort St. Louis, and most of the land of Cajor are supremely adapted for this plant and produce the best possible tobacco that can be expected. It is true, the Negroes manufacture it poorly, since they pound it as soon as it is picked, without curing or drying it, in short, without giving it the form which the Americans gave it even before the Spaniards who seized their country, taught them to give this plant the necessary treatment. The Negroes do nothing of the kind. After they have pounded or beaten the tobacco leaves, they press them and make them into bricks or a kind of twists, which they tie tightly and dry slowly in the shade. This tobacco is none the less excellent in spite of the poor treatment. What would it be if it were worked carefully and regularly? For this it would be necessary to have a larger quantity planted and sell it on the spot to people who would give it the proper treatment and make it into cords, leaves, twists, and torquettes, such as would be demanded by the French manufac-

---

[1] *Ibid.*, p. 327.
[2] J.-B. Labat, *Nouvelle relation de l'Afrique occidentale*, Paris 1728.

turers. This is easy enough, but what is harder is to overcome the laziness of the Negroes. Mr. Brue has tried it several times, but in vain. He has frequently convinced Jean Barre and Jamsec of the great advantage to be derived from the cultivation of this plant, and of other things which they could get from their land. They agreed with him, but when it came to put a hand to the work, their arms dropped, and they said that their ancestors had not done so and consequently they must not undertake it, and this reason, pitiable as it was, kept them in inaction."[1] "They produce a lot of tobacco in this region (at Bievert), whole fields being occupied by it. I have said elsewhere that the Negroes neither take it as snuff, nor chew it, it all being consumed in smoking. They pound it when it is ripe, and put it into bricks. Although they give it little attention even as they lack a number of things necessary for it in other countries, it is none the less excellent. One can imagine what it would be if it were treated as in America."[2]

From the preceding extracts it follows that the tobacco in and near the Mandingo country was of exceptional quality even though it was not properly treated. In other localities the tobacco was apparently of an inferior quality, but precise information on this point is not obtainable. Some American archaeologists point to this inferiority in the treatment of the tobacco as a *prima facie* proof that it was imported to Africa from America, because there it has received a better treatment. This reasoning may be paralleled by the statement that the potato is a native of Maine or Ireland, whence it was imported to Peru, because in Maine or Ireland it receives a better treatment, or that the double roses are native in those countries where they

*Ibid.*, vol. III, p. 202 f.
*Ibid.*, vol. IV, p. 185.

are produced and have been imported into those countries where they grow single and wild. The absurdity of this is self-evident and needs no further discussion.

Labat tells of the Negro pipes as follows: "The *cassots* are pipes, of which the bowl is nicely made of clay, while those of the women are of gold or silver. The stem, which is always at least eighteen inches long, is a reed set in circles of gold, silver, coral, and amber. One sees *cassots* made by Moors which are perfect in beauty."[1] "The Negroes of these regions are the most skilful makers of *cassots* or pipe bowls in the whole country."[2] This *cassot* is obviously the Arabic *qaṣabah* "pipe," which once more shows that the habit of smoking the *tabbāq* was derived by the Guinea Negroes from the Arabs. Other authors, Dapper half a century earlier, and later ones, all agree that the cultivation of a good quality of tobacco was universal in the Guinea region.[3] Bosman, who found the Guinea tobacco stinking, had no higher opinion of the Brazilian kind: "This country produces none of those green Herbs common in Europe, except Tarragon and *Tobacco;* of both which here is great Plenty, especially of the last, which stinks so abominably, that it is impossible for one that is even not very nice to continue near the Negroes when they smoak this devilish Weed; which yet agrees very well with them.

"Some of them have Pipes made of Reeds, which are about six Foot long; to the End of which is fixed a Stone or Earthen Bowl, so large that they cram in two or three Handfuls of *Tobacco;* which Pipe thus filled, they without ceasing can easily smoak out: and they are not put to hold their Pipe, for being so long, it rests on the Ground.

[1] *Ibid.*, vol. III, p. 134 f.
[2] *Ibid.*, vol. IV, p. 53.
[3] Comes, *op. cit.*, p. 130 ff.

"All the Inland Negroes take this *Tobacco*, but those who live amongst us, and daily converse with the Europeans, have Portugueze, or rather *Brasil Tobacco*, which, tho' a little better, yet stinks to a great degree.

"Both the Male and Female of the Negroes, are so very fond of this *Tobacco*, that they will part with the very last Penny which should buy them Bread, and suffer Hunger rather than be without it; which so enhances the Price, that for a Portugueze Fathom, which is much less than one Pound of this Trash, they will give five Shillings, or a Gold Quarter of a Jacobus.

"Let us therefore rather praise those Smoakers (my good friend) who take the noble Spanish or Virginia *Tobacco;* but as for those stupid wretches who content themselves with the Amorsfort Weed, I heartily wish, as a Punishment of their depraved taste, that during their lives they may never smoak better than our Negroes, and Brasil on Sundays and Holidays; yet under Condition they be obliged to keep Company with each other, and be banish'd the Company of genteel Smoakers: But this by the way only.

"The *Tobacco-Leaf* here grows on a plant about two Foot high, and is of the Length of two or three Handsbreadth, and the Breadth of one, bears a small Bellflower; which, when ripe, turns to seed."[1]

Not in the coast region of Guinea, but far in the interior, whether one proceeds from the Senegal or the Gold Coast toward the Niger basin, was the ancient native home of the tobacco, after it may have been transported thither from farther north by the Arabs. The farther one gets away from Arabic influence, the less ancient is the custom of smoking. In the Portuguese Congo, where the smoking must have been known from its association with Brazil, one hears nothing of smoking tobacco until the middle of the XVII.

[1] W. Bosman, *op. cit.*, p. 286 f.

century, when it spreads through the south and east, mostly through the Dutch trade. But smoking of another substance by the Portuguese in Angola is mentioned earlier, in Purchas' rendering of Pigafetta's account of the Congo,[1] where we read: "Signor Odoardo affirmed, that the Portugals have proved it (the sanders) for the head-ache, by laying it on the coales, and taking the smoake of it."

---

[1] S. Purchas, *Hakluytus Posthumus or Purchas His Pilgrimes*, Glasgow 1905, vol. VI, p. 424.

# CHAPTER IV.

## The Sovereign Remedy of the Indians.

It is not necessary to go once more[1] over the American side of the tobacco smoking, since it has become apparent that it is derived from the Negro habit. A few additions, however, can be made that will illustrate the Negro influence. Thevet[2] showed that the tobacco was dried by the Indians in the shade, that is, precisely as it is dried by the Negroes of Guinea. Although Thevet, in the middle of the XVI. century, described the smoking among the Indians of Brazil, yet the custom was only sporadic and, according to an anonymous authority, who wrote after 1568, *"tobacco was not yet raised at that time, nor was its usefulness known."*[3]

In Nicaragua smoking in our sense of the word is already reported in the year 1529: "One Saturday, August 19, 1529, in the square of Nicoya, Don Alonso, otherwise called Nambi, which in his Chorotega language means 'dog,' two hours before it became night, while at one part of the square eighty or one hundred Indians, apparently common or plebeian people, began to sing and dance about in an areyto, the cacique sat down in another part of the square with great pleasure and solemnity upon a duho or small bench, and his chiefs and about seventy or eighty others on similar duhos. And a lass began to bring them drink in small calabashes like plates or saucers, some *chicha* or wine,

---

[1] See the chapter on Tobacco in vol. I.
[2] *Ibid.*, p. 132 f.
[3] "De tabaco se não tratava ainda neste tempo, nem se entendia a sua utilidade," *Revista do Instituto historico e geographico de São Paulo*, vol. III, p. 171.

which they make of maize, and which is very strong and acid, which in color resembles chicken broth, when one or two yolks of eggs are dissolved in it. And when they began to drink, the same cacique brought a handful of *tabacos*, which are a span in length and a finger in thickness, and are made of a certain rolled leaf and tied with two or three cabuya strings, which leaf and plant they raise with great care for the sake of these *tabacos*, and they light them a little at one end; it burns slowly down like an incense stick until it stops burning, which lasts a day; and from time to time they put it in the mouth at the other end from the one at which it burns, and they draw in the smoke for a little while and take it out, and hold the mouth closed and retain the breath for a while, and then breathe forth, and the smoke comes out of the mouth and nostrils. And every one of the Indians mentioned held one of these leaf rolls, which they called *yapoquete*, and in the language of this Island of Hayti or Hispaniola it is called *tabaco*."[1]

Unfortunately no trust can be placed in the whole account, since it is at variance with Oviedo's later statements. I have already shown[2] that in 1535 he knew of tobacco, which he in virtue significantly compared with henbane, only from hearsay accounts, and as falsely recorded by Ramon Pane as being smoked through the Y-shaped fork and through the nose. Besides, *tabaco* was to him the Y-shaped instrument, and not the weed. He also knew at that time that the Negroes of Hispaniola were smoking. In 1547 he still repeated the same account, but, in 1557, when he composed his larger work, he correctly stated that *tabaco* was the thing smoked, "the smoke,"as he puts it. As the account of the year 1529, which refers to Nicoya in Nicaragua (modern Costa Rica), was also written in

[1] G. F. de Oviedo, *Historia general y natural de las Indias*, Madrid 1855, vol. IV, p. 96.
[2] Vol. I, p. 115 ff.

1557, it follows that he was giving here his knowledge of the year 1557, and not that of 1529. Whatever he may have seen at Nicoya in that earlier period did not make an impression upon him until he knew precisely what *tabaco* was. There can be no doubt whatsoever that he had seen the Negroes smoking in or before 1535, but he did not dare to tear himself away from the Columbian myth of smoking, and so perverted the facts, until the universal knowledge of smoking, which was becoming known throughout Europe in the years 1556-1558, especially through Thevet in 1557, who boasted of being the first to bring tobacco seed to Europe, led him to making corrections in the direction of truth, and not of myth.

Now, it would be strange, indeed, if in 1529 the caciques of Nicoya had not been smoking. Nicaragua was opened up in 1513, after Central America had been known for eleven years, through Columbus' discovery, and the city of Panama, not more than three hundred or four hundred miles away from Nicoya, had been founded in 1519. Panama became the distributing centre of Negro superintendents, as we have seen from the specific reference to them in 1535 in Peru,[1] and the Gulf of Nicoya, on the west coast, was the very region where Avila had opened up Nicaragua to Spanish settlement. Even as early as the year 1513 there was a Negro[2] in Balboa's expedition for the discovery of the western ocean. Ever since Gil González de Avila had come to Nicoya, that is, several years before 1529, the Indians of the region had at least nominally turned Christians,[3] and consequently had fallen under Spanish influence.

But the case is far worse still. Negroes were residents in Darien before 1513, that is, before any white

[1] See p. 62 f.
[2] G. F. de Oviedo, *op. cit.*, vol. III, p. 12.
[3] *Ibid.*, p. 111.

men had made permanent settlements there.  Peter
Martyr says: "The Spaniards found Negro slaves in
this province.  They only live in regions one day's
march from Quarequa, and they are fierce and cruel.
It is thought that Negro pirates of Ethiopia established themselves after the wreck of their ships in these
mountains.  The natives of Quarequa carry on inces-
sant war with these Negroes.  Massacre or slavery is
the alternate fortune of the two peoples."[1]  Gómara
similarly remarks: "Balboa found some Negroes,
slaves of the lord.  He asked them whence they got
them, but they could not tell, nor did they know more
than this that men of this color were living nearby, and
they were constantly waging war with them.  These
were the first Negroes that had been seen in the Indies,
and I think no others have been noticed."[2]

Of course, the explanations given by Peter Martyr
and Gómara as to the presence of the Negroes in Darien
and their fierceness are of no consequence, since the
conquerors could not understand the natives.  What is
certain is that Negroes were present in 1513 in Darien
and we shall later see that these or their like were there
in the interest of trade, along the trade route to Peru
and Mexico.  The presence of tobacco in this region
cannot be dated earlier than the presence of Negroes
there, at whatever time they may have come there.
Oviedo mentions *chicha* in the same breath with
tobacco, and here at least the name is of Negro origin.
In another place[3] Oviedo informs us that in Nicaragua
*yaat* was "a certain herb which the Indians hold in their
mouths, and with which, they say, they do not get so
tired as if they did not have it."  The Chorotega language of Nicaragua is a corrupted Nahuatl, and *yaat*

[1] III. 1.
[2] F. L. de Gómara, *La historia general de las Indias*, Anvers 1554, cap.
LXII.
[3] *Op. cit.*, vol. III, p. 106.

corresponds to Nahuatl *yetl* "incense, perfume, tobacco," and *yapoquete* "cigar" is compounded of Nahuatl *yetl* "tobacco" and *poctli* "smoke." This latter tautological compound at once betrays an attempt at popular etymology, where *tabaco*, through *tapaco*, since Nahuatl has no *b*, has become *ya-poqu-ete*. In Nahuatl itself the compound has been inverted and *poc-yetl* has been further transformed to *pic-yetl* "small, crushed incense," which it is not, for Molina's dictionary gives for *picyetl* "a plant like henbane, which is medicinal," thus fully agreeing with Oviedo's definition of *tabaco* in 1535, and with the African plant which was used for the henbane of European medicine. Oviedo is the only early author on America who records the placing of tobacco in the mouth in order to cure fatigue, although this is the common method of using tobacco in East Africa,[1] hence it is more likely that Oviedo confused the tobacco with the coca, even as another time he confused it with the *datura arborea*.

I have already pointed out the fact that *picyetl*, in all probability, was formed from a Maya language.[2] This assumption is greatly strengthened by the fact that in the Maya country we have a compound which is much nearer to *tobaco*, and which at once explains Chorotega *yapoquete* and Nahuatl *piciyetl*. Las Casas quotes a law of the Indians of Vera Cruz: "If a married man sinned with a widow or married woman, he was chastized once or twice, and if they saw him persevere in his sin, they tied the hands of both behind their backs, and so high that they could not reach the ground, and burned beneath them an herb which they called *tabacoyay*, which must have been stinking, and put the smoke through their nostrils for a good while, and then let them go,

[1] Comes, *op. cit.*, p. 152 *et passim*.
[2] Vol. I, p. 150.

advising them to mend their ways."[1]   The law is unquestionably apocryphal, but it is interesting to observe
that in Las Casas' time the name of "tobacco," which
was here not yet used for pleasure smoking, but for a
punishment, was named *tabaco-yay*, the second part
corresponding to *yetl* of the Mexicans, while the first
is obviously the same as *yapoquete*.   I have already
pointed out that *yetl* is, in all likelihood, a "smoke"
word and of Mandingo origin.[2]   This is again shown
by the extraordinary distribution of the word, for we
find it not only in Vera Paz, but also in Chibcha, where
we have *ie* "smoke."

In Venezuela, Oviedo says, "the *boratio* (wizard) says
that he will give his answer after having consulted with
the devil, and for this conversation and consultation
they lock themselves up in a room alone, and here they
make certain smokes (ahumadas) which they call
*tabacos* with such herbs as bereave them of their sense;
and here the *boratio* remains a day, or two, or three, and
sometimes longer, and, after coming out, he says that
the devil has told him so and so, answering the questions
put to him, according to the desires of those whom he
wishes to satisfy; and for this they give the *boratio* some
gold trinket or other things.   For less important matters the Indians have another way.   There is in this
country an herb called *tabaco*, which is a kind of plant
as high as a man's breast, and more or less branching,
which puts forth leaves a palm in length and four fingers
in width, and of the shape of a lance iron, and they are
hairy.   And they sow this herb, and the seed which it
makes they keep for the next year's planting, and they
watch it carefully for the following purpose:   When
they reap it they put the leaves in bunches and dry it

M. Serrano y Sanz, *Historiadores de Indias, Apologética historia de las
Indias, de Fr. Bartolomé de las Casas*, in *Nueva Biblioteca de autores españoles*,
Madrid 1909, vol. I, p. 627.
 [2] Vol. I, p. 154.

in the smoke in bunches, and they keep it, and it is a much appreciated article of commerce among the Indians. In our Hispaniola there is much of it in the ranches, and the Negroes whom we employ value it highly for the effect which it produces by smoking it until they fall down like dead, and thus they are the greater part of the night, and they say that they do not feel the fatigue of the previous day."[1]

This account is of extraordinary importance, since it shows that tobacco was raised in the middle of the century in Hispaniola, where the Negroes were addicted to it, for the trade among the Indians, that is, that the Indians were encouraged by the Whites and Negroes to smoke it, not that it was a common native article among the Indians, precisely as in Nicaragua we are told that only the caciques and their chosen men smoked in 1529. However, Oviedo, as before, is not certain of his grounds. While his description of the tobacco plant is correct for Hispaniola, except as to its soporific effect, he confuses the plant with the action by attaching in the first part the name *tabaco* to the act of smoking. Here the substance smoked is obviously supposed to be different from tobacco. We have in Gómara the same account for New Granada, where we are told, "they offered incense to the gods with herbs; they have oracles with the gods, from whom they seek advice and answer as to temporal wars, suffering, marriage, and such things. For this purpose they put on their joints certain herbs which they call *jop* and *osca*, they take the smoke."[2]

The last sentence runs in the Medina 1553 edition "unas yerbas que llaman *jop, y osca*. Y toman el humo." The Saragossa 1554 edition reads "*jop y osca, y toman el humo*," while the Anvers 1554 edition has it

---

[1] *Op. cit.*, vol. II, p. 298.
[2] Gómara, *op. cit.*, cap. LXXII.

"*jop, y osca.* Toman el humo." The many variations show that we have here a printer's error, most likely for "*tabacos,* y toman el humo," *acos* having pied into *osca,* *tab* into *jop,* while the *y* before "toman" got between the two. However, *osca* has assumed in Chibcha the name for either "tobacco" or *datura arborea.* In the Chibcha dictionary[1] we read "tabaco, borrachero, *hosca,*" and "borrachero" is given in the Spanish dictionaries as the name of the *datura arborea,* "a shrub of South America which grows to the height of from sixteen to eighteen feet; it is very branching, has large hairy leaves, and white funnel-shaped flowers. The whole plant exhales a disagreeable odor, and its food causes delirium, hence its name." Under "borrachero" the Chibcha dictionary gives *tyhyquy,* which is doubled in Oviedo's *tectec.* "There is in this country a plant called *tectec,* which drives one mad, and if a man eats enough of it, it will kill him. To craze a man, they throw it into a pot in which they cook food and if the guests eat of the plant with the meat with which it was cooked they become crazed for three or four days and the madness is according to the quantity thrown in."[2]  Apparently the leaves of the *datura arborea* were used like the tobacco for narcotic purposes, and with this Gómara's references to tobacco are reduced to extremely slim proportions for we have only one in regard to the use of *cohoba* in Hispaniola which is based on Ramon Pane, and this is of no consequence, besides suspiciously resembling the effect of the *datura arborea,*[3] and another, which relates to Darien, where there is merely reference to a smoke offering to the gods.[4]

---

[1] E. Uricoechea, *Gramática, vocabulario, catecismo i confesionario de la lengua chibcha,* Paris 1871.

[2] *Op. cit.,* vol. II, p. 390.

[3] *Op. cit.,* cap. XXVII.

[4] *Ibid.,* cap. LXVIII.

We have already seen that in Mexico no definite account of smoking is contained in the early historians, who simply tell of the use of liquid amber wrapped in tobacco leaves as incense, employed by Montezuma after a repast, in order to induce sleep. This *acayetl*, literally "reed incense," is very frequently depicted in the Mexican manuscripts as an attribute of power, as, for example, in the splendid portraits of Toculpotzin and Quauhtlazacuilotzin, and was held in the hand without being taken into the mouth.[1] Even as late as 1582 very few Indians smoked tobacco, and of these only laborers, that is, such as came in contact with the Negro slaves, while the custom had become universal with the Spaniards.[2] For this reason hardly any pipes have been found in Mexico. But the case is quite different in Michuacan, where the Tarascans were addicted to smoking.

---

[1] "Il ne faut pas confondre l'*acayetl* ou roseau brûle-parfums, avec la pipe proprement dite; dans les premiers temps, ces roseaux parfumés se portaient allumés à la main; ce n'est plus tard qu'ils se convertirent en pipes, c'est-à-dire, qu'on s'avisa d'en aspirer la fumée par une extrémité," E. Boban, *Documents pour servir à l'histoire du Mexique*, Paris 1891, p. 177, and see Tables 66 and 68.

[2] "La yerba que llaman *picietl*, que según dicen es la misma que en España llaman beleño, aprovéchanse de ella para dormir y amortiguar las carnes y no sentir el mucho trabajo que padece el cuerpo trabajando, la cual toman seca, molida y mojada y envuelta con una poca de cal en la boca, puesta entre el labio y las encías, tanta cantidad como cabrá en una avellana, al tiempo que se van á dormir ó á trabajar; aunque muy pocos de los indios que se crían con españoles usan de ella, ni aun de la gente política y ciudadana, sino hombres rústicos y trabajadores. También toman de esta yerba por humo en cañutos de caña, envuelta con liquidámbar, porque atestados de ella los encienden por el un cabo, y por el otro lo chupan, con que dicen que enjugan el cerebro y purgan las reumas por la boca; y está ya tan admitido de los españoles que padecen estas enfermedades, que la usan para su remedio, y se hallan muy bien con ellos; y también usan de ella para ciciones, tercianas y cuartanas, tomándolo por vía de calilla, porque les hace purgar. Asimismo las hojas tostadas y puestas en la hijada, cuando hay dolor se quita con ellas," J. B. Pomar y A. de Zurita, *Relación de Tezcoco*, in *Nueva colección de documentos para la historia de México*, México 1891, vol. III, p. 64 f.

In a XVII. century pictorial account of Michuacan[1]
the caciques are represented as smoking a long pipe, of
which the bowl ends at the bottom in two mastaria.[2]
The pipes have an amazing resemblance to the Roman
pipes, except that instead of one nipple there are two.
This type of pipe is widely distributed through
America. "The remaining pipe of the seven belongs
to a type before referred to by us as common on St.
Francis river, and figured by Holmes as coming from
Arkansas, on which two feet, or supports, project forward from the base of the bowl to enable the pipe to
maintain an erect position when placed on a level surface. It is interesting to note that pipes are on sale at
the present day, having precisely similar supports intended for the same purpose. The pipe here shown by
us has these supports well defined which display flattening on the under surface as if through wear. Some
Arkansas pipes of this type, however, show the projec-
tions as mere knobs, as if conventionalizing had begun."[3]
Holmes[4] reports a number of pipes from the Eastern
part of the United States with "a flattening of the base
as though to permit the bowl to rest steadily on the
ground while the smoking was going on, probably
through a long tube or stem. This flattening is in many
cases accompanied by an expansion at the margins, as
in plate XXXIII a, b, or by a flattish projection beyond
the elbow."[5] As the knob in many of these pipes is
beyond the lower surface, it could not represent a surface to rest upon. Indeed, it would not be possible to

[1] E. Seler, *Die alten Bewohner der Landschaft Michuacan*, in *Gesammelte
Abhandlungen zur amerikanischen Sprach- und Alterthumskunde*, Berlin
1908, vol. III, p. 33 ff.
[2] *Ibid.*, pp. 63, 102.
[3] C. B. Moore, *Antiquities of the St. Francis, White, and Black Rivers,
Arkansas*, Philadelphia 1910, p. 278 f.
[4] *Aboriginal Pottery of the Eastern United States*, in *Twentieth Annual
Report of the Bureau of American Ethnology to the Secretary of the Smithsonian
Institution 1898-99*, Washington 1903, part II.
[5] *Ibid.*, p. 99.

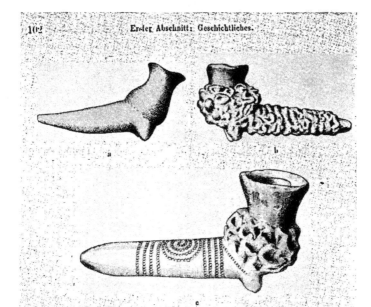

Abb. 11. Thönerne Tabakpfeifen aus *Michuacan*.
*a. b.* Museo Nacional de México.
*c.* Königl. Museum für Völkerkunde, Berlin.

Abb. 42. Tarasische Rechtspflege.
(Handschriftliches Blatt meiner Sammlung.)

From E. Seler's *Gesammelte Abhandlemgen*, vol. III.

FIG. 8.—Pipe of earthenware. Rose Mound. (Full size.)

From C. B. Moore's *Antiquities of the St. Francis, White, and Black Rivers, Arkansas.*

insert a straight reed in such a way as to smoke out of the pipe. The reverse is true, the flat surface being a development of the original knob, which universally appears in old European pipes.

Although the fame of the tobacco plant had been slowly reaching Europe, and Nicot's experiments with the tobacco for medical purposes had been going on for some time, the real sensation was produced only in 1571 when Monardes published the second part of his work dealing with the medicinal plants of the New World. In Mexico the interest in the native plants had been fostered chiefly by Fray Bernardino de Sahagun, who, since 1536, had off and on been connected with the College at Tlatelulco, where he instructed promising young Indians in Latin and European learning.[1] The progress which they made was phenomenal, and many of them entered the learned professions. Here at Tlatelulco he got his information about Mexican plants and medicine from old, illiterate physicians: "This above account of the medicinal plants and other objects mentioned was given by the doctors of Tlatelulco, old men, and very experienced in matters of medicine, since they all cure publicly. Their names and that of the notary who wrote it are as follows, and since they cannot write they asked the notary to put down their names: Gaspar Matias, resident of Concepción; Pedro Destrago, resident of Santa Inés; Francisco Simon and Miguel Damian, residents of Santo Toribio; Felipe Hernández, resident of Santa Anna; Pedro de Requena, resident of Concepción; Miguel Garcia, resident of Santo Toribio; Miguel Motilinia, resident of Santa Inés."[2]

---

[1] B. de Sahagun, *Historia general de las cosas de Nueva España*, in *Biblioteca Mexicana*, Mexico 1896, lib. X, cap. 27 (p. 307).

[2] *Ibid.*, lib. XI, cap. 7, §5 (p. 146).

Icazbalceta[1] says that the ignorance of reading makes it believe that the physicians were not of those who had studied medicine in the college, but natives of the pre-Columbian kind.   But it is not even certain that all the physicians were Indians.  A. de Remesal tells of a quack in Santiago of Guatemala who in the year 1541 had killed many people by his ignorance, and yet, in less than a year, the cabildo of the city "passed an ordinance that, considering that the city has at present no physician who can read and knows medicine, said N. may do as his conscience of a good Christian prompts him, to the best of his knowledge and belief; and if anyone called him to cure him, and some trouble should befall him from such a cure, it should be at the risk of the person who thus called him, and he should from now on be relieved of the fine."[2]   In the city of Mexico conditions were probably better, but the small towns where "the doctors of Tlatelulco" practised were lucky enough to have quacks of the Santiago type, if they had any smattering of medicine.   The college of Tlatelulco, where medicine was taught to the Indians, was in very bad shape between 1546 and 1566, when the school was left entirely in the hands of the Indians,[3] and in 1572 its rector was an Indian, Martín Jacobita.[4]   "The doctors of Tlatelulco" can only mean "those who had studied at Tlatelulco," where they were put through their paces on a minimum of information, apparently by a *viva voce* instruction.   What "the doctors" learned there, was a medley of European medicine and native practices, which Sahagun gave out as the Nahuatl art of medicine.

[1] J. García Icazbalceta, *Bibliografía mexicana del siglo XVI*, México 1886, vol. I, p. 160.

[2] *Ibid.*, p. 163.

[3] *Ibid.*, p. 259.

[4] *Ibid.*

In 1595 a pestilence broke out among the Indians of Tezcuco, and this is the way it was handled by the Spaniards: "The Father Superior of this monastery, Fray Juan Baptista, in the beginning of this pestilence (which had raged for the space of two months) provided himself with such medicines and provisions as seemed proper to him. And when the Indians came to confession (because the moment they fall sick they immediately rush to confession on foot, or carried on their relatives' shoulders, or on stretchers, or the best way they can), he had in readiness barbers who, when they confessed, immediately bled them at the portals of the monastery, and there they remained for a while, and then they were given syrups of cassia and warm water, and soothing syrups, if they coughed a great deal. And of this syrup as much as four large jars or vats each day were used, for there were days when as many as three hundred sick, and usually two hundred to two hundred and fifty, were treated. Pregnant women, who could not be bled, had cups placed on their shoulders, and they received the specific of their disease, which in the language of Mexico is called *cohuanenepilli*, in hot wine manufactured by the Indians, and this cured them. The children had their cuppings on the legs, and they, too, got *cohuanenepilli*. All the sick in general received a purging with a peculiar root called *matlalitzic*, which is far better than the one of Michuacan, or with another root called *ytztic tlanoquiloni*, while others received cassia, whatever each needed, *because the best doctor of the village each time attended to it and ordered it.* These purging medicines were given to them to take home, and they were instructed how to use them. The most needy persons received from the Father Superior quince jam or some other preserve or dainty, which he had ordered in quantity from Mexico. Just think what were in those days the portals and court of the

Tezcuco Monastery, full of so many sick people, some being confessed, others being bled, others syrupped, and others again attended to and consoled! What angels walked in the exercise of this ministry! Otherwise, what number of men would have been sufficient to attend to so many diverse needs, especially since some of the clerics had themselves fallen ill? Besides this, those who were well went out to attend upon Indians from a distance, who could not come to the Monastery, and there were many of them, and they took with them barbers and purges and everything else needed, and at first they confessed them and then they treated them as in the monastery. And for many who suffered from diarrhoea they used other native medicines, such as would cure them fastest. This care and extreme diligence, applied more than ever before, was the second cause why not so many were endangered or died, as in other plagues."[1]

From this account it follows clearly that the village doctors, whether they were Indians or Spaniards, used an eclectic system of medicine from the European and Nahuatl pharmacopoeia. Again and again we hear of the extraordinary capacity for European learning in the Indians, and, on the other hand, Sahagun was so fascinated by the Nahuatl that he not only composed sermons in that language, but also wrote his great history of Mexico in the same, and only later translated it into Spanish. When the protomedic Hernández about the same time composed his work on Mexican plants, he wrote it in Latin, but had it translated into Nahuatl by an Indian, who also was to make a Spanish translation of it.[2] It is, therefore, not safe in any particular case to ascribe to a Nahuatl source what was accepted by Sahagun as of such an origin. I have already shown

[1] G. de Mendieta, *Historia eclesiástica indiana*, México 1870, p. 516 f.
[2] N. León, *Cuatro libros de la naturaleza, extracto de las obras del Dr. Francisco Hernández*, Morelia 1888, p. XIV.

that his *chapopotli* is described in identical terms as the *pissasphaltum* of Belon.[1] Hernández, too, used the same terms. Hence it follows that the passage from Belon had passed through a Nahuatl source at the Tlatelulco Medical School.

Similarly, the European medical practice of smoking, however with a substitution of the newer, and, therefore, reputed better tobacco, was applied by the Mexicans in precisely those cures in which henbane and its substitutes had been used in Europe. Sahagun wrote: "Against continued headache we shall use the following remedies: smell a certain herb called *ecuxo*, or the *picietl*, when it is green; tie the head with a kerchief and take some smoke."[2] "For a cold in the head or catarrh take the herb called in Mexican *yecuxoton*, or *picietl*, and smell it while it is green, and crush it and rub it with the finger inside of the mouth, in order to expel the humors."[3]

Unfortunately Hernández has come down to us only in Ximenez' annotated edition of 1615[4] and the still later Latin edition of Recchi,[5] but Ximenez' text is, in all probability, not far distant from that of Hernández, and, besides, the forty years intervening cannot have made much of a change in the medical concepts of the City of Mexico. In Ximenez' edition we read: "Of the *tauacos*, which they use in Hispaniola, which the Mexicans call *picietl*. In Hispaniola they call *tauacos* certain hollow pieces of cane, one and a half palms in length, which are outside smeared over with coal dust, and inside are full of *tauaco*, liquid amber (or *xochi ocotzotl*), and also of some other hot and fragrant materials, which, being lighted on the side where the filling

[1] See vol. I, p. 181 ff.
[2] *Op. cit.*, lib. X, cap. 28, § 1 (p. 313).
[3] *Ibid.*, (p. 317).
[4] León, *op. cit.*
[5] N. A. Recchi, *Nova plantarvm, animalivm, et mineralivm mexicanorvm historia*, Romae 1651.

is, emit the smoke through the other end, and which, swallowed through the mouth, gently sooth the senses and all labor and fatigue, and, besides, this remedy removes all pains, especially of the head, and the phlegm from the chest, which causes asthma, is rejected, and it comforts the stomach, but its abundant use should be avoided, because it greatly disturbs the liver, charging it with too much heat, which is the cause of cachexy, an ill habit of the body, and other incurable diseases."[1]

This passage shows that only the curative properties of the tobacco, which corresponded to those of henbane, etc., were recognized, and smoking as a pleasure was still considered to be injurious.  In another part of his work Hernández has a much longer and more circumstantial account of tobacco, and makes it clear that he got his story out of Estienne and Liebaut, whose work appeared in 1570, that is, one year earlier than the story of tobacco as given by Monardes.  Hence it will be best to consider the matter in the chronological order in which the tobacco and its properties became known.

[1] *Op. cit.*, p. 245 f.

# CHAPTER V.

## THE REDISCOVERY OF TOBACCO.

In 1557 Thevet had brought some tobacco seeds to France, where no doubt it was grown in gardens, but it did not attract any attention. In 1560 Jean Nicot was the French ambassador in Portugal. On April 26 of that year he wrote to the Cardinal of Lorraine: "I have acquired an herb of India, of marvellous and approved property against the *Noli me tangere* (certain cancerous ulcers) and fistulas, declared incurable by the physicians and of prompt and certain cure among the Moors. As soon as it has produced its seed, I will send it to your gardener, at Marmoustier, and the plant itself in a barrel with the instruction for transplanting and caring for it."[1] Nicot obviously knew that the Moors, that is, the Negroes or Arabs, were using the tobacco in medicine. The Papal Nunzio at Lisbon during the same year was Cardinal Santa-Croce, and he is said to have sent the tobacco seed to Rome. In any case, from Italy a specimen of what seems to be *Nicotiana rustica* was about this time sent to Matthioli in Austria, and he identified the plant with henbane.[2]

Nicot's plant produced a tremendous sensation in France. His name was permanently attached to it, and Dr. Liebaut in 1570[3] extolled its properties to the

[1] E. Falgairolle, *Jean Nicot, Ambassadeur de France en Portugal au XVIe siècle*, Paris 1897, pp. 50 and XC.

[2] Petri Andreae Matthioli senensis medici, *Commentarii in sex libros Pedacii Dioscoridis Anazarbei de medica materia*, Venetiis 1565, p. 1063 f.

[3] J. Liebaut, *L'agriculture et maison rustique de M. Charles Estienne docteur en medecine*, Paris 1570.

sky.   Liebaut's *L'agriculture et maison rustique* was frequently reprinted, and it was translated into several languages.   We shall give here his chapter on the tobacco from the English translation of 1596:[1]   "*Nicotiane*, although it bee not long since it hath been known in Fraunce, notwithstanding deserueth palme and pryce:  and among all other medicinall hearbs, it deserueth to stande in the firste rancke, by reason of his singuler vertues, and as it were almost to bee had in admyration as hereafter you shall vnderstand.   And for that none such as of auncient tyme, or of late dayes haue written the nature of plantes, did neuer make mention thereof, I haue therfore learned the whole historie touching the same, which I learned of a gentleman my very friend, ye first author, inuenter, and bringer of this herb into France: wherfore I thought good to publish it in writing for their sakes, that haue so often heard speaking of this saide hearbe, and yet neyther knewe the hearbe not the effects thereof.

"Thys hearbe is called *Nicotiane*, of the name of him that gaue the firste intelligence thereof vnto this Realme, as many other plantes haue taken their names of certeyne Greekes and Romaines, who hauying beene in straunge Countries (for seruice of their common Weales) haue brought into their countries many plants, which were before vnknowne.   Some haue called thys Hearbe the Queenes Hearbe, because it was firste sent vnto her, as heerafter shalbe declared by the Gentleman, that was the first inuenter of it, and since was by her giuen to diuers for to sow, whereby it may be planted in this lande.   Others haue named it the great Priors hearbe, for that he caused it to multiply in Fraunce, more than any other, for the great reuerence that he bare to this hearb, for the diuine effectes there-

---

[1] N. Monardes, *Joyfull Newes out of the Newfound Worlde*, London 1596, fol. 42 ff.   It is already contained in the edition of 1580, but the Harvard University copy is imperfect.

in contayned.  Many have giuen the name, *Petum*, which is indeede the proper name of the Hearbe, as they which haue trauelled that Countrie can tell.  Notwithstanding, it is better to name it *Nicotiane*, by the name of him that sent it into Fraunce first, to the ende that he may haue the honour thereof, according to his desert, for that hee hath enriched our Countrie, with so singular an Hearbe.  Thus much for the name, and now hearken for the whole Historie.

"Maister John Nicot, Counsellor to the King being Embassadour for his Maiestie in Portugall, in the yeere of our Lorde 1559.60.61. went one day to see the Prysons of the King of Portugall: and a Gentleman being the keeper of the said Prisons presented him with this hearb, as a strange plant brought from Florida. The same Maister Nicot, hauing caused the said hearb to be set in his Garden, where it grewe and multiplyed maruellously, was vpon a tyme aduertised by one of his Pages, that a yong man, of kinne to that Page made a say of that hearbe, brused both the hearbe and the Juyce together, vpon an vlcer, which he had vpon his cheeke neere vnto his nose, comming of a *Noli me tangere*, which began to take roote already at the gristles of the Nose, wherewith he founde himselfe maruellously eased.  Therefore the saide Maister Nicot caused the sick young man to bee brought before him, and causing the said hearb to be continued to the sore eight or ten daies, this saide *Noli me tangere* was utterly extinguished and healed: and he had sent it, while this cure was a woorking to a certeyne Phisition of the King of Portugall one of the greatest fame to examine the further working and effect of ye said *Nicotiane*, and sending for the same young man at the end of ten dayes, the sayde Phisition seeing the visage of the said sicke young man, certified that the saide *Noli me tangere* was vtterly extinguished, as indeed he neuer felt it since.

"Within a while after, one of the Cookes of the sayde
Embassadour hauing almost cutte of his thombe, with
a greate Chopping knyfe, the Steward of the house of
the sayde Gentleman ran to the saide *Nicotiane*, and
dressed him therewith fiue or sixe tymes, and so in the
ende thereof hee was healed: from that tyme forwarde
this hearb began to bee famous throughout Lisheborn,
where the court of the king of Portugall was at that
present, and the vertue of this saide hearbe was extolled,
and the people began to name it the Ambassadours
hearbe.   Wherefore there came certeine dayes after, a
Gentleman of the Countrie, Father to one of the Pages
of the Ambassadour, who was troubled with an vlcer
in his Legge, hauing had the same twoo yeares, and de-
maunded of the sayde Embassadour for his hearbe, and
vsing the same in such order as is before written, at the
end of ten or twelve daies he was healed.   From that
tyme forth the fame of that same hearbe increased in
such  sort,  that  many  came  from  al  places  to  haue
some of it.   Among al others there was a woman that
had her face couered with a Ringworme rooted, as
though she had a visour on her face, to whome the
saide L. Embassadour caused the hearb to be given,
and told how she should use it, and at the ende of eight
or ten daies, this woman was thoroughly healed, who
came and presented her selfe to the Embassadour,
shewing him of her healing.

"After there came a Captayne to present his sonne
sicke of the kinges euill to the saide L. Embassadour,
for to send him into Fraunce, vnto whome there was a
saye made of the sayde hearbe, which in fewe dayes
did begin to shewe great signes of healing: and finally
he was altogether healed therby of the kinges evill.

"The L. Embassadour seeing so great effectes pro-
ceding of this hearbe, and hauing heard say that the
Lady Montigue that was, died at Saint Germans, of an

vlcer bred in her brest, that did turne to a *Noli me tangere*, for the which there coulde neuer remedy be found: and lykewise that the Countesse of Ruffe, had sought for al the famous Phisitions of that Realme, for to heale her face, vnto whom they could giue no remedy: he thought it good to communicate the same into France, and did sende it to king Frauncis the seconde, and to the Queene Mother, and to many other Lords of the Court, with the maner of ministring the same, and how to apply it vnto the said diseases, euen as he had found it by experience, and chiefly to the Lorde of Iarnac, Gouernour of Rogel, with whom the said Lorde Embassadour had great amity for the seruice of the king. The which Lord of Iarnac told one day at the Queenes table, y he had caused the saide *Nicotiane* to be distilled, and the water to be drunke, mingled with water of *Euphrasie*, otherwise called eiebright, to one that was short breathed, who was therewith healed.

"This hearbe hath the stalke greate, bearded and slimie, the leafe large and long bearded slimye, it groweth in branches halfe foote to halfe foote, and is very ful of leaues, and groweth in height foure or fiue foot. In hot countries it is nyne or tenne monethes in the yeere laden, in one selfe tyme, with leaues, flowers and Coddes, ful of rype graynes, which is when they are waxed blacke and to be ripe, which is when they are yet greene. It sproutes foorth neere the roote muche, and reuyueth by a great quantitie of buddes, notwithstanding the graine is the least seede in the worlde, and the rootes be like small threeds.

"*Nicotiane* doth require a fat grounde finely digged, and in colde Countreyes very well dunged, that is to saye, a grounde in the which the dung must be so wel mingled and incorporated, that it be altogether turned into earth, and that there appeare no more dung.

"It requireth the south Sunne, and to be planted by a wal, which may defende it against the North winde recouering the heat of the Sunne against it, being a warrant vnto the said hearbe against the tossing up of the winde, because of the weaknes and highnes thereof.

"It groweth the better being often watered, and re-uiueth it selfe by reason of the water in time of droughts. It hateth the colde, therefore to preserue if from dying in the Winter time, it must be either kept in caues made of purpose within the said gardens, or els couered with a double matte, and a Penthouse of Reede made on the Wall ouer the hearbe, and when the South Sunne shineth, the dore of the place must be opened where the hearbe is on the Southside.

"For to sowe it, there must bee made a hole in the ground with your finger, as deepe as your finger can reache, then cast into that hole 40. or 50. graines of the sayde Seede together, stopping againe your hole, for it is so small a Seede, that if there bee put in the hole but three or four graynes thereof, the earth would choke them, and if the weather be drye, the place must be watered lightly during the time of fifteene dayes after the sowing thereof: it may also be sowen like vnto Lettis and other such hearbes.

"And when the hearbe is out of the ground, for so muche as euerie graine thereof will bring foorth his Twigge, and that the little threeds of the Roote are the one within the other, you must make with a great knife a greate compasse within the earth rounde about the sayde place, and lift up the earth together with the Seede, and cast it into a payle of water, so that the earth be separated, and that the little twigges may swimme about the water, then shal you take them without breaking, the one after the other, and you shal plant each of them again by themselves, with the selfe same earth, and shall set them three foote from the wall, leauing foure foote space from one Twigge to another, and if the earth which is neere vnto the wall, be not so good as it ought to bee, you shall prepare and amende it as aforesaide, helping the sayd Twigges so remoued by often watering.

"The time to sowe it is in the middest of April, or at the beginning: As touching the vertues, it will heale *Noli me tangere*, all olde Sores and cankered Vlcers, hurts, Ringwormes, great Scabbes, what euill soeuer be in them, in stamping the leaues of the said hearbe in a cleane Morter, and applying the hearbe and the Juyce together vppon the griefe, and the parties must abstaine from meate that is salt, sower, and spiced, and from strong wine, except that it be well watered.

"The leafe of this hearbe being dried in the shadow, and hanged vp in the house, so that there come neither Sunne, winde, nor fire therunto, and being cast on a Chaffyng dish of Coales to bee burned, taking the smoke thereof at your mouth through a fonnel or cane your head being wel couered, causeth to auoide at the mouth great quantitie of slimy and flegmatike water, wherby the body will be extenuated and weakened, as though one had long fasted, thereby it is thought by some, that the dropsie not hauing taken roote, will be healed by this Perfume.

"Moreouer the inhabitantes of Florida doe nourish themselues certaine times, with the smoke of this Hearbe, which they receiue at the mouth through certayne coffins, such as the Grocers doe vse to put in their spices. There be other oyntmentes prepared of the saide hearbe, with other simples, but for a truth this only simple hearbe, taken and applyed as aforesaide, is of greater efficacie, notwithstanding one may make therof an oyntment, which is singular, to cleanse, incarnate, and knit together all manner of woundes: the making of the sayde Oyntmentes, is thus. Take a pounde of the freshe Leaues of the sayde Hearbe, stampe them, and mingle them with newe Ware, Rosine, common oyle, of each three ounces, let them boyle altogether, vntill the Juice of *Nicotiane* be consumed, then adde therto three ounces of Venise Turpentine, straine the same through a Linen cloth, and keepe it in Pottes to your vse.

"Loe, here you haue the true Historie of *Nicotiane*, of the which the sayde Lorde Nicot, one of the Kinges Counsellers first founder out of this hearbe, hath made mee priuie aswel by woorde as by writing, to make thee (friendly Reader) partaker thereof, to whome I require thee to yeeld as harty thankes as I acknowledge myself bound vnto him for this benefite receiued."

Monardes had twice brought out a book on the plants coming from the West Indies, namely in 1565 and 1569, but tobacco was not among them. In 1571 he published a second part, chiefly on tobacco and sassafras, and in the introduction to this work he said: "These dayes past I wrote a booke of all thinges which come from your Occidentall Indias, seruing for the vse of Medicine, and surely it hath beene taken in that estimation, that the thinges which in it are intreated of doe deserue. And seeing the profite that it hath done, and how manny haue beene remedyed and healed with those remedies, I dyd determine to proceede forwardes, and to write of the thinges, which after that the first part was written, haue come from those countries of the which I haue vnderstood, that no lesse vtilitie & profite shal come, then of those which are past, for there shalbe discouered newe thinges and secrets, which will bring admiration, neuer to this day seene nor knowne before. And seeing that these medicinall thinges which we doe treate of, and the Realmes, and countries from whence they come, belong vnto your Maiestie, and he also that writeth of them, is your

Maiesties subject: I doe desire your Maiestie, to receiue this trauell into your protection, and that the
rewarde may be such, as for the like works dedicated
to your Maiestie is accustomed to be given.''[1]   As
tobacco was unquestionably known in Spain in 1569,
as it was in Portugal, Monardes can only mean that
the attention to tobacco was directed to him by the
very Liebaut in his famous work which is always quoted
by the name *La maison rustique*, that is, it was only
Nicot's published experiments that made it necessary
to emphasize the marvellous qualities which of right
should be claimed for a plant from the Spanish colonies.
His account of the tobacco in the English translation
of 1596 runs as follows : "Of the Tabaco, and of his
great vertues.—This Hearbe which commonly is called
*Tabaco*, is an Hearbe of much antiquitie, and knowen
amongst the Indians, and inespecially among them of
the newe Spaine, and after that those Countries were
gotten by our Spaniards, being taught of the Indians,
they did profite themselues with those thinges, in the
woundes which they received in their Warres, healing
themselves therewith to their great benefite.

"Within these few yeeres there hath beene brought
into Spayne of it more to adornate Gardens with the
fairenesse thereof, and too giue a pleasaunt sight, than
that it was thought to haue the meruelous medicinable
vertues which it hath, but nowe we doe vse it more for
his vertues, than for his fairenesse.   For surely they
are such which doe bring admiration.

"It is growing in many partes of the Indias, but ordi-
narilie in moyst and shadowie places, and it is needefull that the grounde where it is sowne, be well tilled,
and that it be a fruiteful grounde and at all times it is
sowen, in the hot Countries.   But in the colde Coun-

---

[1] *Ibid.*, fol. 33a.

tries it must bee sowen in the Moneth of Marche, for
that is may defende it selfe from the frost.

"The proper name of it amongst the Indians is
*Picielt.* For the name of *Tabaco* is giuen to it by our
Spaniards, by reason of an Island that is named *Tabaco.*

"It is an hearbe that dooth growe and come to bee
very greate: many times too bee greater then a Lem-
mon tree.   It casteth foorth one steame from the roote
which groweth vpright, without declining to any parte,
it sendeth foorth many Bowes, straight, that well neere
they bee equal with the principall steame of the tree:
his Leafe is wel neere like to the Leafe of a Citron tree,
they come to bee verie great, and be of colour greene,
the Plant it heauie, they be in the Garden as Cytrons
and Orenges are, for all the yeere they are greene, and
haue leaues, and if any whyther they be those that are
lowest.   In the highest parte of all the Plante, there
doth growe out the flower, the which is after the manner of white Campanillia, and in the middest of Carna-
tion colour: it hath a good shew when it is drie, it is
like to blacke Poppie seede, and in it is shut vp:  the
seede is very small, and of the colour of a dark Tawny.

"The Roote is great, conformable to the greatness of
the Plante, deuided into many partes, and it is like to
wood in substaunce, the which being parted, it hath
the hearte within, like vnto the colour of Saffron, and
beeying tosted, it hath some bitterness with it.   The
Rinde cometh away easilie, we knowe not that the
roote hath any vertue at all: Of the Leaues onely we
know the vertues, which we will speake of, although
that I belieeve that the roote hath medicinall vertues
enough, the which time shall discouer.   And some will
say that it hath the vertue of Ruibarbe, but I haue not
experimented it as yet, they doo keepe the leaues after
they be drie in the shadow, for the effects that we wil
speake of, and they be made into pouder, to be vsed of

them in place of the Leaues, for it is not in all partes.
The one and the other is to bee kept a great time, without corrupting.  The complexion thereof is hot and
drie in the second degree, it hath vertue to heate and
to dissolue, with some bynding and comforting, it glew-
eth together and sodereth the fresh wounds and healeth
them:  the filthy wounds and sores it doth cleanse and
reduce to a perfect health, as it shal be spoken of hereafter, and so likewise wee will speake of the vertues of
these hearbes, and of the thinges that they are good
for euery one perticulerly.

"This hearbe *Tabaco*, hath perticuler vertue to heale
griefes of the heade and in especially comming of colde
causes, and so it cureth the headake when it commeth
of a cold humor, or of a windy cause.  The leaues must
be laid hotte to the griefe, and multiplying them the
tyme that is nedeful vntill the griefe be taken away.
Some there be that doo annoynt them with the Oyle
of Orenges, and so they performe a verie good woorke.

"If any manner of griefe that is in the body or any
other part thereof it helpeth, proceeding of a cold
cause, and applyed thereunto, it taketh it away, not
without great admiration.

"In griefes of the brest it worketh a maruellous effect
and inespecially in those that doo cast out matter and
rottenness at the mouth, and in them that are short
breathed, and in anie other olde euilles making of the
hearbe a decoction, or with Sugar a Syrope, and being
taken in little quantity, it doth expel the Matters, and
rottenness of the brest maruellously, and the smoke
being taken in at the mouth, doth cause that the matter
be expelled out of the brest of them that doo fetch
their breath short.

"In the griefe of the stomack, caused of colde, or
winde, the leaues being put very hot, it dooth take it
away, and dissolueth it by multiplying the vse, vntil it

be taken away. And it is to be noted, that the leaues are to be warmed better than any other, amongst Ashes or Embers very hotte, thrusting the hearbes into them. and so to warme them wel, and although they be layde to with some ashes, they make the worke better, and of more strong effectes.

"In Opilations of the stomacke, and of the inner partes principally, this hearbe is a great remedie: for that it dooth dissolue, and consume them, and this same it dooth in any other manner of Opilations or hardness that are in the belly, the cause being of a colde humor, or of windiness.

"They must take the hearbe greene, and stampe it, and with those stamped leaues rubbe the hardness a good while, and at the tyme as the hearbe is in the Morter a stamping, let there be put to it a fewe droppes of Vinegar, that hys worke may be made the better: and after the place is rubbed where the paine is, then lay vpon it one leafe or two leaues of the *Tobaco* being hotte, and so let it alone til the next day, and then do the like againe, or in place of the leaues vse a Linnen cloth wet in the hotte iuice. Some there bee, that after they haue rubbed it with the stamped leaues, do annoint it with oyntments, made for the like euils, and vpon it they lay the leaues for the iuyce of the *Tabaco*. And surely with this cure they haue desolued great and hard opilations, and very old swellings. In the griefe of the stone of the kidneies and Reines, this hearbe woorketh great effects, by putting the Leaues into Ashes, or Embers, hotte, that they may warme wel, and then being laid vpon the griefe, multiplying the vse of it as often as it is needfull. It is necessarie in the seethinges that are vsed to bee made for Glisters to put into them with the other things, the Leaues of this hearbe, for that they shal profit much: and likewise for Fomentations and Plaisters, that they shall make.

"In griefes of windes they woorke the like effect, taking away the paines that come of the windinesse, applying the leaues after the same sort as is aboue saide.

"In the griefe of women, which is called the euill of the Mother, laying too one leafe of this hearbe *Tobaco* very hotte, in the manner as it is saide, it dooth manifestly profit and it must be layde vppon the Nauell. And vnder it some do vse it first of all, thinges of good smell vppon the Nauel, and then vpon that they lay the leafe. In that which they finde most profite, is to lay the Tacamahaca, or the oyle of liquid Amber, and Balsamo, and Caranna, or any of those vnto the Nauel, and to keep it to it continually, that it may cleane vnto it, and this worketh manifest profit in griefes of the Mother.

"In one thing, the women that dwel in the Indias do celebrate this hearbe, that is, in the euil breathing at ye mouth of children, when they are ouer filled with meat, and also of olde people, anoynting their bellies with lampe oyle, and laying some of those leaues in ashes hotte to their bellies, and also to their shoulders, for it doth take away their naughtie breathing, and maketh them go to the stoole, applying it vnto the fundement at what time it is needfull, and if the leaues be ashed it is the better.

"Wormes, of all kindes of them, it killeth, and expelleth them maruellously, the seething of the hearbe made into a Syrope delicately, being taken in very little quantitie, and the iuyce thereof put on the nauel. It is needful after this be done to giue a Glister, that may auoide them, and expell them out of the guttes.

"In griefes of the Joyntes comming of a colde cause it maketh a maruellous worke, the Leaues of this *Tabaco* being laid hotte vpon the griefe the like doth the Juyce layd vpon a little cloth hotte, for that it doeth dissolue the humor, and taketh away the paines therof.   If it come of a hot cause it doth hurt, sauing when the humor hath bene hot, and the subtill part is dissolued, and the grosse remaineth, then it doeth profite as of the cause were colde, and it is to be vnderstood, that the leaues being layde, where as is griefe of the sayde cause, in any part of the bodie, it profiteth much.

"In swellings or in cold Impostumes, it doth dissolue and vndoe them, washing them with the hot Juyce, and laying the beaten leaues, after they be stampt, or the leaues being whole of the said *Tabaco*, vpon it.

"In the Toothache, when the griefe commeth of a colde cause or of a colde Rumes, putting to it a little ball made of the leafe of the *Tabaco*, washing first the tooth with a smal cloth wet in the Juyce, it taketh away the paine, and stayeth it, that the putrification goe not forwarde: in hot causes it doth not profite, and this remedie is so common that it healeth euerie one.

"This hearbe doth meruellously heale Chilblaines, rubbing them with the stamped leaues, and after putting the hands and Feete in hot water, with Salt, and keping them warme:  this is done with great experience in many.

"In venom and venomous wounds our *Tabaco* hath great commendation, which hath beene knowne but a short time since: for when the wilde people of the Indias, which eate mans fleshe doe shoote their Arrowes, they annointe them with an hearb or Composition made of many poysons, with the which they shoote at al things that they would kill, and this venom is so strong and pernicious, that it killeth without remedie, and they that bee hurte die with great paines and accidents, and with madnes, vnless that there be found remedy for so great an euill.   A fewe yeeres past they laid to their wounds Sublimatum, and so were remedied, and surely

in those partes they haue suffered much with this
vexation of poyson.

"A little whiles past, certain wilde people going in
their Bootes to S. John De puerto Rico, to shoote at
Indians, or Spaniards (if that they might find them)
came to a place and killed certain Indians and Spaniards, and did hurt many, and as by chaunce there was
no Sublimatum at that place to heale them, they remembered to lay vpon the wounds the Juice of the
*Tabaco*, and the leaues stamped.   And God would, that
laying it vpon the hurts, the griefs, madnes, and accidents wherewith they died, were mittigated, and in
such sorte they were deliuered of that euill, that the
strength of the Venom was taken away, and the wounds
were healed, of the which there was greate admiration.
Which thing being known to them of the Ilande, they
vse it also on other hurtes and woundes, which they
take when they fight with the wilde people, now they
stand in no feare of them, by reason they haue founde
so great a remedie, in case so desperate.

"This Hearbe hath also vertue against the hearbe
called of the Crosseboweshooter, which our hunters doe
vse to kill the wilde beastes withall, which hearbe is
Venom most strong, and doth kill without remedie,
which the Kinges pleasure was to proue, and com-
maunded to make experience therof, and they wounded
a little dogge in the throate, and put forthwith into the
wound the hearbe of the Crosseboweshooter, and after
a little whyle they powred into the selfe same wound
that they had annointed with the Crosseboweshooters
hearbe, a good quantitie of the Juice of *Tabaco*, and layde the stamped leaues vpon it, and they tied vp the
dogge and he escaped, not without great admiration
of all men that saw him.   Of the which, the excellent
Phisition of the Chamber of his Maiestie, Doctor
Barnarde in the margent of this booke, that saw it, by

the commaundement of his Maiestie, writeth these
wordes: I made this experience by the commaundment
of the kinges Maiestie.   I wounded the dogge with a
knife, and after I put the Crosseboweshooters hearbe
into the wound, and the hearbe was chosen, and the
dogge was taken of the hearbe, and the *Tabaco* and his
Juyce being put into the wounde, the dogge escaped
and remained whole.

"In the venomous Carbuncles, the *Tabaco* being applied in manner as is aforesaid doth extinguish ye malice
of the venom, and doth that which all the workes of
Surgerie can doe, vntill it be whole.   The same effect
it worketh in bytings of venomous beastes, for it killeth
and extinguisheth the malice of the venom and healeth
them.

"In woundes newely hurt, and cuttes strokes prickes,
or any other manner of wounde, our *Tabaco* worketh
maruellous effectes, for that it doeth heale them and
maketh them sound.   The wound must be washed with
wine, and procure to annoynt the sides of it, taking
away that which is superfluous, and then powre into
it the Juice of this hearbe, and lay vpon it the stamped
leaues, and being wel bound it shall continue on vntill
the next day that thou shalt return to dresse it.   After
the same fashion the pacientes shall keepe good order
in their meate, vsing the diet necessary, and if it be
needful of any euacuation by stoole, the cause being
greate, let be done what shall be conuenient.   And
with this order they shalbe healed without any need
of any more Surgerie then this hearbe only.   Here in
this Country, and in this City they know not what
other to doe, hauing cut or hurt themselues, but to
runne to the *Tabaco*, as to a most ready remedie.   It
doth meruellous workes, without any need of other
Surgery, but this only hearbe.   In restraining the fluxe
of blood of the wounds it procureth most maruellous

workes, for that the Juyce and the Leaues being stamped, are sufficient to restraine any fluxe of blood.

"In olde Sores it is maruellous the woorkes and the effects that this hearbe doeth, for it healeth them wonderfully, making cleane and mundifying them of all humors that are superfluous, and of the rottennes, that they haue, and bringeth vp the flesh, reducing them to perfite health, the which is so common in this Citie, that euery man doeth knowe it: and I hauing ministred it to many people as well men as women, in greate number, and being grieved often, and of twentie yeeres, haue healed olde rotten sores in legges, and other partes of the body, with this remedy only to the great admiration of all men.

"The order of the cure that is to bee wrought with thys hearbe is this following. For the old rotten sores although they may be cankered, let the sicke man bee purged with the counsell of a Phisition, and let him blood if it bee needefull and then take this hearbe and pounde it in a Morter, and wring out the Juyce, and pur it into the sore, and then after the manner of a playster lay the stamped leaues vpon it, which are the Leaues that the Juyce is taken out of, and this doe once euerie day eating good Meates, and not exceeding in any disorder, for other wise it will not profit. And doing this it wil make cleane the euil flesh that is rotten, and superfluous, vntil it come to the whole flesh, and it is not to be maruelled at, if the wounde be made very great. For the euil must be eaten vp, vntil it come to the good, and in the same cure putting in lesse quantitie of iuyce, it wil incarnate, and reduce it to perfit health, in such sort, that it accomplisheth all the workes of Surgery, that all the Medicines of the world are able to doo, without hauing neede of any other manner of Medicine.

"This worke dooth cure old Sores, with very great
admiration: and not only in men but in bruite beastes
also.   As at this day in all partes of the Indias, where
there are any cattell hauing wounds or gaules: and the
countrey being hotte and moyst ouer muche, dooth
soone rotte them, an very quickly they come to bee
cankered. and for this cause many great cattel doo die:
To remedy this and the wormes that doo increase in
the sores, they had for remedy to put into the sores
Sublimatum, for that in this remedy they dyd finde
more benefite then in any other, that they had vsed.
And for that the Sublimatum beares there so high a
price, manytimes it was more worth then the cattell
that it healed.   For this cause and for hauing founde
in the *Tabaco*, so muche vertue too heale newe woundes
and rotten, they did accorde and agree togeather to vse
the *Tabaco*, in the healing of beastes, as they had done
in the cure and remedy of men, powring the Juyce of
the *Tabaco* into the wounds, and washing them therewith, and laying vpon them the stamped leaues of the
*Tabaco*, after that the Juyce is taken from them.   And
it is of so great efficacie and vertue, that it killeth the
wormes, and maketh cleane the sore, eating away the
euill fleshe, and ingendering newe vntill it be whole, as
in the other thinges which we haue spoken of.   The
like it doth in the gaules of the beasts of Cariege, the
iuice being powred in, and the beaten leaues wherout
the iuice commeth of the *Tabaco* as it is sayde: although
they may be cankered it doth make them cleane and
incarnate them, and cureth and helpeth them.   And
so the Indians doo carrie it, when they iourney, for this
purpose and effect, and it procureth the profite that
the iuyce doeth.

"I sawe a man that had certeyne old sores in his nose,
wherby he did cast out from him much matter, which
dayly did rotte and canker inwarde, and I caused him

to take at his nose the iuyce of this *Tabaco*, and so he
did: and at the seconde tyme, he caste out from him,
more than twenty little wormes, and afterwards a fewe
more, vntyl that he remained cleane of them, and vsing
it so certeyne dayes, hee was healed of the sore, that
he had in the inner part of his nose: and if he had tar-
ried any longer, I thinke that there had remained
nothing of his nose, but all had been eaten away, as it
happeneth to many, which we see without them. And
beeing wryting of this, a daughter of a Gentleman of
this Cittie, had many yeares a certeyne kinde of skabbes,
or wel neere skuruie in her head. I had her in cure and
did vnto her many benifits vniuersal, and perticuler:
and also Maisters of Surgerie had done their diligence,
and all did not profite. And a Gentlewoman, which
had the charge of her, as shee heard mee speake one
day much good of the *Tabaco*, that it was good and
profitable, for so many infirmities, she sent for it, and
did rubbe hard the disease that the wench had, and
that day she was very euill as though shee had beene
foolishe: and ye gentle woman did not let (in seing
her after that sort) to rubbe her harder, and then the
wench did not feele so muche griefe, but the dry
skabbes began to fall, and the white scurffe of her head
in such sorte, that it made cleane and healed her head,
with dooing so certeyne dayes, so that shee was healed
of her skuruie disease very well, without knowing what
she did.

"One of the meruelles of this hearbe, and that whiche
bringeth most admiration, is, the maner howe the
Priests of the Indias did vse it, which was in this manner: when there was amongst the Indians any manner
of businesse, of greate importaunce, in which the
chiefe Gentlemen called Casiques or any of the principall people of the Countrey, had necessitie to consult
with their Priests in any businesse of importance:

then they went and propounded their matter to their chiefe Priest, foorthwith in their presence, he tooke certeyne leaues of the *Tabaco* and cast them into ye fire, and did receiue the smoke of them at his mouth, and at his nose with a Cane, and in taking of it, he fell downe vpon the ground, as a Dead man, and remaynyng so according to the quantity of the smoke that he had taken when the hearbe had done his worke he did reuiue and awake, and gaue them their aunsweares according to the visions, and illusions which he sawe, whiles hee was rapte in the same manner, and he did interprete to them, as to him seemed best, or as the Diuell had counselled him giuing them continually doubtful aunswers, in such sorte, that howsoeuer it fell out, they might say that it was the same, which was declared, and the answere that he made.

"In like sort the rest of the Indians for their pastime, do take the smoke of the *Tabaco*, to make themselues drunke withall, and to see the visions, and things that represent vnto them, that wherein they do delight: and other times they take it to know their businesse, and successe, because conformable to that which they haue seene, being drunke therwith, euen so they iudge of heir businesse.  And as the deuil is a deceiuer, and hath the knowledge of the vertue of hearbs, so he did shew the vertue of this Hearb, that by the meanes thereof, they might see their imaginations, and visions, that he hath represented vnto them, and by that meanes deceiue them.

"To haue hearbes that haue the like vertue, is a common thing, and in the booke of the Phisition, Dioscorides dooth say, that one Dramme of the roote of Solatro, beeyng taken in wine, which roote is very straunge and furious, prouoketh sleepe greatlie, and maketh him that taketh it, to dreame of thinges variable, and dooth represent vnto hym terrible imaginations, and visions.

Others doe giue delectation and pleasure.   Of the Anis
seed they say, being eaten at the houre, when that any
shal sleep, it maketh a pleasant, and delectable dreame.
The Radish doth make them greeuous and very heauie,
and so likewise of many other hearbs, which would be
ouer large to speake of, as of this matter, the auncient
writers report.

"Diego Gratia de Guerta, in the booke that hee wryt-
eth of the Spicerie and drugs of the Orientall Indias,
reporteth that in those parts there is an hearbe, which
is called *Bague*, which being mingled with thinges of
sweet smell, there is made of it a confection of excellent
smell and taste: and when the Indians of those parts,
will depriue themselves of iudgement, and see visions
that giue them pleasure, then they take a certayne
quantitie of this confection, and in taking of it, they
remaine depriued of all iudgement, and while the vertue of theyr Medicine dooth endure, they receiue muche
delight, and see thinges, whereby they receive pleasure,
and be glad of them.   There was a mightie Emperor,
being Lorde of many Realmes, sayde vnto Martine
Alfonso de Sosa, who was the vice Roy of the East
India, that when he woulde see Realmes, and Cities,
and other thinges, of the which he did receiue pleasure,
that hee should then take the Bague, made in a certeyne confection, and that in dooing so, he did receiue
pleasure.   The vse of this confection is very common,
and very muche vsed amongst the Indians of those
parts, and they do sel it in the publice market, for that
purpose.

"The Indians of our Occidentall Indias, doo vse the
*Tabaco* to take away wearinesse, and for to make light-
somnesse in their Labour, for in their daunces they bee
so much wearied, and they remaine so wearie, that they
can scarcely stirre: and because that they may labour
the next day, and returne to that foolish exercise, they

receiue at ye mouth and nose, the smoke of the *Tabaco*, and remain as dead people: and being so, they be eased in such sorte, that when they be awakened out of their sleepe, they remain without wearinesse, and may returne to their labour as much as before, and so they doe alwaies, when they haue need of it: for with that sleepe, they receiue their strength, and be much the lustier.

"The blacke people that haue gone from these partes to the Indias, haue practised the same manner and vse of the *Tobaco*, that ye Indians haue, for when they see themselues weary, they take it at the nose, and mouth, and it happeneth vnto them, as vnto our Indians, lying as though they were dead three of foure houres, and after they remayne lightened, without wearinesse, for to labour againe: and they do this with great pleasure, that although they bee not weary yet they are verie desirous to doe it: and the things is come to suche effecte, that their Masters chasten them for it, and doe burne the *Tabaco*, because they shoulde not vse it: whervppon they goe to the desertes, and secrete places to doe it, because they may not be permitted, to drinke themselues drunke with Wine, and therfore they are gladde to make themselves drunken with the smoke of *Tabaco*, I haue seen them doe it here, and it happened to them as is saide. And they say, that when they come out of the same traunce or dream they finde themselues very lusty, and they reioyce to haue beene after the same sort and manner, seeing that therby they doe receiue no hurt.

"Thees barbarous people do vse ye like things to take away weariness; and not only this custom is vsed in our Occidental Indias, but it is also a common thing in the Oriental Indias. And also in the Portugall Indias, for this effecte, they doe sell the Opio in their Shoppes, euen as they sell Conserua, with the which the Indians vse to ease themselves, of their labour that they take, and to be merrie, and not to feele paines of any greate labour of the bodie, or mynde that may come vnto them, and they call it there amongst themselves Aphion. This Aphion the Turkes doe vse for this effecte. The Souldiers and Captaines that goe to Warres, when they labour muche, after the time that they be lodged, that they may take their rest, they receiue Aphion, and sleepe with it, and remaine lightened of their labour. The most principall people take Bague, and it hath a better taste, and a better smel, for there is put to it much Amber, and Muske and Cloues, and other spices. And surely it is a thing of admiration, to see howe these Barbarous people doe take such Medicines, and how many of them doe take them, and that they doe not kill them, but rather they take them for health and remedie for their necessities.

"I sawe an Indian of those partes, that in my presence did aske an Apothecarie for a quart of Opio, and I demanded of him wherfore he would haue it: and he told me that he tooke it to put away weariness, when he felt himself ouer much grieued, and afflicted with labour, and he tooke the halfe of that which he caried, for the Apothecary gaue hym more then a pint for twelue pence, and therewith he slept so soundly, that when he awoke from sleepe, hee founde himselfe verie much eased of his wearinesse, in suche sorte, that he might continue his labour. I meruelled at it, and it seemed to me a thing of Mockerie, seeing that fiue or sixe graines, bee the most that wee can giue to a sicke Person howe stronge soouer hee bee, which beeing very well prepared, doeth cause many times Accidentes of Death. And many yeeres after standing in the Shoppe of an other Apothecary of this Citie, there came an other Indian, of the same Orientall Indias, and he asked of the Apothecarie for some Opio called Aphion, the which

Apothecarie vnderstoode him not. And I remembring my selfe of the other Indian, caused him to shewe vnto the Indian Opio, and in shewing it to him, hee said that is was that which he asked for, and he bought a quarter of a Pinte of it, and I asked of the Indian, wherefore he would haue it, and he tolde me the same that the other Indian did, that it was because he might labour: and ease himselfe of his wearinesse, for that hee did beare burdens, and should helpe to discharge a shippe: wherefore he sayde hee would take the one halfe, that he might therwith labour, and the other halfe after he had laboured, that therwith he might take ease, and rest. Then I gave him credite to the first Indian, of that he sayd vnto me, and since I haue beleeued that which I haue seene and read, in those partes to bee a thing in common vse, for the like effectes. And truely it is a thing worthy of greate consideration, that fiue graines of Opio do kill vs, and threescore doe giue them health and rest.

"The Indians doe vse the *Tabaco*, for to suffer drieth, and also to suffer hunger, and to passe daies without hauing neede to eate or drinke, when they shal trauel by any desert or dispeopled countrie, where they shal finde neither water, nor meate. They receiue thereof little balles, which they make of the *Tabaco*. For they take the leaues of it, and chew them, and as they goe chewing of them, they goe mingling with them certaine pouder, made of the shelles of Cockels burned, and they mingle it in the mouth altogether vntil they make it like dowe, of the which they frame certaine little Balles, little greater then Peason, and lay them to drie in the shadow, and after they keep them, and vse them in this forme following.

"When they vse to trauel by the wayes, where they finde no water nor meate, they take a little ball of these, and out it betweene the lower lippe and the teeth, and goe chewing it all the time that they trauell, and that which they chew, they swallow downe, and in this sort they journey three or foure dayes, without hauing neede of meate, or drinke, for they feel no hunger, drieth nor weaknesse, nor their trauel doth trouble them. I thinke that to iourney after this sort, is the cause they goe chewing continually the little balles: for they bring Fleume into the mouth, and swallow it into the stomacke, the which doth retaine the naturall heate, which it doth consume, and so they maintain themselues therby, the like wherefor wee see to happen in many beastes, for that a great part of the winter, they be shut vp in their Caues, and hollows places of the earth, and passe their time there without any meate, for that they haue to consume the naturall heate, of the fatnes, which they had gotten in the Summer. The beare being a great and fierce beast, much time in the Winter remaineth in his Caue, and liueth without meate or drink, with onely chewing his pawes, which perhaps he doeth for the sayd cause. This is the substance which I haue gathered of this hearb, so celebrated and called *Tabaco* for that surely it is an hearb of great estimation, for the excellent vertues that it hath, as wee haue sayde."[1]

Monardes' discussion of tobacco consists of two parts. The account of the use of tobacco by the Indians and Negroes is taken out from Peter Martyr, Oviedo, and other contemporary writers, but even here we have a touch of personal experience, when Monardes says that he saw the Negroes in Spain use tobacco for the same purposes. The rest of the story is dealing with experiments in the application to diseases, and here we get the whole list of virtues, anciently applied to viscous substances, by Ibn-al-Baitār specifically referred to *tubbāq* in Syria, Egypt, and Africa. But the

---

[1] *Ibid.*, fol. 33b to 41b.

chief virtue, according to Monardes, is in the healing of cankerous sores, that is, of the very *noli me tangere*, to which Nicot directed the attention, and which was the subject of Liebaut's discussion.  If Monardes did not get this suggestion directly from Nicot or Liebaut, they must all have received it from the same source, to which Nicot refers, namely the Negroes.

From Oviedo we learned that tobacco was raised by Negroes in the Spanish plantations for the trade with the Indians.  We also know that early in the XVI. century Arawaks from the West Indies crossed over to Florida, hence a relation must have subsisted between the two countries.  Jacques Cartier tells us of the travels of Indians from the Great Lakes somewhere to the Gulf of Mexico, ostensibly in order to meet European traders, and I have already suggested that the mounds of the Mound-builders were constructed by the Indians or the traders as fortifications, to secure the trade.  It will now be shown that tobacco was one of the articles which was carried along these routes by persons who were acquainted with the African stockade posts.

De Soto distinctly refers to the mounds as built for defence:  "The Chief's house stood near the beach, upon a very high mount made by hand for defence."[1]  Biedma tells the same:  "It is the custom of the Caciques to have near their houses a high hill, made by hand, some having the houses placed thereon."[2]  Just such a hill is described by Marees, who says that here they gather on Tuesdays, which is their Sunday, for religious services,[3] and a comparison of the Peul African stockade[4] with Le Moyne's drawing of a Florida stockade, made

[1] B. Smith, *Narratives of the Career of Hernando de Soto in the Conquest of Florida*, New York 1866, p. 23.
[2] *Ibid.*, p. 251.
[3] P. de Marees, *op. cit.*, p. 67.
[4] F. Moore, *Travels into the Inland Parts of Africa*, London 1738, p. 35.

AFRICAN MOUND, from P. de Marees' *Beschryvinge....van Gunea.*

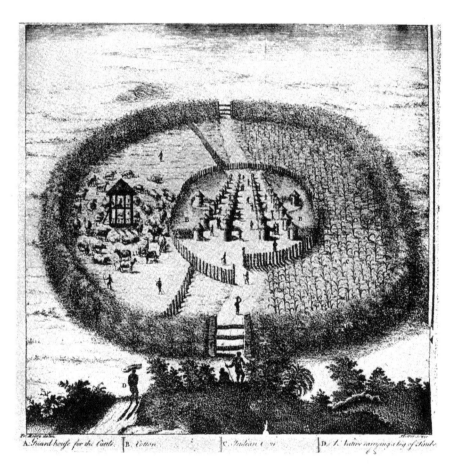

A. Guard house for the Cattle. | B. Cotton | C. Indian Corn | D. A Native carrying a log of Timber

AFRICAN STOCKADE, from F. Moore's *Travels into the Inland Parts of Africa*.

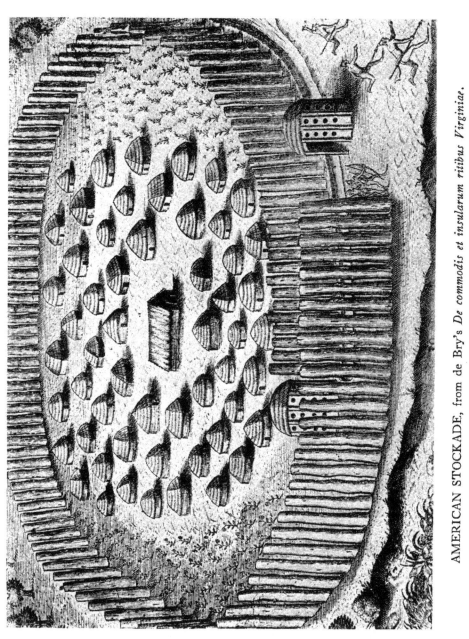

AMERICAN STOCKADE, from de Bry's *De commodis et insularum ritibus Virginiae.*

INDIAN FUMIGATION, from de Bry's *De commodis et incolarum ritibus Virginiae.*

in 1564,[1] is most striking.  Both are circular, built of
heavy upright posts, have a similar gate entrance, contain rows of circular huts, and within the stockade
there are two fields.

Cabeza de Vaca, who traversed North America from
1528–1536, found tobacco already in use among the
Indians: "In this whole country they make themselves drunk by a certain smoke for which they give
all they have."[2]  In Le Moyne's illustration the smoke
is taken both in the form of fumigation or through a
pipe,[3] but in either case it is merely as a medical practice, and not as a universal habit.  The very fact that,
according to Cabeza de Vaca, the Indians gave their
all for a smoke shows that tobacco was hard to obtain
and expensive.  When Hariot, in 1587,[4] described the
tobacco of Virginia, he not only mentioned it as cultivated, but finished his account with the words, "and
these are all the commodities for sustenance of life that
I know and can remember vse to husband:  all else
that followe are found growing naturally or wilde," by
which he showed that tobacco was not known to him
as growing wild.  Again, Strachey, in the beginning of
the XVII. century,[5] remarked that tobacco was taken
in proportion to the number of wives a man had, that
is, according to his wealth, which once more shows that
smoking was an expensive luxury still.  Even as late
as the year 1600 Champlain thought of St. Domingo,
that is, Hispaniola, as the great exporting place of

[1] Th. de Bry, *Admiranda narratis fida tamen, de commodis et incolarum ritibus Virginiae*, Francofurti ad Moenum 1590.

[2] F. Bandelier, *The Journey of Alvar Nuñez Cabeza de Vaca*, New York 1905, p. 124.

[3] De Bry, *op. cit.*

[4] See vol. I, p. 141 ff.

[5] *Ibid.*, p. 143.

tobacco.[1]  Champlain only once mentions tobacco as in use in Canada, when at a *tabagie*, or festive occasion, the Great Sagamo exchanged a smoke with Sieur du Pont-Graué of Saint Malo and himself,[2] that is, tobacco was used, as in Mexico, Nicaragua, Darien, only by the rich who could afford it.   Nowhere, except near Spanish plantations, where Negroes raised the tobacco, do we hear of the generality of Indians as smoking. The further we go away from this, the more solemn is the occasion at which tobacco is smoked.   It took a whole century for tobacco to become popular and universal, and then, after Nicot and Monardes had raised it to the dignity of a sovereign remedy, the English and Dutch, at the end of the XVI. century, began a furious rivalry to spread the precious product of Virginia and Guiana to all the corners of the earth.   Only then did people begin to take notice of the smoking, which before was not even referred to, except in America, because of the notoriety given to it by Peter Martyr and Oviedo.

It must be remarked that Champlain's *tabagie* has nothing whatsoever to do with "tobacco" and is an additional proof of the African influence upon Indian matters.   Lescarbot devotes a whole chapter to the Indian *tabagie*,[3] but all we learn from him is that *tabagie*, Indian *tabaguia*, is 'a banquet." No Indian language seems to have the word, but it is found everywhere in Guinea, where the French writers got it.   Alvares d' Almada says that the great feast among the Wolofs is called *tabasquio*.[4]   Indeed, the Wolof dictionary re-

---

[1] "Il faut que ie dye encore qu'à costé dudict canal de Bahan, au sudsuest, l'on voict l'isle St Domingue, dont i'ay parlé cy dessus, qui est fort bonne & marchande en cuirs, gingembre & casse, *tabac*, que l'on nomme autrement petung, ou herbe à la Royne, que l'on faict seicher, puis l'on en faict des petits tourteaux.   Les mariniers, mesme les Anglois, & autres personnes en vsent & prennent la fumée d'iceluy à l'imitation des sauuaiges," C.-H. Laverdière, *Oeuvres de Champlain*, Québec 1870, p. 50 f.
[2] *Ibid.*, p. 71.
[3] *Op. cit.*, vol. III, chap. XIV.
[4] *Op. cit.*, p. 19.

cords *tabaskia* "the December feast," and we have Mandingo *tabaski*, Peul *tabaske, taaske, taske* "feast of the sacrifices," from Berber *tafaske, tafeske* "feast of the sacrifices." It is only accidental that in French tobacco was connected with *tabaquia*, leading to *tabagie* "a place where tobacco is smoked."

# CHAPTER VI.

## Tobacco and the Sciences.

We can now summarize the history of tobacco smoking from its inception to the end of the XVI. century. Smoking for medicinal purposes is very old, and goes back at least to Greek medicine. A large number of viscous substances, especially henbane and bitumen, were employed in fumigation and taken through the mouth, sometimes through the nose, for certain diseases, especially catarrh, toothache, and pulmonary troubles. This fumigation took place through a funnel which very much resembles a modern pipe, but by its knob-like end at the bottom of the bowl shows its derivation from the distilling cap of the alchemist's retort. The large number of pipes found in Roman or early mediaeval graves show by the lids on the bowls that the distilling cap was employed, as today, by inverting its position on the alchemist's retort.

The Arabic sources make it clear that in Persia and Syria a substance, *tubbāq*, obviously the tobacco of our day, was employed for the same purpose for which the henbane and bitumen were used in the Graeco-Roman medicine, and that in Africa another plant of the same kind was in use by the Arabic physicians. These two plants are unquestionably the *Nicotiana tabacum* and *Nicotiana rustica*. Among the Negroes the narcotic quality of the tobacco also led to a sacerdotal use of the same, and this will be discussed in full in my next volume. From Africa the tobacco found its way into America, half a century, possibly a century, before the so-called discovery, chiefly in its sacerdotal significance.

As a vice, smoking was in America for a long time and everywhere confined at first to caciques and the rich, and in North America tobacco could be obtained only at great cost.

Although smoking among Indians and Negroes is recorded in America from the beginning of the XVI. century, it is clear, from the statements made by Oviedo, that the white planters of Hispaniola and, later, of Venezuela, encouraged their Negro slaves to raise tobacco, to be used in the barter trade with the Indians, and that nearly a century passed before the habit of smoking became universal among the Indians and Europeans. In Mexico, where tobacco was, in the middle of the XVI. century, included in the Nahuatl pharmacopœia, the whole medical science was a creation of the Aztecophile Spaniards in the College of Tlatelulco.

In 1557 Europe for the first time became acquainted with tobacco, through Thevet's importation, though, no doubt, locally it may have been known earlier. Nicot, who learned of its medicinal properties at Lisbon. specifically tells us that the Moors, that is, the Arabs or Mohammedan Negroes, employed this weed in their therapeutics, which once more confirms the fact that, although tobacco was reimported from America, it had its origin in Arabic medicine. The experiments, carried on by Nicot, received full publicity in Liebaut's *La maison rustique*, in 1570, and only next year, Monardes, influenced by the prevailing notion in Mexico that the College of Tlatelulco taught a native medical science, perpetuated the error, which from then on became universal, that America was the original home of smoking. From that time on the dozen or more editions of *La maison rustique* and a host of newer works set the pace for the popularity of tobacco, especially that from Virginia, where, we are definitely informed, it did not grow wild.  Since then the accumulated errors of Peter Martyr, Oviedo, Sahagun, Monardes, as to the American origin of tobacco smoking, have become so firmly embedded in the belief of philologists, botanists, and archaeologists, that they are blinded to the obvious proof to the contrary.  It, therefore, becomes necessary to pass in review these indurated errors, and point out their obvious fallacies.

One of the commonest philological arguments resorted to by botanists and archaeologists, to prove the origin of a plant in the Old or New World, is to point to the universality of a word as a sign of importation, and to a diversity of names for a particular plant as a sign of its native origin.  No experienced philologist would for a moment countenance such a procedure, because he knows that while the distribution of the same root word does point to a common origin, the absence of such a common word is proof of nothing whatsoever. The use of the word *automobile* over a vast territory is a *prima facie* evidence that it spread from some focus into all directions, but the fact that there is no common word for *potato* or *buckwheat* in the European languages is *not* a proof of their nativity in Europe.  The potato, which is known in England from the Spanish name for "sweet potato," in Germany as *Kartoffel*, from the French name for "truffles," in French as *pomme de terre* and, in the culinary language, simply as *pomme*, in Yiddish as *bulbe*, in Polish as *ziemniak*, etc., etc., is none the less not a native of Europe.  Buckwheat, in French known as *sarassin*, that is, "the *Saracen* plant," in Russian as *grečikha*, "the *Greek* plant," was imported into Europe by the Arabs, and "maize," in spite of its name of *kukuruza* in Russian, and similar divergen-names in the other languages, comes from America.

On the other hand the appearance of a common root, even in isolated locations, speaks volumes for the relat tionship of the idea or object, at least in these isolated positions. The Japanese *bargande*, for "sales," from the English "bargain day," is clear evidence of the derivation of the Japanese idea from England or America, even though no other language possesses this term. Not a thousand quotations from other languages, where no such term exists, even distantly affects the conclusion from the Japanese and English. Meringer has clearly shown the absurdity of any generalization from the absence of common terms in the Indo-European vernaculars as to the existence of the object or idea in the original language, from which these vernaculars are derived. He pointed out the highly amusing result from such type of philology that the Indo-European ancestors must have possessed feet but not legs, hands but not arms, fathers but not sons, and so on.

When two civilizations come into contact, a number of things may happen philologically. In the first impact of such a conflict, the lower civilization may accept without hesitancy any foreign term for any object that even in a slight degree differs from the native state, hence, while the Anglo-Saxons had pigs, sheep, and cows, they, during the Norman invasion, adopted "pork," "mutton," and "beef" as terms for the same as transformed by the foreign culinary art. For the same reason, words, literally by the thousand, have been transferred from Greek and Latin into the European languages, for the new religious, scientific, political terms, forced upon them by the superior culture. But soon the lower type of civilization accomodates itself to the level of the higher, and it borrows the ideas without taking over the words. Thus the German *Erziehung* and *Begriff* are clearly transferences of Latin *educatio* and *comprehensio* into the German vernacular. At this stage the ascertainment of the cultural borrowing becomes increasingly more difficult, although the borrowing is just as obvious, when the proper precautions have been observed.  Now, this accomodation of the lower civilization to the level of the higher in many cases begins amazingly early after the first impact.

Some native languages are, by their peculiar structure, very resistent to mere borrowings, and employ various means to disguise them.  The Chinese, on account of its monosyllabic structure, changes foreign polysyllabic words into a semblance of native monosyllabic compounds, where popular etymology and native sounds play frightful havoc with the foreign words.  Something similar may be observed in the case of the almost monosyllabic Otomi in Mexico and, to some extent, in the Maya languages, while the highly analytical Nahuatl generally scorns borrowings and disguises the foreign idea so completely that it may be taken for a native from the start.  Only a very few years after the conquest of Mexico, the Nahuatl used *pesouia* for "to measure, weigh," etc., although it is obviously a borrowing from the Spanish *peso*.

The universality of a term depends entirely upon the impact of its introduction.  "Automobile, telephone, aviation" have come too fast, to show many variations.  Similarly, as Oviedo has shown, the banana spread with tremendous rapidity over Central and South America, hence the word is well-nigh universal, although frequently much corrupted, over an enormous territory.  Wherever the white man came in contact with the Indian, the horse and cow were at once made familiar to the natives, hence Spanish *caballo* and *vaca* lie at the base of the peripheral contact of the two races, but in the interior, where the horse and cow were not received by the first impact, the terms are generally of native origin, generally borrowings, with proper variations, from native names for supposedly similar animals, the

riverhorse and stag. From this it follows that the
philology of the periphery is frequently different from
the philology of the interior, and this must constantly
be kept in mind, if errors are not to be perpetuated.

Even thus, the mere philological data are insuf-
ficient to establish the relationship of words, because
of the possibility of accidental resemblance, and because, in the case of plants, names have a tendency to
shift from one to another.   For this reason, I long ago
wrote:   "Phonetic studies are not the end of etymolo-
gical investigation of these words but merely an assistance
in the chronological data of sources.   Loan-words must
mainly be studied historically."[1]   And again: "Philology cannot dissociate itself from the history of civilization in the treatment of the origin of words, for words
are carried along roads of communication with the
things which they represent, and it is idle to speculate
on any prehistoric history until all the roads of communication have been traced and mapped out.   These
prehistoric histories base their conclusions on the
universality of certain words in a linguistic group, but
this is no more indicative of the presence of the things
represented by these words in the original stock from
which the group is derived than the universal use of the
word 'automobile' is indicative that the aborigines of
Europe had invented this machine, just as the absence
of a common word for 'hand' cannot lead to the conclusion that the Indo-Germanic primitive man had
not yet emerged from the quadruped stage."[2]

We shall soon see that neither botany nor archaeology possesses a decisive method for the solution of the
history of cultivated plants, hence their *ultima ratio* is
invariably philology.   Thus de Candolle tried to settle
the American origin of tobacco by philological con-

[1] *Modern Language Notes*, vol. X, No. 1, col. 10 ff.
[2] *The Quarterly Journal of Economics*, vol. XXV, p. 241.

siderations: "The common names of tobacco confirm
its American origin.  If there had been any indigenous
species in the old world there would be a great number
of different names; but, on the contrary, the Chinese,
Japanese, Javanese, Indian, Persian, etc., names are
derived from the American names, *petum*, or *tabak*,
*tabok*, *tamboc*, slightly modified.  It is true that Pid-
dington gives Sanskrit names, *dhumrapatra* and *tamra-
kouta*, but Adolphe Pictet informs me that the first of
these names, which is not in Wilson's dictionary, means
only leaf for smoking, and appears to be of modern
composition; while the second is probably no older,
and seems to be a modern modification of the American
names.  The Arabic word *docchan* simply means
smoke."[1]

De Candolle is right in assuming that the wide distribution of *petum* and *tabak* words in the Old World
indicated a borrowing from a common source, but the
same wide distribution of *petum* words in Brazil, Chile,
and Can_da, and of *tabak* words along the periphery,
where Europeans first came in contact in America with
the Indians, similarly proves that the Indian words
are not of native origin.  I have shown by historical
and documentary proof that Latin *bitumen* and Arabic
*tubbāq* were the medical terms for the sovereign remedy
taken through a pipe in the form of smoke, hence the
*petum* and *tabak* words, whether in America, Africa, or
Europe, go back to the Graeco-Arabic medicine, no
matter at what time, whether at the discovery of America or earlier, such habit was introduced by Negroes
under Arabic influence.

Schweinfurth, whose standing as a botanist cannot be
denied, draws the conclusion from the same philological data: "Of all the plants which are cultivated by
these wild people, none raises a greater interest than

[1] A. de Candolle, *Origin of Cultivated Plants*, New York 1885, p. 144.

tobacco, none exhibits a more curious conformity of habit amongst peoples far remote. The same two kinds which are cultivated amongst ourselves have become most generally recognized. These kinds are the Virginian tobacco (*Nicotiana tabacum*) and the common tobacco (*N. rustica*). It is little short of a certainty that the Virginian tobacco has only made its way into the Old World within the few centuries since the discovery of America. No production more than this has trampled over every obstacle to its propagation, so that it has been kept to no limits; and it must be matter of surprise that even Africa (notorious as it has ever been for excluding every sort of novelty in the way of cultivation) should have allowed the Virginian tobacco to penetrate to its very centre.

"It is a great indication of the foreign origin of this plant that there is not a tribe from the Niger to the Nile which has a native word of their own to denote it. Throughout all the districts over which I travelled, the Niam-niam formed the solitary exception to this by naming the Virginian tobacco 'gundeh;' but the Monbuttoo, who grow only this one kind and are as little familiar with *N. rustica* as the Niam-niam, call it '*Eh-tobboo.*' The rest of the people ring every kind of change upon the root word, and call it '*tab, tabba, tabdeet,*' or '*tom.*' The plant is remarkable here for only attaining a height of about eighteen inches, for its leaves being nearly as long as one could span, and for its blossoms being invariably white.

"Quite an open question I think it is, whether the *N. rustica* is of American origin. Several of the tribes had their own names for it. Here amongst the Bongo, in distinction from the '*tabba,*' it was known as '*masheer.*' The growth it makes is less than in Europe, but it is distinguished by the extreme strength and by the intense narcotic qualities which it possesses. It is different in this respect from what is grown in Persia, where it is used for the narghileh or water-pipes, and whence there is a large export of it, because of its mildness and aromatic qualities. Barth has given his opinion that the tobacco is a native of Logane (Mosgoo.) At all events, the people of Africa have far surpassed every other people in inventing various contrivances for smoking, rising from the very simplest apparatus to the most elaborate; and thus the conjecture is tenable, that they probably favoured the propagation of the foreign growth, because smoking, either of the common tobacco (*N. rustica*) or of some other aromatic weed, had in some way already been a practice amongst them. To such a hypothesis might be opposed the important fact that on all the monuments of the ancient Egyptians that afford us so clear an insight into the details of their domestic life, there has never been found a written inscription or pictorial representation that could possibly afford a proof that such a custom was known to exist. In conclusion, it deserves to be mentioned that the pagan negroes, as far as they have remained uninfluenced by Islamism, smoke the tobacco, whilst those who have embraced Mohammedanism prefer the chewing of the leaf to the enjoyment of a pipe."[1]

Schweinfurth correctly assumes, like de Candolle, that the wide distribution of *tabba* words in Africa indicates that it proceeds from some common source. His mistake in placing it in America is due to the accepted theory that it was first used there, but my investigation of the medical method of fumigation makes it certain, beyond any dispute, that the *tubbāq* of the Arabs spread throughout Africa without any reference to America. Schweinfurth's argument that the *Nicotiana rustica* may be native in Africa, because of the variety

[1] G. Schweinfurth, *The Heart of Africa*, New York 1874, vol. I, p. 254 f.

of names for it, is, of course, inconclusive, for the same variety of tobacco names in the many American families of languages has with similar logic and inconclusiveness been used to prove that native origin of tobacco in America.[1]  We have already seen from the statements of the Arabs that in Africa a different plant was used for the *tubbāq* of the Arabic pharmacopœia; hence there was no restraining principle in the preservation of native names or the formation of native words for a foreign plant, but the variety of names does not permit of any solution whether the *Nicotiana rustica* was originally native in Africa or not, though it most likely was.   But the definite use of *tubbāq* for the sovereign remedy, recorded not only in Ibn-al-Baitār, but also specifically referred to by Nicot as of Moorish origin, leaves no doubt behind that the *Nicotiana tabacum* was introduced in Africa either by the Arabs or natives and was popularized by a common name through the Arabic medical science, which substituted the viscous plant for the bitumen, henbane, or other viscous plants of the Graeco-Roman pharmacopœia. Engler says: "It is amazing how rapidly tobacco spread in the interior of Africa, that is, if one accepts the very likely justified assumption (falls man der wohl sicher berechtigten Ansicht beipflichtet), that at least the Virginian tobacco reached the Old World only after the discovery of America."[2]  "Since this *Nicotiana rustica* nearly always has varying native names, while the Virginian tobacco is designated by derivatives from *tumbaco*, the assumption is satisfied that the latter plant is a new introduction, while the *Nicotiana rustica* has been at home there for a long time.  The hypothesis established by some that the plant was native in Africa before the discovery of America, might

[1] *The American Anthropologist*, vol. XXIII, p. 19 ff.
[2] *Die Pflanzenwelt Ost-Afrikas und der Nachbargebiete*, Theil B., Berlin 1895, p. 255.

be going too far, if it were based only on the variant names (dürfte wohl, wenn einzig auf die verschiedenen Namen basirt, etwas zu weit gehen), since other plants, unquestionably introduced at a later time, as, for example, maize, have assumed different names in the African Babel of languages."[1]

Engler, one of the great authorities in botany, has only philological arguments for the antiquity of tobacco in America, but is more cautious than either de Candolle or Schweinfurth, from whom he gets the philological data.   He is not at all certain that *Nicotiana rustica* is not a native of Africa, although he is inclined to believe that it was introduced into Africa from America as late as the undoubtedly American maize. But here his philology goes astray.   In what way does a later introduction produce a variety of names when an earlier introduction did not do so?   No such criterion is of the slightest value, since length of time has nothing whatsoever to do with the various treatment of the two species.   Not a thousand years could have changed matters.   If a late introduction of maize could bring about a multiplicity of names, then there must have been a corresponding period when the *N. tabacum* had variant names.   When and how were they all of a sudden abandoned for the one name?   Engler obviously felt uncomfortable with his modified view of de Candolle's and Schweinfurth's opinion, and so expressed himself in the hypothetical forms which nullify his conclusions.

We turn to the botanical methods of ascertaining the original home of tobacco, and here again we find that botany can approach this question only hypothetically.   The limitations imposed by climate and soil conditions may help somewhat in narrowing down the possible early habitat of a plant, so that one could not

[1] *Ibid.*, p. 261.

look for palms in the temperate zone.  But the reverse
process of migration from the temperate zone to the
tropical regions is by far a more difficult proposition:
"It can not be said that the vegetation of the principal
land areas shows that the movements of species are
chiefly from colder to warmer regions, yet it is obvious
that in any series of experiments species from cool regions may be more easily established in warm places
than the reverse, and montane plants may come to the
seashore more easily than the plants of maritime zones
may spread over a mountain.  Disseminational movements are seen to be freer when they are from regions
presenting climatic extremes to more equable climates,
as amply illustrated by the success of so many species
from the Atlantic states and Arizona highlands on the
Pacific seashore.  Possibly the occurrence of the suc-
culent Opuntia in Saskatchewan may be considered as
an example of this as the predominant feature in dissemination."[1]  Where plants, either naturally or by
main action, are transferred from one habitat to another,
variations, sometimes of startling character, may spring
up immediately, and the new favorable environment
generally causes a multiplication of the species unknown in its original habitat: "The experiments
again make it plain that the habitat in which a plant
may be found, or in which it may have originated, may
not furnish the most favorable environmental complex,
as amply illustrated by the behavior of species that
have become weeds.  In other words the fitness of a
species for its native habitat may not be so close as its
fitness for other, as yet untried conditions."[2]  "The
nuts from trees at the lower and higher levels taken to
the Coastal plantation develop into trees easily separ-

---

[1] D. T. MacDougal, *The Reactions of Plants to New Habitats*, in *Ecology*,
vol. II, (1921), p. 19.

[2] *Ibid.*, p. 20.

able as to form and behavior."[1]   "The transferrals
resulted in a development of rootstocks, shoots and
flowers which in some cases were notably different from
that exhibited by the species in their native habitats.
The behavior and formation of an extra leaflet by
Arisaema has been mentioned above.   *Fragaria california* taken to the warmer and more arid climate of
Tucson developed one or two extra leaflets.   *F. ovalis*
from the Montane region showed a similar departure
both at Tucson and at the Coastal plantation.   *F.
virginiana* did not make extra leaflets at the Montane
plantation, but did so under the stimulating environment at the coast, also showing some ascidial leaves.
*F. california* from the coastal region likewise formed
ascidial leaves when under the influence of unaccus-
tomed conditions, including high temperatures and
aridity, at the Desert Laboratory."[2]   "The plants
transferred developed in some cases rootstocks, shoots,
and flowers notably different from those of their native
habitats."[3]   When, therefore, the same or closely al-
lied species are found in two continents, say in Africa
and South America, we have but the slimmest chance
of determining the original home by "botanical" means.
Did we not otherwise know that the cardoon and milk
thistle are of European origin, the interminable tangles
which these weeds form in some spots in South America
would lead to the supposition that they started here.
Hence a botanist can only cautiously refer to the direction of migration or may entirely refrain from sug-
gesting it.   Engler has pointed out the identity or
close relationship of nearly two hundred species or
even families in Africa and America.   Of these some
are ascribed to a conscious introduction into Africa

[1] *Ibid.*, p. 17.
[2] *Ibid.*, p. 11.
[3] *Ibid.*, p. 20.

from America,[1] but the majority are supposed to have been carried in the ooze of the bottoms or in some other way, and the direction is not indicated.

The rapidity with which new varieties and species arise in new surroundings, by climatic or soil influences, has already been pointed out. To this must be added the endless and striking possibility of hybridization which takes place, not only under cultivation but naturally in new circumstances. This has been demonstrated by Focke[2] and others, who have given long lists of new varieties and species, many of which have retained permanent characteristics. No plant has in this respect yielded such remarkable results as the genus *Nicotiana:* "The genus *Nicotiana* has become especially important for the knowledge of the plant bastards. It formed the point of issue for the epochal investigations of Kölreuter, and has later held the attention of the investigators of hybrids, because its varieties enter into combinations with each other with astounding ease. Plant forms which are so unlike to each other that ordinarily one could hardly think of a possibility of their crossing, in the genus *Nicotiana* often produce bastards without any difficulty."[3] Focke classes all the species of tobacco under three heads. The varieties and species which contain in their midst *N. rustica* he denominates as *Chlorotabacum,* those that contain *N. tabacum* as *Eutabacum,* and those which contain *N. suaveolens* of New Holland *Petuniopsis.* Focke remarks that *N. suaveolens* "is the only New Holland species which in its native home is unusually rich in form and variety; the authors of the *Flora Australis* know of no significant difference between it and the American *Nicotiana*

[1] *Ueber floristische Verwandtschaft zwischen dem tropischen Afrika und Amerika,* in *Sitzungsberichte der Königlich Preussischen Akademie der Wissenschaften,* Berlin 1905, p. 225.

[2] W. O. Focke, *Die Pflanzen-Mischlinge, ein Beitrag zur Biologie der Gewächse,* Berlin 1881.

[3] *Ibid.,* p. 271.

*acuminata*, while the forms of both cultivated in
Europe differ considerably."[1]   There is no way of
determining whether the *Nicotiana suaveolens* is a very
old plant in Australia or a late sport from an American
or African variety.   A vast number of crosses have
been produced by botanists and gardeners, many of
which have developed permanent characteristics.
Every once in a while a new variety springs up, of whose
pedigree nothing is known.   Thus, in 1905, a beautiful
garden plant, *Nicotiana forgetiana*, was brought out of
Brazil, and a hybrid from this, *Nicotiana Sanderae*,
was advertized by a gardening firm.[2]   A *Nicotiana
torreyana* was in 1916 announced from Montana, the
Yellowstone and Wyoming.[3]   The number of varieties
in America is very large, but of their antecedents next
to nothing is known.   We shall confine ourselves to
one of them, *Nicotiana glauca*, found in Brazil, Argen-
tine, Chile, Mexico, Texas, and California.   Kuntze
records it growing wild in the whole Mediterranean
region, in Granda, Monaco, Alexandria, Tripolis,
Greece, Morocco, Sicily, Sardinia, in the Canary and
Cape Verde Islands, and in the Herero country.[4]   His
preconceived notion that it must originate from America
leads him to state that it *apparently* spread in late times,
but of this there naturally is no certainty.   We have
already seen that both *Nicotiana tabacum* and *rustica*

[1] *Ibid.*, p. 286.
[2] Curtis's *Botanical Magazine*, London 1905, No. 8006.
[3] *Botanical Gazette*, vol. LXI, p. 43 f.
[4] "*Nicotiana glauca.*   Diese hochstrauchige amerikanische Art hat sich
anscheinend erst in neuerer Zeit im ganzen Mittelmeergebiet (ich fand sie
bei Granda und Monaco eigeburgert, habe sie von Alexandrien (Schweinfurth), Tripolis (Ruhmer) gesehen, nach gefl. Mittheilungen des Herrn
Prof. Knecht kommt sie in Griechenland vor, nach Herrn Rector Rensch
in Marocco, nach Borzi in Sicilien, nach Ascheron in Sardinien) verbreitet,
nach Christ wächst sie auf den Canaren, nach Urban auf den Capverdischen
Inseln (leg. Kurtz) und jetzt ist sie auch aus Sudwestafrika bekannt,"
Kuntze, *Plantae Pechuelianae Hereroenses*, in *Jahrbuch des Königlichen
Botanischen Gartens*, Berlin 1886, p. 268.   See also his *Revisio generum
plantarum*, Leipzig 1891, pars II, p. 451.

have been found growing wild in Africa, and they are mentioned by H. Pobéguin as indigenous in French Guinea.[1]

It is clear from the botanical data that the original home of tobacco cannot be ascertained otherwise than historically and philologically, as the botanical data prove nothing and are correct either way. But some archaeologists reck neither philology, history, nor botany, and boldly proclaim the antiquity of tobacco and the pipe in America on the basis of archaeological data. In the chapter on cotton I show how insecure and absolutely wrong the data derived from archaeology may be. The guano test has completely collapsed under close scrutiny, and chronology is in consequence demoralized. Some American archaeologists make the inexcusable blunder of generalizing archaeological data arrived at in Egypt, Babylonia, or Greece, to conditions in America. In the first place, Egyptian and Babylonian chronology has been shifted by centuries and even milleniums, even though we have documentary and inscriptional evidence for a large number of data. In America we have, with a few insignificant exceptions, no written documents for pre-Columbian times. Besides, the stratifications formed in the soil of Egypt or Babylonia lead to no result whatsoever, if applied to Peru, Mexico, or Arizona. We see, in the chapter on cotton, how burials and reburials completely upset the orderly geological formations, and how the guano deposits show no tendency whatsoever for regular average increments. Long and painful studies in soil changes in Arizona may some day determine whether anything like a regular increment of soil deposits is formed there. The chances are against it, for in the region of the sandstorms one season may transform a region as much as decades and centuries.

[1] *Côte occidentale d'Afrique*, Paris 1906, p. 332.

Suppose that here successive layers of various cultures are found. No matter how different these may be, we have not even distantly any criterion for the length of each cultural period, which may count by milleniums, centuries, or decades. The fact that a layer of Basket-makers' culture is found beneath a layer of cotton textile culture helps us little, since even the stone age is found side by side with the copper and iron age. The vagaries of special cultural ages are very puzzling and disconcerting, and unless chronological data are obtained independently from archaeology the latter becomes the most elusive and dangerous of all the sciences. Suppose a tobacco pipe filled with the substance smoked is found twenty or forty feet below the ground, in what is supposed to be a layer of Basket-makers' culture. Let us assume that the contents of the pipe are analyzed chemically and no trace of nicotine is found in it. This does not prove that tobacco was not smoked at that period. Let us assume that nicotine is found in it. This would show that tobacco was smoked then, but we should still have to ascertain the date of the Basket-makers' culture, and here we would be let loose in a sea of uncertainty, without even a distant chance of solution. The twenty or forty feet of soil above the pipe may have originated in a vast number of ways, as, indeed, we have found burials in Peru in deep wells and in guano, where the depth may be of human formation. It would take a great deal more than the word of an explorer to ascertain the position of an object *in situ* before the exploration, and thus the whole archaeological argument disappears as before.

Only when archaeological data are checked by historical and philological considerations is there the least chance of arriving at the truth. Where these fail us, archaeology is nothing more than guesswork, and the conclusions drawn from it are not worth the paper they are written on.   In the case of tobacco, not a single authenticated archaeological datum has been brought forward in America to prove that in which even botany falters, while philology and history alone furnish us the unmistakable data for smoking and pipes in Europe, centuries and, possibly, milleniums before the discovery of America.

The hypothetical case of the Basket-maker culture was based on the vagaries of an archaeologist.   Since writing it there have come to my notice two works bearing on the subject.[1]   The authors in an elaborate and, on the whole, satisfactory manner have investigated the Basket-maker caves in Arizona, and we shall here analyze the references to tobacco pipes.

In the earlier expedition "pipes of stone were found at Sayodneechee (two examples), and in Cave I (one example).   One of the Sayodneechee pipes is of very soft, red sandstone and is in fragmentary condition (A-1911).   The shape is very squat and the walls thick; what is left of the bowl is lined with a heavy 'crust' deposited by the smoke.   The stem hole, very small in proportion to the size of the bowl, holds the rotted remains of a wooden mouthpiece.   The other Sayodneechee pipe (fig. 94, b) and the one from Kinboko (fig. 94, a) are much alike in size, shape, and material. The bowls are made of fine-grained limestone, banded horizontally and darkened by long use.   The outer surfaces are polished, but not highly enough to obliterate entirely the marks of the pecking tool with which they were originally roughed out.   The rims are thick, in one case flat, in the other rounded.   The bowl of each

---

[1] A. V. Kidder and S. J. Guernsey, *Archeological Explorations in Northeastern Arizona,* in *Smithsonian Institution, Bureau of American Ethnology,* Washington 1919, Bulletin 65; and S. J. Guernsey and A. V. Kidder, *Basket-Maker Caves of Northeastern Arizona, Report on the Explorations, 1916-17,* in *Papers of the Peabody Museum of American Archaeology and Ethnology, Harvard University,* Cambridge 1921, vol. VIII, No. 2.

is heavily encrusted with the carbonized remains of the smoking mixture. The relative size and shape of bowl and stem hole is best shown in the illustration. In the stem hole of the Kinboko specimen may be seen remnants of the gum that once fastened the stem in place, and the same material was used to mend an incipient crack in the bowl. The dimensions of this example are: Length, $1^7/_{16}$ inches; greatest diameter, $1^1/_4$ inches; thickness of rim, three-sixteenths inch; diameter of stem hole, one-eighth inch.

"Two pipes of clay may perhaps best be described here. They were the only pottery objects found by us that are surely identifiable as Basket Maker products. One (fig. 94, *d*, Cave I) is crudely modeled from a bit of dark-gray clay; the surface is lumpy and carelessly finished. The second (A-1967, Sayodneechee) is also very poorly made and the surface is irregular. While both these specimens are longer and slimmer than the stone pipes, they are, nevertheless, much squatter than the long, tubular cliff-dwelling type; they differ from it also in having a distinct bowl much larger than the orifice which receives the stem. Although we recovered no example with the mouthpiece preserved, its nature is illustrated by a pipe in the Deseret Museum, Salt Lake City, probably from Cottonwood Canyon, Utah, which has a short, straight stem made from a 2-inch section of hollow bird bone. The bowl is of horizontally banded limestone, heavy, squat, and flat-lipped; in every way similar to our specimens. A Basket-maker pipe with wooden stem is figured by Montgomery in Moorehead's 'Stone Age in North America,' vol. II, p. 38, fig. 436."[1] One stone pipe and part of a clay pipe come from Cist E, of which the authors say: "Cist E, a circular slab

---

[1] Kidder and Guernsey, *Archeological Explorations in Northeastern Arizona*, p. 187 f.

inclosure, had evidently been plundered; there remained in it, however, a stone pipe, part of a clay pipe . . ."[1] Plundered graves cannot form the starting point for any chronology or the ascertainment of culture to which the objects belong, since these pipes may have gotten much later into the opened graves. Besides, as, by the authors' own statement, pottery has not been definitely ascribed to the Basket-makers,[2] no clay pipe can be definitely ascribed to them. Again, since "a (tubular) clay pipe was found on the surface of a small ruin on the top of the mesa at the mouth of Sagi Canyon,"[3] which they do not ascribe to the Basket-makers, there is no reason to give another chronology for the first clay pipe. One stone pipe was found in Cist B at Sayodneechee where skeletons of nineteen persons were packed together, and the origin or fate of this cist was a puzzle to the authors.[4] I cannot locate in the book the remaining stone pipe, but as it is identical in shape with others, nothing new is learned from it. In their later work the authors asserted that "no specimens of true pottery, either vessel or sherd, have yet been found by us under circumstances indicating that it was a Basket-maker product. All but one of the several jars discovered came from the surface sand overlying the Basket-maker deposits; they are of common cliff-house ware, and were undoubtedly cached in the caves at a comparatively late date. The exception is a pot found in Sunflower Cave in 1915, lying below a cliff-house floor. This was figured in our previous report and referred to as possibly of Basket-maker origin. It is of plain black ware, uncorrugated; in shape it is almost spherical. No further evidence that the Basket-makers produced ves-

[1] *Ibid.*, p. 82.
[2] *Ibid.*, p. 208 f.
[3] *Ibid.*, p. 144.
[4] *Ibid.*, p. 29 f.

sels of this type has since come to light, and we are inclined to consider it early Puebloan."[1]   This once more excludes the clay pipe, and, indeed, "no pipes were found in 1916-1917."[2]   "The Casa Grande people used in smoking perforated tubes of clay or stone resembling pipes.   The cane cigarette also was commonly used as shown by rejected canes found in great abundance in some of the rooms of Compound A.   A large number of these canes are found also in shrines or other sacred places of the Hohokam, where they were placed by the ancients.

"A broken pipe made of clay was excavated at Casa Grande and another was found on the ground.   The former object has a slight enlargement of the perforation at one end.   Although much of the stem is missing, there is no doubt that this pipe belongs to the type called the straight-tube variety, which is considered by the best authorities to be the prehistoric form in the Southwest."[3]   We have here, in the same region, but not in Basket-maker territory, the same tubular pipe, obviously a development of the Mexican *yetecomatl*, when tobacco became common in Mexico.   From here the specifically Mexican tubular pipe spread to the North-west.   It is found abundantly in British Columbia, where "as late as 1891 there were Indians who still used the straight tubular pipe."[4]   With these facts before us, the proof of the antiquity of tobacco smoking in North America turns out to be of a piece with the proof of the antiquity of cotton in South America, as based on the guano deposits.

[1] Guernsey and Kidder, *Basket-Maker Caves of Northeastern Arizona*, p. 98.
[2] *Ibid.*, p. 95.
[3] *Twenty-eighth Annual Report of the Bureau of American Ethnology to the Secretary of the Smithsonian Institution*, (1906-1907), Washington 1912, p. 135 f.
[4] H. I. Smith, *The Archaeological Collection from the Southern Interior of British Columbia*, Ottawa 1913, p. 33.

# PART III: BEAD MONEY.

# CHAPTER I.

## The Cowries.

The 154th Chinese radical is 貝 *pei*, which, in the older rounded form, is 貝: "A cowrie, a small shell used for money in China in early feudal times. They were current together with the coppers invented later on, till under the Ch'in Dynasty (3rd Century B. C.); then the cowries were left out. The character represents the shell, and the feelers with which it moves. It is the 154th radical of characters relating to values and trade."[1] The very large number of derivatives from this character relating to barter, and the presence of these derivatives in the ancient classics make it certain that the shell of certain marine animals was employed more than a millenium before the Christian era as currency. Indeed, it is already mentioned under the Hia dynasty (2000-1550 B. C.),[2] and in the *Pen-tsao* the compounds *pei-tze, pei-tch'i* are used for the cowries of the Eastern Sea, that is, south-east of the Shantung peninsula,[3] but the modern *ho-pei*[4] also goes back to an earlier form, as we shall later see. In the second century B. C. there are also references to *tze-pei* "purple shell,"[5] which was two or three inches long and "was formerly found on the shores of the prefecture

[1] L. Wieger, *Chinese Characters*, trans. by L. Davrout, Ho-kien-fu 1915, vol. I, p. 323.

[2] S. Lane-Poole, *Coins and Medals*, London 1894, p. 192.

[3] *Ibid.*, p. 194.

[4] *The Journal of the Royal Asiatic Society of Great Britain and Ireland*, London 1888, vol. XX, p. 432.

[5] Lane-Poole, *op. cit.*, p. 194.

of Teng-tchou, north of the Shantung peninsula."[1]   In mediaeval Chinese works dealing with the trade in the East Indies, the cowries are mentioned as *pei, pei-tze,* and *tze-pei.*

The earliest European account of Chinese cowries is contained in Marco Polo, where their use as currency is mentioned in the province of Carajan: "Their money is such as I will tell you.   They use for the purpose certain white porcelain shells that are found in the sea, such as are sometimes put on dogs' collars; and 80 of these porcelain shells pass for a single weight of silver, equivalent to two Venice groats, i. e. 24 piccoli.   Also eight such weights of silver count equal to one such weight of gold."[2]   The Italian version[3] has "*porcellane* bianche" for "white porcelain shells."   The French version has for it "*pourcelaines* blanches,"[4] but the old Spanish translation writes "lur moneda es *porçellas* qui se troban en la mar et LXXX daquellas *porcellanas* valen un peso."[5]   From these it is clear that Marco Polo's *porcellanas* was understood in the XIV. century as being in some way derived from *porco* "pig."   This is also brought out in the Genoese inventories of 1389 and 1390, where there is reference to "conchetta una nigra *purzelette*, conchette due de *porcelleta*, conchete quatuor *porcellete*,"[6] where, whatever the word may have been, it is freely derived from *porcellana*, just as in the case of the Span. *porcella*. Marco Polo asserted that these *porcellane* were not native to Carajan, but were brought from India.[7]

[1] *Ibid.,* p. 193.

[2] H. Yule, *The Book of Marco Polo,* London 1871, vol. II, p. 39.

[3] G. B. Baldelli-Boni, *Il Milione di Marco Polo,* Firenze 1827, vol. I, p. 110 f.

[4] M. G. Pauthier, *Le livre de Marco Polo,* Paris 1865, p. 389.

[5] H. Knust, *El libro de Marco Polo,* ed. by R. Stuebe, Leipzig 1902, p. 44.

[6] *Atti della Società Ligure di Storia Patria,* Genoa 1866, vol. IV, p. 184.

[7] Yule, *op. cit.,* vol. II, p. 45.

Marco Polo also mentions the manufacture of porcelain at Tyunju in China, using the same word for it as for the cowrie shell: "Let me tell you also that in this province there is a town called Tyunju, where they make vessels of porcelain of all sizes, the finest that can be imagined. They make it nowhere but in that city, and thence it is exported all over the world. Here it is abundant and very cheap, insomuch that for a Venice groat you can buy three dishes so fine that you could not imagine better."[1] A later edition of the Italian text has an amplification of the story, according to which the porcelain is found in a mine, from which it is brought out into the open, to weather for forty years, in order to refine it. Consequently the porcelain is gathered up so that only the children or grandchildren are benefited by it.[2] The confusion between "cowrie shell" and "porcelain" in Marco Polo is due to a double popular etymology, one Chinese, the other Italian. Marco Polo heard in southern China the common diminutive *pei tsz*, where it sounds *puitsz* "cowrie shell," which reminded him of Ital. *porce*. At the same time the "white porcelain," which is called *pai ts'z*, in Canton *pak ts'z*, at Fu-Kien, where he saw the porcelain, was pronounced almost as the word for the "cowrie shell."[3] Marco Polo also knew that Ital. *porcellano* was used for *puzzolana*, as at

---

[1] *Ibid.*, p. 186.

[2] "E dove si parte dall' alveo maestro vi è la città di Tingui. Della quale non si ha da dir altro, se non che in quella si fanno le scodelle e piadene di *porcellane* in questo modo, secondo che li fu detto. Raccolgono una certa terra come di una miniera, e ne fanno monti grandi, e lascianli al vento, alla pioggia e al sole, per trenta, e quaranta anni, che non li muovono. E in questo spazio di tempo la detta terra si affina, che poi si può far dette scodelle, alle quali danno disopra li colori che vogliono, e poi le cuocono nella fornace. E sempre quelli, che raccolgono detta terra, la raccolgono per suoi figliuoli, o nepoti. Vi è in detta città a gran mercato, di sortechè per un grosso veneziano si averà otto scodelle," Baldelli-Boni, *op. cit.*, vol. II, p. 354 f.

[3] "Selon la Géographie impériale, on y fabriquait anciennement des 'vases en *porcelaine* blanche' (*pĕ-tsĕ-k'i*); quand la blancheur en était pure, sans tache, ils étaient très-recherchés," Pauthier, *op. cit.*, p. 532.

Genoa,[1] and since to him porcelain was some kind of cement, and the shells had a glaze similar to that of porcelain, he with easy conscience chose *porcellana* to express both ideas.

The confusion of the Italian editor of Marco Polo, who told of the long time it took for the mined porcelain to weather, is due to an exaggeration of the Arabic account of Ibn-Batutah, according to whom the material which was mined in a mountain had to be burnt and weathered for a month, in order to produce the whitest of porcelain.[2] This apocryphal story took possession of the authors who had read Marco Polo, and, from the latter's use of *porcellana* both for "cowrie" and "porcelain," arose the story of the manufacture of porcelain from cowrie shells. Damiano a Goes, at the end of the XV. century, wrote, "scutellae mira arte ex calce concharum fictae, quas *porcellanas* vocant."[3] "Barbosa wrote about 1516, 'They make in this country a great quantity of porcelains of different sorts, very fine and good, which form for them a great article of trade for all parts, and they make them in this way. They take the shells of sea-snails, and egg-shells, and pound them, and with other ingredients make a paste, which they put underground to refine for the space of

[1] We have also Catalan *porcellana* "puzzolana, cement."

[2] "On ne fabrique pas en Chine la porcelaine, si ce n'est dans les villes de Zeïtoûn et de Sîn-calân. Elle est faite au moyen d'une terre tirée des montagnes qui se trouvent dans ces districts, laquelle terre prend feu comme du charbon, ainsi que nous le dirons plus tard. Les potiers y ajoutent une certaine pierre qui se trouve dans le pays; ils la font brûler pendant trois jours, puis versent l'eau par-dessus, et le tout devient comme une poussière ou une terre qu'ils font fermenter. Celle dont la fermentation a duré un mois entier, mais pas plus, donne la meilleure porcelaine; celle qui n'a fermenté que pendant six jours, en donne une de qualité inférieure à la précédente. La porcelaine en Chine vaut le même prix que la poterie chez nous, ou encore moins. On l'exporte dans l'Inde et les autres contrées, jusqu'à ce qu'elle arrive dans la nôtre, le Maghreb. C'est l'espèce la plus belle de toutes les poteries," C. Defrémery and B. R. Sanguinetti, *Voyages d'Ibn Batoutah*, Paris 1879, vol. IV, p. 256.

[3] W. Heyd, *Histoire du commerce du Levant au moyen-âge*, Leipzig 1886, vol. II, p. 678.

eighty or a hundred years, and this mass of paste they leave as a fortune to their children.' In 1615, Bacon said, 'If we had in England beds of porcelain such as they have in China, which porcelain is a kind of plaster buried in the earth and by length of time congealed and glazed into that substance; this were an artificial mine, and part of that substance.' Sir Thomas Browne, in his *Vulgar Errors*, asserted, 'We are not thoroughly resolved concerning Porcellane or China dishes, that according to common belief they are made of earth, which lieth in preparation about an hundred years underground; for the relations thereof are not only divers but contrary; and Authors agree not herein.' These fables were refuted at the end of the sixteenth and seventeenth centuries by travellers who had occasion to make observations on the spot. Juan Gonzalez de Mendoza, who wrote in 1585, reiterated Barbosa's story, and (in the early English translation) called its validity into doubt; for, if it were true, the Chinese, in his opinion, could not turn out so great a number of porcelains as is made in that kingdom and exported to Portugal, Peru, New Spain, and other parts of the world. J. Neuhof, who accompanied the embassy of the East India Company of the Netherlands to China from 1655 to 1657, scorns the 'foolish fabulists of whom there are not a few still nowadays who made people believe that porcelain is baked from egg-shells pounded and kneaded into a paste with the white of an egg, or from shells and snail-shells, after such a paste has been prepared by nature itself in the ground for some hundred years.' The Jesuit, L. Le Compte, rectified this error by saying that 'it is a mistake to think that there is requisite one or two hundred years to the preparing of the matter for the porcelain, and that its composition is so very difficult; if that were so, it would be neither so common, nor so cheap.' These two authors

were seconded by E. Ysbrants Ides.  The analogy of
the beliefs in the origin of murrines and porcelain is
striking; and this fancy has doubtless taken its root in
the Orient, whence crafty dealers propagated it in the
interest of their business."[1]

From the IX. century on we have many references
in the Arabic authors to the cowries in Asia and Africa.
Suleiman says: "Their (the Maldivians') money consists of cowries (ودع *wada'*).  The queen stores these
cowries in her treasuries."  "The cowries come up to the
surface of the water, and contain a living creature; a coco-
tree branch is thrown into the water, and the cowries
attach themselves to it.  The cowry is called *kabath*."[2]
The foreign name is a transcription of Sinhalese *kavadiya* or Malayalam *kavadi*.  Mas'ūdī tells very nearly
the same story:  "The queen has no other money but
cowries, which are a kind of molluscs.  When she sees
her treasure diminishing, she orders her islanders to
cut coco-branches with their leaves, and to throw them
upon the surface of the water.  To these the creatures
attach themselves, and are then collected and spread
upon the sandy beach, where the sun rots them, and
leaves only the empty shells, which are then carried to
the treasury."[3]  Albiruni (A. D. 1030) calls the islands
*Divah Kauzah* (or *Kavzah* or *Kuzah*) "the island of
cowries, because there they gather cowries from the
branches of the coco-nut palms, which they plant in
the sea."[4]  Edrisi (1099-1186) writes:  "Commerce is
carried on by means of shells.  They are distant from
one another about six miles.  Their king preserves

---

[1] B. Laufer, *The Beginnings of Porcelain in China*, in *Field Museum of Natural History*, Publication 192 (Anthropological Series), vol. XV, No. 2, p. 135 f.
[2] A. Gray and H. C. P. Bell, *The Voyage of François Pyrard* (The Hakluyt Society), London 1890, vol. II², p. 429.
[3] *Ibid.*, p. 430.
[4] *Ibid.*, p. 431.

these shells in his treasury, and he possesses the greater
portion of them  .  .  .  They say that the shells
which compose the royal treasure are found on the surface of the water in calm weather.  They throw into
the sea pieces of coco-wood, and the shell-fish attach
themselves thereto.''[1]  They are called رك , obviously
a mispointed *kavadi*, as before.

Ibn Batutah (c. 1350) is of especial interest in connection with the cowries, because of his reference to their
use as ballast and sale in Africa.  "The money of the
islanders consist of *waḍaʻ*.  This is the name of a mol-
lusc, collected in the sea and placed in pits dug out on
the beach.  Its flesh decays and only the white shell
remains.  A hundred of them is called siya, and 700
fál; 12,000 are called kotta, and 100,000 bostú.  Bar-
gains are struck through the medium of these shells,
at the rate of four bostú to a dînâr of gold.  Often they
are of less value, such as twelve bostú to a dînâr.  The
islanders sell them for rice to the people of Bengal,
where also they are used for money.  They are sold in
the same way to the people of Yemen, who use them
for ballast in their ships in place of sand.  These shells
serve also as a medium of exchange with the negroes
in their native country.  I have seen them sold, at
Máli and at Jújú, at the rate of 1,150 to a dînâr.''[2]  Indeed, João de Barros, in the beginning of the XVI.
century, confirms the earlier Arabic accounts of the
cowries in the Maldive Islands and their export to
Africa, and adds the important item that the cowries
were exported from Asia to Portugal, and from there only
to Guinea: "There is also a kind of shellfish, as small
as a snail, but differently shaped, with a hard, white,
lustrous shell, some of them, however, being so highly
coloured and lustrous that, when made into buttons
and set in gold, they look like enamel.  With these shells

[1] *Ibid.*, p. 432.　　　　[2] *Ibid.*, p. 444.

for ballast many ships are laden for Bengal and Siam, where they are used for money, just as we use small copper money for buying things of little value. And even to this kingdom of Portugal, in some years as much as two or three thousand quintals are brought by way of ballast; they are then exported to Guinea, and the kingdoms of Benin and Congo, where also they are used for money, the Gentiles of the interior in those parts making their treasure of it. Now the manner in which the islanders gather these shells is this:—they make large bushes of palm leaves tied together so as not to break, which they cast into the sea. To these the shellfish attach themselves in quest of food; and when the bushes are all covered with them, they are hauled ashore and the creatures collected. All are then buried in the earth till the fish within have rotted away. The shells (*buzios* as we, and *Igovos* as the negroes, call them) are then washed in the sea, becoming quite white, and so dirtying the hands less than copper money. In this kingdom (Portugal) a quintal of them is worth from three to ten cruzados, according as the supply from India is large or small."[1]

Cowries were still in use in the Sahara oases in the XIX. century: "Small wares are sold by the *wadah*, which are the currency of the Sudan, while those of a greater value are bartered for gold dust. The *wadah* of the Christian countries are not the only ones which are current; they fish for some in the Niger by throwing in the skins of freshly flayed cattle and taking them out the next day, when they remove the shells caught in the night."[2] Daumas pronounces the word *uda*, and Cherbonneau *ude*.[3]

[1] *Ibid.*, p. 484 f.
[2] E. Daumas, *Le Sahara algérien*, Paris 1845, p. 300.
[3] "*Oudé*, coquillage de mer bigarré, en forme de grain de café et fendu par le milieu (porcelaine de mer)," *Définition lexigraphique de plusieurs mots usités dans le langage de l'Afrique septentrionale*, in *Journal asiatique*, ser. IV, vol. XIII, p. 70.

In the beginning of the XVI. century, Pacheco Pereira told of the use of cowries as currency in South Africa: "In the Goat Islands the Negroes gather certain small snails (*buzios*), which are not larger than pine-nuts with their shells and which they call *zimbos*. These pass in Manicongo for money, and fifty of them they give for a chicken, and three hundred are the price of one goat, and similarly other things; and when Manicongo wants to do a favor to some of his noblemen or to pay for a service done him, he orders a certain number of these *zimbos* to be given him, in the same manner as our princes give a money favor in our Kingdom to him who deserves it, and many times to him who does not deserve it; and in the land of Beny they use snails for money, which are somewhat larger then the *zimbos* of Manicongo and which they call in Beny *iguou*."[1]

Pigafetta, at the end of the XVI. century, described the same sea-shells in Congo: "This island (Loanda) furnishes the money used by the King of Congo and the neighbouring people; for along its shores women dive under water, a depth of two yards and more, and, filling their baskets with sand, they sift out certain small shell-fish called *Lumache*, and then separate the male

[1] "Duas ilhas pequenas, baixas e rrasas, de pouco aruoredo, que chamam as ilhas das Cabras, e estas estam muito perto de terra e sam pouoradas dos negros do senhorio de Maniconguo; e ainda vay adiante a terra de Conguo; e nestas ilhas apanham os ditos negros huũs *buzios* pequenos, que nam sam maiores que pinhoeẽs com sua casca, a que elles chamam '*zinbos*', os quaes em terra de Maniconguo correm por moeda, e sincoenta d'elles dam por hũa galinha, e trezentos valem hũa cabra, e asy as outras cousas segundo sam; e quando Manicongo quer fazer mercê a alguũs seus fidalguos ou paguar alguũ serviço que lhe fazem, manda-lhe dar certo numero d'estes *zimbos* pello modo que os nossos principes fazem mercê da moeda d'estes Reynos a quem lha merece, e muitas vezes a quem lha nam merece; e na terra do Beny, de que ja he escrito no quarto item do setimo capitolo do segundo liuro, husam huũs *buzios* por moeda, hum pouco mayores que estes *zimbos* de Maniconguo, aos quaes *buzios* no Beny chamam '*iguou*', e todalas cousas por elles compram, e quem mays d'elles tem, mais rico he," *Esmeraldo de situ orbis*, in *Boletim da Sociedade de geographia de Lisboa*, Lisboa 1904, 22ª. ser., p. 346 f.

from the female, the latter being most prized for its colour and brightness. These *Lumache* are found along all the coasts of Congo, but those of Loanda are finest, being transparent, and in colour somewhat like the chrysolite, with other kinds, not as greatly valued. It must be remembered that gold, silver, and other metals are not valued, nor used as money in these countries; and so it happens that with gold and silver in abundance, either in mass or in coin, yet nothing can be bought except with *Lumache*. In this island are seven or eight towns, known in the language of the country as Libata. The principal one, called il Santo Spirito, is where the Governor resides, who is sent from Congo to administer justice, and amasses riches from these *Lumache*."[1]  Nearly a century later Dapper gave their Bantu name as *cimbo*, which appears in Ogilby's translation as "*simbo*, or little horn-shell." "They have two sorts of *Simbo's*, which serve in lieu of Money, viz. pure *Simbo's*, taken under the Island of Lovando, and used for Trade in Punto; and impure, or Brazile, brought from Rio de Janero, and used in Songo and Pinda, and in the Countreys of Anna Xinga, beyond Massingam, and among the Jages. The *Simbo's* of Lovando are also of two sorts, a finer and a courser, separated by Sifting, the latter they name *Simbos Sisado's*; the other; *Fonda* and *Bomba*. Both these they send to Congo, being carried thither upon the Heads of the Blacks, in Sacks made of Straw, every Sack weighing two Aroba's, that is, threescore and four Pound."[2] "They have no Coyn'd Money, either of Gold, Silver, or Copper; but, as we have often mention'd, make all their Markets with little Shells, call'd *Simboes*, which

[1] M. Hutchinson, *A Report of the Kingdom of Congo, and of the Surrounding Countries; Drawn out of the Writings and Discourses of the Portuguese, Duarte Lopez, by Filippo Pigafetta, in Rome, 1591,* London 1881, p. 18 f.

[2] J. Ogilby, *Africa: Being an Accurate Description of the Regions of Aegypt, Barbary, Lybia, and Billedulgerid, the Land of Negroes, Guinee, Aethiopia, and the Abyssines,* London 1670, p. 561.

pass here as Current, but in other Countreys of no esteem or value: And the Portuguese use them in their Passage, when they or their Pomberoes, that is Slaves, are sent with Merchandise to Pombo, and other Places lying up the Countrey, out of Angola, Lovando, Sante Paulo, through Congo."[1] Cavazzi says that the *zimbi*, as he calls them, were taken out of the sea at Benguela,[2] as well as at Loanda, where the "lumachette" or "chiocciolette," that is, "little snails," were more dim in color and so more esteemed;[3] but the most precious came from Cabocco.[4] In Kimbundu, of Angola, *njimbu* still has the meaning of "conch, shell,"[5] but in Kongo, *njimbu* means "beads, money, blue currency,"[6] in a dialect of this language, Kikongo, *nzimbu* "currency, blue beads,"[7] in Fiote, *nzimbu* "necklace of beads."[8]

According to Knivet, the native money was (*gull*) *ginbo* "a shell of a fish that they find by the shore-side; and from Brazil the Portugals do carry great store of them to Angola."[9] In 1782 one hundred thousand of

[1] *Ibid.*, p. 536.

[2] "Alle spiaggie si pescano i *Zimbi*, de' quali, dicemmo valersi la gente in vece di moneta, spenden doli à numero, & à misura," *Istorica descrizione de' tre' regni, Congo, Matamba, et Angola*, Bologna 1687, p. 11 (I. 20).

[3] "Dirimpetto alla Città distante un quarto di miglio stendesi nel Mare un' Isola lunga cinque leghe, e larga, al più, un miglio scarso: quì pescansi *lumachette, ò chiocciolette*, che per essere di colore più oscuro, liscie, et sottili, sono in maggiore stima, e corrono frà Neri in vece di moneta ne loro contratti," *ibid.*, p. 17 (I. 32).

[4] "In Cabocco, Terra dell' istessa Prouincia, trouansi *Lumachette* di gran prezzo appresso la gente del Congo, ascendendo il valore di una collana di queste al cambio di uno Schiauo; se ne seruono le Persone di condizione, e singolarmente le femmine per ornamento, cingendosene tutto il corpo; & è mercanzia, dalla quale gli habitatori cauano considerabile emolumento," *ibid.*, p. 19 (I. 37).

[5] J. D. Cordeiro da Matta, *Ensaio de diccionario kimbúndu-portuguez*, Lisboa 1893.

[6] W. H. Bentley, *Dictionary and Grammar of the Kongo Language*, London 1887, 1895.

[7] R. Butaye, *Dictionnaire kikongo-français, français-kikongo*, Roulers [1909].

[8] A. Visseq, *Dictionnaire fiot-français*, Paris 1890.

[9] E. G. Ravenstein, *The Strange Adventures of Andrew Battell of Leigh, in Angola and the Adjoining Regions* (The Hakluyt Society), London 1901, p. 96.

these *nzimbu* formed a *cofo*, that is, "box," but the term *cofo* was already employed in 1516.[1]  In the XVII. century the *nzimbu*, like the *nsanga*, was the common coin in Congo: "There are Shells they call *Zimbi* which come from Congo, for which all things are to be bought as if they were Mony; two thousand of them are worth a Maccute.  The People of Congo value these Shells, tho they are of no use to them, but only to trade with other Africans who adore the Sea, and call these Shells which their Country does not afford, God's Children:  For which reason they look upon them as a Treasure, and take them in exchange for any sort of Goods they have.  Among them he is richest and happiest who has most of them."[2]

The Chinese *Cypraea moneta* "was derived chiefly from the Pescadores Islands, between Formosa Sea and the mainland," from which region not less than 44 species of cowries are recorded.[3]  But it is clear, not only from the Chinese sources, but also from Dapper, Cavazzi, and others, that the darker kind was more highly valued in Africa, which is merely a preservation of the relative values of the Chinese *tsze-pei* and *pei*, the "purple shell" and the ordinary "shell," as existing for milleniums.  It is not easy to determine the original pronunciation of Chinese *pei*, but since the pearl oyster was in Athenaeus given as βεϱϐεϱι, in Mas'ūdī as *balbal*,[4] while in the Maldives the name of the *Cypraea moneta* still is *boli* or *boḷi*, the original form of *pei* was, in all probability, *par* or *per*.  Pyrard de Laval has the following references to the word: "At

---

[1] L. Cordeiro, *Memorias do Ultramar. Viagens, explorações e conquistas dos Portuguezes*, Lisboa 1881, p. 8.

[2] J. Churchill, *A Collection of Voyages and Travels*, London 1704, vol. I, p. 620.

[3] Terrien de Lacouperie, *The Metallic Cowries of Ancient China*, in *The Journal of the Royal Asiatic Society*, London 1888, vol. XX, p. 439.

[4] C. B. de Meynard and P. de Courteille, *Les prairies d'or*, Paris 1861-77, p. 328 f.

first, when our people came there, a Portuguese ship
of 400 tons was at anchor in the roads, having come
from Cochin with a full cargo of rice, to take away
*bolys*, or shells, to Bengal, where they are in great
demand."[1]  "From the house to the place of burial
they scatter over the road *bolys* (which are little shells,
of which I shall speak in their place), to the end that the
poor may collect them and make a profit."[2]  "There
is another kind of wealth at the Maldives, viz., certain
little shells containing a little animal, large as the tip of
the little finger, and quite white, polished, and bright:
they are fished twice a month, three days before and
three days after the new moon, as well as at the full,
and none would be got at any other season.  The
women gather them on the sands and in the shallows
of the sea, standing in the water up to their waists.
They called them *Boly*, and export to all parts an
infinite quantity, in such wise that in one year I have
seen thirty or forty whole ships loaded with them without other cargo.  All go to Bengal, for there only is
there a demand for a large quantity at high prices.  The
people of Bengal use them for ordinary money, although they have gold and silver and plenty of other
metals;  and, what is more strange, kings and great
lords have houses built expressly to store these shells,
and treat them as part of their treasure.  All the
merchants from other places in India take a large quantity to carry to Bengal, where they are always in demand;  for they are produced nowhere but at the Maldives, on which account they serve as petty cash, as I
have said.  When I came to Malé for the first time,
there was a vessel at anchor from Cochin, a town of the
Portuguese, of 400 tons burthen;  the captain and
merchants were Mestifs, the others Christianised

[1] Gray, *op. cit.*, vol. I, p. 78.
[2] *Ibid.*, p. 157.

Indians, all habited in the Portuguese fashion, and they had come solely to load with these shells for the Bengal market. They give 20 coquetees [?kegs] of rice for a parcel of shells: for all these *Bolys* are put in parcels of 12,000, in little baskets of coco leaves of open work, lined inside with cloth of the same coco tree, to prevent the shells falling out. These parcels or baskets of 12,000 are negotiated there as bags of silver are here, which between merchants are taken as counted, but not by others: for they are so clever at counting, that in less than no time they will take tally of a whole parcel. Also in Cambaye and elsewhere in India they set the prettiest of these shells in articles of furniture, as if they were marbles or precious stones."[1] "The next greatest trade is carried on with Bengal, and the merchandise carried there most frequently is the little shells of the Maldives, wherewith every year many vessels are laden. The Maldive people call them *Boly*, but the other Indians call them *Caury:* in these they make a marvellous profit all over India."[2] To this must be added the Malay *beya*, *biya* "cowrie shell, duties, toll, taxes," which is also found in Sundanese and other Malay languages. This is either a derivative from the Sinhalese *bella* or the Chin. *pei*. The latter is more likely, however, since we have also Siamese *bia* "cowrie." In any case, the "cowrie" words in Asia so far discussed are all derived from one source.

Samuel Braun, in the beginning of the XVII. century, says that the Dutch bought *accary*, precious beads, at Benin and Amboy, giving in exchange "little white horns and snails with which horse bridles are adorned," and which the natives call *abuy*.[3] Nearly a century

---

[1] *Ibid.*, p. 236 ff.
[2] *Ibid.*, p. 438.
[3] G. Henning, *Samuel Braun, der erste deutsche wissenschaftliche Afrikareisende, Beitrag zur Erforschungsgeschichte von Westafrika*, Basel 1900, p. 60.

later Barbot gives an English word *boejies*, which, he says, has the same sound in Wolof and Peul, and at the Gold Coast.[1] The absence of the word in the modern Negro languages shows that it was not of native origin and did not succeed in maintaining itself. The history of the *abuy* words is best studied in their chronological order.

We have already met with the Portuguese term *buzio* for "cowrie." Ramusio quotes a Portuguese pilot in 1520 to the effect that in Ethiopia, that is, in the interior of Africa, money was represented by the shells which in Italy were called *porcellette*, in Portugal *buzios*.[2] Two years earlier Barbosa told of the small *buzios* of the Maldive Islands, which were current in Cambay and Bengal and were cleaner than copper coin.[3] Another Portuguese account, of about the same time, found its way into Ramusio. Here we have a very detailed statement as to the Maldive shell currency of India.[4]

[1] Churchill, *op. cit.*, vol. V, p. 417.

[2] G. B. Ramusio, *Delle navigationi et viaggi*, Venetia 1588, vol. I, fol. 117a.

[3] "Daquy leuaom tambem hũus *buzios* pequenos, que he grande mercadoria pera ho regno de Cambaia e Bengala, honde corem por moeda baixa, e hamna por mais limpa e melhor que ha do cobre," *Livro de Duarte Barbosa*, in *Collecção de noticias para a historia e geografia das nações ultramarinas*, Lisboa 1867, vol. II, p. 348.

[4] "Ciascuno pou vale 80, *buzios*, cio è *porcellette*, di sorte che ciascuno caho vale 1280. *porcellette*, vale ciascuno Tamcat 9870. *porcellette ò Buzios*; & un Calaim è 458. che è il prezzo, per il quale danno una gallina buona. & per questo si potra sapere quello che potranno comprare per quelle. chiamansi li *Buzios* in Bengala *Curi*. questi *Buzios* corrono per moneta in Orixa, & in tutto il Regno di Bengala, & in Arquam, & in Martabane, & per tutto il regno di Pegu. li *Buzios* di Bengala sono maggiori, & tengono un segno giallo per il mezzo, li quali vagliono per tutta la terra di Bengala, li pigliano in gran quantità di mercantie cosi come oro, & in Orixanon vagliono tanto come in altre parti sono apprezzati, massimamente in questi duoi luoghi di Pegu, & Araquam. gli eletti & migliori vengono portati dalle isole di Diua in gran quantità," *op. cit.*, vol. I, fol. 334a. "La moneta piccola di pegu sono *Buzios* piccoli bianchi: generalmente vagliono in Martabane quindicimila una viza, che sono x. catais, quando è buon mercato sedecimila, quãdo sono molto cari quattordicimila, il generale quattordicimila, vale in calain millecinquecento *Buzios*, & per quattrocento ò cinquecento danno una gallina: (che viene al modo di Venetia un marchetto;)

In the XVII. century Dapper referred to *boesjes* as used instead of money at Benin,[1] and Ogilby, who borrowed his material chiefly out of Dapper, spoke soon after of "East-India little horns, or Shells, which they use in stead of Money."[2]   Still later Barbot called these shells in English *boesjes, bousies, boejies,* and in French *bouges:* "Two *Bousies,* or *Cauries,* East-India shells, which serve for ornaments in necklaces, and go for money at Fida and Ardra."[3]   "At the common price of three *Boesjes* (or *Cauris*) a sort of little white shells, of the Maldivy islands in the East-Indies, which are there the current money, and those three *Cauris* may perhaps cost us about a farthing."[4]   "For an instance of their great dexterity herein, tho' some factors have their *Boejies,* in small barrels, sewed up in sacks, the Blacks, as they carry them along the way, cut the sacks, and dig out the *Boejies,* at the chinks of the barrel, with an iron chissel."[5]   "Besides which, there is a crown, or five shillings a head duty for every slave that is sold for goods;  but the collectors of it, cheat their prince considerably, by agreeing underhand with those who sell these slaves, so that a small matter comes into the treasury, only for such as are sold for *Boejies:* this being the money of the land, it is always paid in the king's presence, and out of that, he takes three crowns for every slave; and yet, some are so sly, as to fetch the *Boejies* from us in the nighttime, or at some other unseasonable hours, to cheat the prince of his customs."[6]

---

& per questo prezzo danno le cose à queste simiglianti, & per questa maniera corre in Araquem. vengono questi *Buzios* dall'isole di Diua, doue fanno li mantili fortilissimi in gran copia: & similmente dell' isole di Bandam & di Burnei le portano à Malaca, & di li sono portati à Pegu," *ibid.,* fol. 335a.

[1] "*Boesjes,* of Oostindische horentjes, die by hen in stede van gelt gebruikt worden," *op. cit.,* part 2, fol. 126; see also fols. 218 and 139.

[2] *Op. cit.,* p. 474.

[3] Churchill, *op. cit.,* vol. V, p. 264.

[4] *Ibid.,* p. 247.

[5] *Ibid.,* p. 332.

[6] *Ibid.,* p. 335.

"The *Boejies* or *Cauris*, which the French call *Bouges*, are small milk-white shells, commonly as big as small olives, and are produced and gathered among the shoals and rocks of the Maldivy islands, near the coast of Malabar in the East-Indies; and thence transported as ballast to Goa, Cochin, and other ports in the East-Indies, by the natives of those numerous islands: and from the above-named places, are dispersed to the Dutch and English factories in India; then brought over to Europe, more especially by the Dutch, who make a great advantage of them, according to the occasion the several trading nations of Europe have for this trash, to carry on their traffick at the coast of Guinea, and of Angola; to purchase slaves or other goods of Africa, and are only proper for that trade; no other people in the universe putting such a value on them as the Guineans; and more especially those of Fida and Ardra have long done, and still do to this very day. And so, proportionably to the occasion the European Guinea adventurers have for those *Cauris*, and the quantity or scarcity there happens to be of them, either in England or Holland, their price by the hundred weight is higher or lower. I can give no reason why they are usually sold by weight, and not by measure.

"These *Cauris* are of many different sizes, the smallest hardly larger than a common pea; and the largest, as an ordinary walnut, longish like an olive; but of such great ones there is no considerable quantity in proportion to the inferior sizes; and are all intermixt, great and small. They are commonly brought over from the East-Indies, in packs or bundles, well wrapp'd, and put into small barrels in England or Holland, for the better conveniency of the Guinea trade.

"Having given this account of the nature of these *Boejies*, it remains to observe the use made thereof, by the Guineans.

"At Fida and Ardra, where, as I have hinted before, they are most fond of them, they either serve to adorn their bodies, or as current coin.  At Fida the natives bore a little hole through each *Boejie*, with an iron tool made for that purpose, and thread them, forty *Boejies* in a string, which they call Toques in Portuguese;  and in their natural language Cenre.

"Five such strings, or Cenres, of forty *Boejies* each, make a certain small measure, called a Galinha, and in their own language a Fore.  Two hundred *Cauris*, and fifty such Fores, make an Alcove, or a Guinbotton, in their language;  the word Alcove being Portuguese, as well as that of Galinha, but as frequently used by the Blacks, as the other names of Fore and Guinbotton, of their own language.  This Alcove measure weighs, as I have before observed, about sixty pounds, and contains four thousand *Boejies*.

"With these strings, or Toques, or Cenres, of forty *Boejies*, they buy and sell all sorts of goods among themselves, as if they were silver or gold money;  and are so very much taken with them, as to tell us they are preferable to gold, both for ornament and traffick;  insomuch, that a handful of them is better for those purposes, than an ounce of fine gold: and it is a general rule there, to reckon a man's wealth by the number of the Alcoves of *Boejies*, and the quantity of slaves he possesses."[1]

We find in Pyrard de Laval the Maldive name of the cowries as *boli, bolli*.  This is given by Christopher[2] *boli, boḷi* "shell, in the general, also the name of the money cowry."  The first *l* is pronounced "as in English, sometimes it is liquid, as in million," while the second is pronounced "with the tongue reverting to the palate."  The first would, therefore, appear to an

[1] *Ibid.*, p. 338 f.
[2] *Vocabulary of the Maldivian Language*, in *The Journal of the Royal Asiatic Society of Great Britain and Ireland*, vol. VI (1841), p. 66.

Italian like *bogli*, and this we shall meet later; while the second would be heard with a soft rasping sound, leading to Port. *buzio*, Fr. *bouge*, or would have the *l* entirely omitted as in Dutch *boejie*, which is mentioned as *abuy* in Africa.   While the latter has not survived in Wolof or Peul, it appears in Benin, according to Duarte Pacheco, as *iguou*, and, according to Barros, as *igovo*. Modern Yoruba *owo*, Ewe *agaga*, possibly Neule *negbie*, Dahome *akwe* "cowrie, money" indicate that the Benin word was approximately *igwo*.   In Dahome *akwe* has received the largest development, for here we find *akweho* "value," *akwejo* "tribute," *akweno* "rich," etc. As *b* is a rare sound in Dahome and *gb* is generally substituted for it,[1] the original *abuy* for "cowrie" would appear in Dahome as *agbwy*, which at once explains Dahome *akwe* and the other related forms.   Thus we are still under the influence of the Maldivian word, due to the importation of the Maldivian cowries into Africa, as mentioned by the Arabic writers.

The Bantu *zimbo*, *nzimbo* is clearly a Bantuized plural form of the same *abuy*.   There is in Bantu a class of nouns which has *in, n, i,* in the singular, and *zin, jin, sin,* in the plural.   "The classifier *in* or *n* may originally have been no other than the indefinite adjective *-mue* 'one, another, some.' "[2]   We actually have Kongo *mbiya* "a single bead," which unquestionably belongs here.   But single cowries were never in use, although forming the lowest unit of the currency, and only the plural of an original *imbuy*, namely *zimbuy*, could survive.   This *zimbuy*, as we have seen, is distributed south of the Gold Coast over a wide territory. In some regions it has assumed the meaning "iron" in a peculiar way.   In Kaffir we have *in-tsimbi* "beads, a bell, iron in bars," in Zulu *in-simbi* "metal, iron,

[1] M. Delafosse, *Manuel dahoméen*, Paris 1894.
[2] J. Torrend, *A Comparative Grammar of the South-African Bantu Languages*, London 1891, p. 86.

appearance." The word is the same as Luganda *en-simbi*, Nyamwesi *lu-simbi* and the "cowrie" words in the other Bantu languages. The change of meaning is due to the fact that iron bars were introduced by the Europeans as currency among the Negroes, especially to the south of the Gold Coast. Dapper speaks of "*staven yzer*, tot de lengte van een, twee, en drie voeten,"[1] "*staven yzers* van acht-en-twintigh en dertigh staven in het duizent pont,"[2] which Ogilby translates "*iron bars* of one, two, or three foot long,"[3] "bars of iron, of which eight and twenty or thirty make a thousand Weight."[4] Although the Bantu word for the cowrie seems to be a pluralized form of original Chinese *pei*, it is more likely, since in the Bantu languages the word generally means "blue currency, blue beads," that it represents Chinese *tsze-pei* "purple shell," as introduced by Arab or Portuguese traders.

The Chinese *ho-pei* for "cowrie" was originally pronounced something like *ka-par*, and this is, no doubt, the origin of the Sanskrit *kaparda* "a small shell or cowrie, used as a coin and a die in gambling, *Cypraea moneta*." This produced Hindustani *kaurī*, *kauḍi*, Marathi *kauḍā*, *kauḍī*, Guzerati *koḍā*, etc., and in the Dravidian languages Kannada *kavaḍi*, *kavaḍe*, Tulu *kouḍi*, etc. We have already met with the "cowrie" words in Arabic, but ودع *waḍa'* is more likely the Dravidian *woḍa* "shell," than a corruption of *kavaḍi*, although the African languages, which have borrowed the term from the Arabic, frequently have the shorter and the longer term side by side. We meet it first in Zanzibar, where we have *kauri* "cowrie," and in Madagascar, where we get Hova *akorany*, Betsileo *akorane*, Taukarana *ankaora*,

---

[1] *Op. cit.*, part 1, fol. 419.
[2] *Ibid.*, fol. 411, and again, part 2, pp. 10, 118.
[3] *Op. cit.*, p. 357.
[4] *Ibid.*, p. 350.

Taimarona *akorá.*[1]   The Hausas, who are the great mercantile people of the Sahara, have *wuri*, plural *kurdī*, *kudi, kawara, al-kawara* "cowrie, money, price."   The first is, no doubt, a form of Arabic ودع *'uḍe*, while the rest are all Arabic forms or adaptions of Arabic forms for the Hindustani *kaurī*.   We find also the Arabic word in Wolof *khorre* "cowrie," Bambara, Dyula *wari*, Malinke *wori* "money."   But we have also Malinke *kurŭn*, Bambara *kuro* "cowrie."   Thus it is clear that while the *abuy* words for "cowrie" came up with the ocean traders from the Maldive Islands, the *kauri* words are chiefly due to an overland trade connecting Zanzibar with the north of Africa and the Western Sudan.

[1] A. Jully, *Manuel des dialectes malgaches*, Paris 1901.

# CHAPTER II.

## The Onyx.

In the Arabic apocryphal stories about Solomon there is frequently reference to the onyx which he caused to be strung by a white worm.[1] For this reason the mottled onyx, a variety of the carnelian, is known among Mohammedan nations as "Solomon's stone," and is accredited with certain magical qualities. He who carries an onyx remains calm during a dispute or laughter; it whitens teeth, sweetens the breath, etc. Mohammed was supposed to have said: "He who carries a carnelian seal in his ring is constantly blessed and fortunate."[2] No wonder, then, that it formed as important an amulet as the cowries, which were known under the name of ودع *waḍa'*, جزء *ǵaz'*, خرز *ḥaraz*, and with which the ancient Arabs used to adorn their idols, even as is the case with the Mohammedan Negroes.[3] It is significant that *ǵaz'* is also the current name for the onyx, but the onyx is usually classed with the carnelians as an عقيق *'aqīq*.

In Persian the onyx is known as *sang-i-sulaimānī*, literally "stone of Solomon," although the Persian dictionary[4] says: "An onyx, agate imported from Sulaimāniya, whence the name, and used for amulets;" but neither Yākūt nor Al-Bakri records such a place name. The anomalous *sulaimānī* for *sulaiman* is due to

---

[1] M. Grunbaum, *Neue Beiträge zur semitischen Sagenkunde*, Leiden 1893, p. 218.
[2] E. Doutté, *Magie et religion dans l'Afrique du Nord*, Alger 1909, p. 83 f.
[3] *Ibid.*, p. 82.
[4] F. Steingass, *A Comprehensive Persian-English Dictionary*, London [1892].

the Arabic adjective سليماني *sulaimānī*, for عقيق سليماني
*'aqiq sulaimānī* "Solomon's carnelian," that is, "onyx."
The Persian word is found also in Hindustani, where we
get *sulaimānī*, or *sulaimānī patthar* "onyx," literally
"Solomon's stone," *sang-e-sulaimānī* "agate, onyx."
Toward the west, Pers. *sang* became generalized as "gem,
bead" in general, since the chief purpose of the *sang-i-
sulaimānī* was to furnish beads. But in Arabic it produced a number of words, in which the original meaning
of "stone" can be discovered only by a careful analysis.

We have here سنجه صنجه *sangah*, *ṣangah* "scale for weighing." We shall later see that small onyx balls were actually used as weights, hence the Persian name for "stone
(of Solomon)" received the meaning "scale for weighing." But we have also several times سنجه *sangah* used
as "small metal ball, a small ball dropped hourly by
a clock," where the reference to the onyx weights is
still more obvious. Again, Arab. سنجه *sungah* means
"blackness mixed with speckles of white, and of red,
and of yellow in an animal," which is the description
of the color of the onyx. But there is also an Arab.
سنيح *sanīḥ* "pearls, the string upon which they are to
be strung, ornaments of a woman, of moulded metal,
stones, gold, silver, or jewels, or gems," which, in all
probability, is a derivative from the same Persian
word.

The Persian word found its way into Africa, from
Zanzibar or further down the coast. We have, in
Zanzibar, Swahili *ushanga* (plural *shanga*, *mashanga*)
"a bead; beads are sold in the interior, being imported
in large variety of shape and color to suit the peculiar
taste and demand of different localities."[1] Among the
Warundi, on the opposite shore, a string of beads used

[1] A. C. Madan, *Swahili-English Dictionary*, Oxford 1903.

as a monetary unit is known as *urusanga*. The Swahili *ushanga* was carried down the coast into Portuguese territory, when we get Inhambane *urañga*, Sofala *vusañga*, Tette *ūsanga*, Sena *ūsañga*, Quellimane *nsañga*, Cape Delgado *usañga* "beads," and, since the favorite bead was blue, we get Quellimane *a-misañga* "blue-glazed,"[1] from the plural for bead, which also produced Port. *missanga* "glass bead, string of glass beads, trifle." In Kongo we get *nsanga* "string of beads, a string of 100 blue beads of the currency,"[2] in Fiote *m'sanga*, pl. *misanga*, "small pearl."[3] Kongo *nsungu* "cowrie shell" is unquestionably related to these words. As we get away from the direct influence of the traders, the original *sanga* gets more and more corrupted. Thus we have Bemba *ubulungu*,[4] where the relation to *sanga*, through the form *urañga*, as in Inhambane, and Kongo *nsungu*, is still obvious. The same is true of Lala-Lamba *uulungu*;[5] but in Sindebele *ulu-cu* "a string (of beads)"[6] the first syllable has itself become a class prefix, leaving *cu*, from the original *sanga*, to do the work of the Persian word.

In the very beginning of the XVI. century beads were imported into Africa from Cambay in India, by the way of Mozambique: "There went also in the little ship some honourable merchants of Mozambique, who carried with them cloth of Cambaya and red beads, these being the principal articles used in that trade. Sancho de Toar took also for the king a present of pieces of crimson silk, mirrors, caps, trappings for hawks, little bells from Flanders, small transparent

[1] W. H. J. Bleek, *The Languages of Mozambique*, London 1856.
[2] W. H. Bentley, *op. cit.*
[3] *Dictionnaire francais-fiote, dialecte du Kakongo*, Paris 1890.
[4] W. G. Robertson, *An Introductory Handbook to the Language of the Bemba-People*, London 1904.
[5] A. C. Madan, *Lala-Lamba-Wisa and English, English and Lala-Lamba-Wisa Dictionary*, Oxford 1913.
[6] W. A. Elliott, *Notes for a Sindebele Dictionary and Grammar*, Bristol [19 –].

glass beads, and other things to be had in that country,
and which delight the people of Sofala."[1] Duarte
Barbosa, who described Africa and Asia in 1518, frequently refers to Cambay and the beads manufactured
there. At Sofala he met Moors who brought beads
from the east coast, whither they were carried from
Cambay: "And the manner of their traffic was this:
they came in small vessels named zambucos from the
kingdoms of Quiloa, Mombaça, and Melynde, bringing many cotton cloths, some spotted and others white
and blue, also some of silk, and many small beads, grey,
red, and yellow, which things come to the said kingdoms
from the great kingdom of Cambaya in other greater
ships. And these wares the said Moors who came
from Melynde and Mombaça [purchased from others
who bring them hither and] paid for in gold at such a
price that those merchants departed well pleased;
which gold they gave by weight."[2] "The road thereto
[Zimbaoche] goes inland from Çofala towards the
Cape of Good Hope. In this town of Benametapa is
the King's most usual abode, in a very large building,
and thence the traders carry the inland gold to Çofala
and give it unweighed to the Moors for coloured cloths
and beads, which are greatly esteemed among them;
which beads come from Cambaya."[3] "Further on,
leaving this Cuama, a hundred and forty leagues from
it, skirting the coast, is a very great town of Moors
called Angoya [which has its own king]. In it dwell
many merchants who deal in gold, ivory, silk and
cotton cloths and Cambay beads as those of Çofala
were wont to do."[4] The Melinde, Zanzibar, and Maga-
doxo Moors carried on an active trade with Cambay:

[1] Theal, *op. cit.*, vol. II, p. 26.
[2] M. L. Dames, *The Book of Duarte Barbosa* (The Hakluyt Society),
London 1918, vol. I, p. 6 ff.
[3] *Ibid.*, p. 11 f.
[4] *Ibid.*, p. 14 f.

"They are great barterers, and deal in cloth, gold, ivory, and divers other wares with the Moors and Heathen of the great kingdom of Cambaya; and to their haven come every year many ships with cargoes of merchandize, from which they get great store of gold, ivory and wax. In this traffic the Cambay merchants make great profits, and thus, on one side and the other, they earn much money."[1] "The kings of these isles [Zanzibar] live in great luxury; they are clad in very fine silk and cotton garments, which they purchase at Mombaça from the Cambaya merchants. The women of these Moors go bravely decked, they wear many jewels of fine Çofala gold, silver too in plenty, earrings, necklaces, bangles and bracelets, and they go clad in good silk garments."[2] "The place [Magadoxo] has much trade in divers kinds, by reason whereof many ships come hither from the great kingdom of Cambaya, bringing great plenty of cloths of many sorts, and divers other wares, also spices: and in the same way they come from Adem. And they carry away much gold, ivory, wax and many other things, whereby they make exceeding great profits in their dealings."[3]

Apparently Aden Arabs and Jews carried on the most active trade with Cambay, whence came the *alaquecas*, that is, the carnelians: "To the harbour of this city come ships from all parts, more especially from the port of Juda, whence they bring copper, quicksilver, vermilion, coral and woollen and silken cloths, and they take thither on their return great store of spices and drugs, cotton cloths and other wares of the great kingdom of Cambaya. From Zeila and Barbora too come many ships with food-stuffs in abundance; [in return they take back Cambay cloth and beads both large and small, and all the goods in which they trade

[1] *Ibid.*, p. 22 f.
[2] *Ibid.*, p. 27 f.
[3] *Ibid.*, p. 31.

for Arabia Felix and Preste Joam's country also come here, as do the ships of Ormuz and Cambaya] and those of Cambaya come laden with cloth of many kinds; so great is the number of them that it seems an astonishing thing! And, as I have already said, they bring cotton, drugs (great quantity), gems, seed pearl in abundance, *alaquequas*, and to the said kingdom of Cambaya they take back madder, opium, raisins of the sun, copper, quicksilver, vermilion and great store of rosewater, which is made here. They also take much woollen cloth, coloured Meca velvets, gold in ingots, coined and to be coined (and also some in strings), and camlets, and it seems an impossible thing that they should use so much cotton cloth as these ships bring from Cambaya."[1] These carnelians were found beyond Cambay, at Limodara: "Beyond this city of Cambaya, further inland is a town called Limadura. Here is found an *alaquequa* (carnelian) rock, which is a white, milky or red stone, which is made much redder in the fire. They extract it in large pieces, and there are cunning craftsmen here who shape it, bore it and make it up in divers fashions, that is to say; long, eight-sided, round and olive-leaf shapes, also rings, knobs for hilts of short swords and daggers, and other ways. The dealers come hither from Cambaya to buy them, and they [thread them, and] sell them on the Red Sea coast whence they pass to our lands by way of Cairo and Alexandria. They take them also to Arabia and Persia, and to India where our people buy them to take to Portugal. And here they find great abundance of *babagoure*, which we call *calsadonia* (chalcedony), which are stones with grey and white veins in them, which they fashion perfectly round, and after they are bored the Moors wear them on their arms in such a manner that they touch the skin, saying that

[1] *Ibid.*, p. 55 f.

they are good to preserve chastity: as these stones are plentiful they are not worth much."[1]

At about the same time, the factor at Sofala informed King Don Manuel of the importation of "red beads of Cambaya three and a half quintals nine pounds, which cost in Diu eight hundred and forty reis the farazola, which, when they are good, are valued in the factory at fifty miticals and more."[2]  Even as late as the middle of the XVI. century there seemed to be no beads in South Africa except those which were imported from India, for the wearing of a bead necklace by a Kaffir was taken by shipwrecked people as a proof that they were within the territory frequented by European traders: "Among them was one of whom the rest seemed to make the most account, and he it was who answered our questions, which he understood as little as we did his, and though there was no pomp or dignity about his person, being naked like the rest, yet he was distinguished from them by wearing a few beads red in colour, round, and about the same size as coriander seeds, which we rejoiced to see, it seeming to us that these beads being in his possession proved that we were near some river frequented by trading vessels, for they are only made in the kingdom of Cambaya, and are brought by the hands of our people to this coast."[3]  At the end of the century the red beads were also manufactured at Negapatam and imported into South Africa by the Portuguese: "The dress of these negroes is similar to that of the negroes of Tizombe, but they wear red beads in their ears, which the others do not. Nuno Yelho asked the Kaffir to whom he gave the lid where these were obtained, and he saw from their appearance that they came from the land of the Inhaca, who is king of the people living by the river of Lour-

[1] *Ibid.*, p. 142 ff.
[2] Theal, *op. cit.*, vol. I, p. 104 f.
[3] *Ibid.*, p. 225.

enço Marques. These beads are made of clay of all
colours, of the size of a coriander seed. They are made
in India at Negapatam, whence they are brought to
Mozambique, and thence they reach these negroes
through the Portuguese who exchange them for ivory."[1]
Beads were also imported from Chaul, whence they
came in bars: "Above Sena to the eastward, which
is the other side of the river, along it and in the interior
there is much cotton, and of it the inhabitants weave
the cloth for the machiras, which are very plentiful in
all that province; and that country is called Bororo.
The beads for which these machiras are bartered are
bought in Chaul, generally at fifty pardaos a bar,
each bar containing four quintals. This bar, however,
in Sena, with the expenses, may be worth one hundred
cruzados, which is the highest rate at which it can be
estimated. There of one bar of beads they make a
thousand to a thousand four hundred montanas, which
are bundles of strings of beads held together in the
fashion of a horse's tassel. These montanas in Bororo
are worth two machiras each, and thus they make two
thousand four hundred and more from the bar. These
machiras are sold to the negroes on the western bank
of the river, who are called Botongas, at a mitical of
gold apiece, which there is the weight of a cruzado and
a testoon. In this way one hundred cruzados may well
be made to yield three thousand cruzados, if order is
kept, and Portuguese are not allowed to go about
spoiling the trade, as they did on our departure."[2]
Some beads were made of potter's clay, and at the
end of the XVI. century Kaffir traders, in the employ
of the Portuguese, carried them far inland: "They
also take for this trade some small beads made of
potter's clay, some green and others blue or yellow,

[1] *Ibid.*, vol. II, p. 303.
[2] *Ibid.*, vol. III, p. 234.

with which the necklets are made that the Kaffir women wear round their necks, like our rich necklaces. These beads are threaded on fibres of macosi, which is like the leaves of the palm, and they make necklets of ten or twelve rows, each being a palm's length. They call them metins, which is a weight in use with them. Ten of these metins they call a lipate, and twenty a lipote, which is worth a cruzado and costs in that place about forty reis. All these things are sold forthwith, and double or more than double the money is made."[1]

*Alaquecas*, that is, Arab. عقيق *'aqīq* "agate, onyx," are mentioned on the west coast of Africa even before Duarte Barbosa,[2] but these do not seem to have been introduced there directly from Cambay or through Melinde, but indirectly from Europe. There is no evidence of any trade relation between Cambay and the west coast of Africa above Angola.

Barbosa distinguishes between the carnelians and *bābāgūrī*, which he calls "chalcedony." In Cambay the Guzerati name for "onyx" is still *bawaghori*,[3] and the usual Turkish word for "agate, onyx" is *bābāqūrī*. We do not meet with any earlier references to this word than in Barbosa, but a Turkish author, Sidi 'Ali Kapudān, mentions it in 1554: "In this country (Guzerat) is a profusion of *bābāghūrī* and carnelians; but the best

---

[1] *Ibid.*, vol. VI, p. 368.

[2] "*Alaquequas*, que sam hūas pedras a que nós chamamos de estancar sangue," D. Pacheco Pereira, *Esmeraldo de situ orbis*, in *Boletim da Sociedade de Geographia de Lisboa*, 22ª. série (1904), p. 88; "em toda esta terra na costa do mar há ouro, hainda que he em pouca cantidade, o qual custumamos resguatar por *halaquequas* e por contas amarellas e verdes," *ibid.*, p. 162; also pp. 139, 166. See also F. Hümmerich, *Quellen und Untersuchungen zur Fahrt der ersten Deutschen nach dem portugiesischen Indien, 1505-6*, in *Abhandlungen der Königlich Bayerischen Akademie der Wissenschaften, philosophisch-philologische und historische Klasse*, vol. XXX, part 3, p. 79 ff.

[3] "The *mora* or *bawa ghori* onyx is of two kinds, one dark with white veins, the other greyish white with dark veins," *Gazetteer of the Bombay Presidency*, vol. VI, p. 199.

of these last are those coming from Yaman.''[1]   In 1592
grain weights of *bābāghūrī* were made in northern India,
to be used in weighing,[2] especially of jewels,[3] and in
one Persian author the veins of the eye are compared
with *bābāgūrī* threads.[4]

Of the origin of the carnelian manufacture at Cambay little is known.  "So far as has been traced, the
Musalmán travellers of the ninth and tenth centuries
make no mention of an agate trade at Cambay.  Marco
Polo (1290) says nothing of a special agate trade, either
in his description of Cambay or in the notices of the
Arabian and African ports then connected by commerce
with Gujarát.  The fifteenth century travellers make
only a casual reference to the agate as one of the products of Cambay.  Early in the sixteenth century, the
agate trade seems to have risen to importance.  Var-
thema (1503-1508) speaks of two mountains, one of
carnelians about seventy, the other of diamonds about
one hundred miles, from Cambay.  About this time,
according to a tradition of the Cambay agate workers,
an Abyssinian merchant came to Gujarát, and established an agate factory at Nándod in Rájpipla.  At
first the stones were prepared by Musalmáns, but the
Kanbis were not long in learning the craft.  The merchant died at Nándod, and his tomb is near the well
known tomb of Báwa Ghor at the ford of that name
across the river Narbada.  After some time, according
to the same account, the Kanbi agate workers left
Nándod and came to settle in Broach, and from Broach
went to Cambay.  The Sidi merchant is still remembered by the Hindu agate workers.  Each year on the day
of his death Shrávan sud purnima (July-August full-

[1] H. Yule, *Hobson-Jobson, a Glossary of Colloquial Anglo-Indian Words and Phrases*, new ed. by William Crooke, London 1903.
[2] H. Blochmann, *Āīn i Akbarī*, in *Bibliotheca Indica*, published by the Asiatic Society of Bengal, new series, No. 149, p. 35.
[3] *Ibid.*, p. 615.
[4] *Ibid.*

moon), they offer flowers and cocoanuts at his tomb. As it is far to go from Cambay to Báwa Ghor, they have in Cambay a cenotaph, takiya, in his honour, and those of them who are settled in Bombay have brought with them this memorial of the founder of their craft. The Cambay agate workers assert that the well known shrine of Báwa Ghor was raised in honour of their patron. According to their story, while wandering from place to place as a religious beggar, the Báwa did business in precious stones, and, becoming skilled in agates, set up a factory at Nimodra. Here he prospered and died rich. The local legend of the saint of Báwa Ghor makes no mention of his success as an agate dealer."[1]

"About the middle of the fifteenth century (1437), when the Bahmani dynasty became independent of Delhi and intercourse with north India ceased, the fashion arose of bringing to western India large numbers of Abyssinians and other East Africans. These men, from the Arab El Habish the people of north-east Africa, were known as Habshis, or more often as Sidis, which was originally a term of respect, a corrupt form of Syed. Though most Habshis came to India as slaves, their faithfulness, courage, and energy often raised them to positions of high trust in the Bahmani court. According to Orme the successful Abyssinians gathered round them all of their countrymen whom they could procure either by purchase or invitation, including Negroes from other parts of Africa, as well as Abyssinians. From their marriages, first with natives of India and afterwards among their own families, there arose a separate community, distinct from other Musalmáns in figure, colour, and character. As soon as they were strong enough they formed themselves into an aristocratic republic, the skill and utility of the lowest

[1] *Gazetteer of the Bombay Presidency*, vol. VI, p. 206.

orders giving them influence, and influence fostering a
pride in their name which made them among the
most skilful and daring sailors and soldiers in Western
India."[1]

From these accounts it follows that the modern agate
trade of Cambay was started by Abyssinians, who
derived the name of the mottled onyx or agate from a
patron saint, *Bābāgūr*. The real onyx, known as
*sulaimānī*, was brought to Cambay from Jabalpur,[2] and
the *bābāgūrī* was apparently inferior only to the *sulaimānī*, if it was not identical with it. In any case one
would expect the Abyssinians, like the Arabs, to con-
nect the Cambay onyx with their patron saint, King
Solomon, from whom they claimed descent, through
the Queen of Sheba.[3] Now, one of the mystic names
of King Solomon is *Agūr*, from Proverbs XXX. 1,
where these proverbs are ascribed to him. The explanation of this name was that he was called so because
he "gathered," אגר, the words of the Law.[4] Hence the
Latin Vulgate translates Heb. אגור of Proverbs
XXX. 1 by "congregans." The Syriac version left
*Agūr* untranslated, but Barhebraeus derived the word
from אגר "he hired out," "Solomo seipsum vocat
*Aghur*, utpote qui se sapientiae locaverit." It is most
likely, therefore, that the Abyssinians got their story
of "Bāba *Agūr*," instead of "Bāba Salāmā," from
some Jews, with whom they were associated in Abyssinia and at Aden, in order to explain the relation of
King Solomon to the onyx, which he "gathers," as in
the Arabic story.

It is a curious fact that *Bābāgūr* is not only the
Abyssinian patron saint, but, as *Gūr-bābā*, is also wor-

[1] *Ibid.*, vol. XI, p. 433 f.
[2] *Ibid.*, vol. VI, p. 199.
[3] E. Littmann, *Bibliotheca abessinica; The Legend of the Queen of Sheba
in the Tradition of Axum*, Leyden, Princeton, N. J. 1904.
[4] Grunbaum, *op. cit.*, p. 207.

shipped by the Bhils and other native races in the
neighborhood of Cambay and further away.[1] "The
familiar *Gor Bāba*, a deified ghost of the aboriginal
races, has in many places become a new manifestation
of Siva, as *Goreswara*."[2]  That this is not a chance
transference is proved by the fact that the milkstone,
or chalcedony, which we have so far found as *sulaimānī* and *bābāgūrī*, is recorded in an XVIII. century
Sanskrit dictionary as *Siva-dhātu*, that is, "Siva's
mineral."  Of course, the Hindustani *gaur, gorā*, from
Prakrit *goraō*, Sanskrit *gaura* "white, of fair complexion," which is also an epithet of Siva, caused the
confusion of *Bābāgūr* with Siva on one hand, and with
the white onyx on the other, even as it led to the popular *Gor bāba* "white spectre," but this confusion is of
late origin and would not have taken place so readily,
if it had not been for the importance of the agate bead
and its magical powers.  It is even possible that
Hindustani *guriyā* "glass bead, bead or stones of a
rosary or necklace" owes its form to the same "agate"
word, instead of being derived from Sanskrit *guṭikā*
"round ball," from which comes Hindustani *goṭī*
"round pebble, bead."

[1] Dames, *op. cit.*, p. 144.
[2] W. Crooke, *The Popular Religion and Folk-Lore of Northern India*,
Westminster 1896, vol. I, p. 84.

# CHAPTER III.

## AGGRY BEADS.[1]

Duarte Pacheco, who wrote his *Esmeraldo de situ orbis* in 1506, mentions at Elmina blue beads called *coris*:[2] "At Rio dos Forcados, in Benin territory, barter takes place, chiefly in slaves, cotton cloth, and a few leopard skins, and palm oil, and certain blue beads with red lines, which they call *coris*. These things we buy for brass and copper armrings, and all this is of value at the Castle of Jorze da Mina, and our chief's factor sells it for gold to the Negro merchants."[3] A similar statement was made soon after by a Portuguese pilot: "In this place (Elmina) a large number of Negroes congregate with gold found in the river and the sand, and trade with above mentioned factors, taking from them all kinds of things, mostly beads made of glass and another kind of beads made of a blue stone, I will not say lapis lazuli, but some other mineral, which our king gets from Manicongo, where this stone grows; and these beads are made in the form of slender pipes and are called *coril*, and for these they give con-

---

[1] For general literature on Aggry Beads see: G. P. Rouffaer, *Waar kwamen de raadselachtige Moetisalah's (Aggri-Kralen) in de Timor-groep oorspronkelijk van daan?*, in *Bijdragen tot de Taal-, Land- en Volkenkunde van Nederlandsch-Indië*, 's-Gravenhage 1899, vol. VI, pp. 409–675, and A. W. Nieuwenhuis, *Kunstperlen und ihre kulturelle Bedeutung*, in *Internationales Archiv für Ethnographie*, vol. XVI (1904), pp. 136–153.

[2] "Estes leuam d'esta casa muitas mercadorias asy como lambẽs, que he a principal d'ellas, de que já no noveno item do quarto capitolo d'este segundo livro falamos, e pano vermelho e azul e manilhas de latam e lenços e coraes e hũas conchas vermelhas, que antre elles sam muito estimadas, asy como nós ca estimamos pedras preciosas; isso mesmo val aquy muito ho vinho branco e hũas contos azues, a que elles chamam 'coris,' e outras muitas cousas de desvairados modos," *op. cit.*, p. 253.

[3] *Ibid.*, p. 313.

238 AFRICA AND THE DISCOVERY OF AMERICA

siderable gold, because they are greatly esteemed by all
the Negroes, who put them into the fire, to see that
they are not counterfeit, since many are imported that
are made of glass, which resemble them greatly, but
will not stand the fire test."[1]

In Benin the name of these beads is still "*koli*, a
kind of precious beads or coloured stones, worn as
ornament by the natives of this coast and paid by the
same weight of gold. It is said, that they are digged
out of the ground all along the Slave-coast and found
in ordered strings, as the bones of a decayed snake or
as if formerly bound together, the string being decayed.
Some suppose that they are of animal origin (such is
the idea of the natives themselves), some that they
were manufactured in Egypt, some thousand years
ago and brought here by the first settlers, and some
that they were formerly manufactured in Venice and
the art lost."[2] There is a great diversity of opinion
as to the material from which these beads were made.
"The wearing of coral was a royal privilege, which the
king conferred on his subjects. Where the office of
the holder was not hereditary, as, for instance, with the
fiadors, the bunches of coral had to be returned to the
king on the holder's decease. According to Bold,
coral beads 'are the intrinsic treasures of the rich, being
held in the highest estimation, and from their rarity,
are only in the hands of a few chiefs, whose avidity for
them is immeasurable; the species admired are the
pipe beads of various dimensions, and are valued at
ten large jars of oil an ounce, of the smaller sort, and
so on in proportion for the larger sized.' Mr. Punch
informs me that 'as a matter of fact, the King of Benin
had few, if any, of the large coral beads such as Nana,
Doré, Dudu, and the Jekri chiefs obtained from the

---

[1] Ramusio, vol. I, fol. 116a.
[2] J. Zimmermann, *A Grammatical Sketch of the Akra- or Gā-Language*,
Stuttgart 1858, p. 157.

merchants in Benin River. His coral was insignificant pipe coral, and was only striking when made up into vests and hats. The Binis valued more the agate beads, and especially the dull kind. A necklet of this dull agate was a king's gift, and no one could wear such a necklet, unless it were given him by the king. It was death, in fact, to wear it otherwise. The shiny chrystalline agate, with white quartz veins, anyone could use. Such coral as the Binis had was obtained through Jekri traders, either from the Benin River or Lagos. The Binis said it was dug up at the "back of Benin," but everything, in the days I am speaking of, 14-15 years ago, which was at all mysterious came from the back of Benin.'

"Nyendael describes the coral beads as made of 'pale red coctile earth or stone and very well glazed,' and says they are very like 'speckled red marble.' While no doubt the material of which the so-called coral beads are made varies, all the beads which have come into my hands are either red coral or agate beads, the former having the characteristic structure and composition of coral, while the latter show the concentric zones of chalcedony, some red and some white. Vast numbers of artificial beads go to the African market, but the above specimens are all natural. At the famous agate works at Oberstein in Rhenish Bavaria, large numbers of trivial ornamental articles are specially made for the African trade. In Burton's time the red coral was brought from the Mediterranean."[1] But Dapper assumed that *akori* was a bluish coral growing in the water: "The Commodities, which the Europeans and other Whites Trade for in the River of Benyn, are Cotton-Cloathes, Jasper-Stone, and Women-Slaves, Leopard-Skins, some Pepper and

[1] H. L. Roth, *Great Benin, its Customs, Art and Horrors,* Halifax 1903, p. 26 f.

*Akori*, which is a certain bluish Coral, growing like a Tree in the Water. This *Akori*, carried to the Gold-Coast, the Women wear for an Ornament in their Hair."[1]

*Akori* is obviously a generic name for "bead," made of a large variety of material. The word is actually used in this sense elsewhere, as in Neule *gri* "beads," and is unquestionably identical with the "cowrie" words, which on the Ivory Coast and among the Mandingos have assumed the meaning "money." This is made certain by the fact that Mandingo *wari*, *wori* is found in the Baule country as *worye* "blue bead."

The common story that these beads were dug up from ancient graves has led Delafosse to investigate such a necropolis in the Baule country,[2] where these beads are called *worye*. Delafosse found these made of glass, but, as he thought, of a manufacture common to ancient Eygpt or Assyria. The same deposits of blue beads are found at Zanzibar. "Besides carnelian beads, pierced amethysts and garnets and great quantities of glass beads are also found at certain states of the tide at the ruined towns in Pemba. They are generally considered to be of Arabian or Persian manufacture, and to date from the twelfth to the fifteenth century; although some specimens may be considerably older and date from the Ptolemaic period.

"The most common bead found at Ndagoni is a large, irregularly shaped, bluish-green glass bead of a distinctive character. After heavy rain they may be picked up on the sea-beach by hundreds. That they are of somewhat archaic manufacture is evident from the irregularity of their shape and size. Many of them appear to have become distorted in the process of being made.

[1] J. Ogilby, *op. cit.*, p. 473.
[2] *Sur des traces probables de civilisation égyptienne et d'hommes de race blanche à la Côte d'Ivoire*, in *L'Anthropologie*, Paris 1900, vol. XI, p. 677 ff.

"The question is often asked how the existence of such quantities of beads in the sea-sands of Pemba can be accounted for.

"The suggestions generally put forward in reply are:

"1. That they formed a portion of a cargo of a wrecked ship.

"2. That they have been washed out of ancient graves by the encroaching sea.

"3. That they are the remains of some propitiatory or thank-offering made by the former inhabitants of the ruins, to the sea.

"4. That a bead factory or depot existed at the towns where beads are now found, and that the encroaching sea has liberated the beads.

"With reference to the above propositions, it will be realised of course that beads formed until quite recent times—and in fact to some extent form still—the chief currency of native Africa: and everything from a tusk of ivory to a cob of Indian corn had to be paid for in beads, cloth, and in more recent times by brass wire and gunpowder, so there is nothing inherently extraordinary that beads should be found at the sites of these ancient and deserted trading-stations. The only surprising thing about them is that they should be found concentrated in particular spots on the sea-shore.

"With regard to the above suggestions as to how the beads came in their present position, all are reasonable except perhaps the first. It would be too remarkable a coincidence that ships had run ashore, and been wrecked exactly opposite most of the towns of Pemba and Zanzibar. It is, moreover, reasonable to suppose that had they run ashore as is suggested, the cargo would have been saved and taken out of them, for all the sites where beads are found are on the shore of a harbour, and the sea in these sheltered tropical waters is never rough enough to break up a ship. At these 'bead-sites,' the sea is seldom rougher than the Serpentine.

"The fourth explanation seems the most probable, and it possesses none of the objections of the previous ones. It not only accounts for the glass beads, but also for the glass fragments, some of which, especially at the Ndagoni ruins, appear to be, not pieces of glass vessels, but melted fragments and slag from crucibles used in the manufacture of the blue beads.

"It is worthy of note that at Mogdishu, in Italian Somaliland, one of the oldest Persian or Arab settlements on the coast, complete apparatus for the manufacture of glass beads, such as crucibles, paste for making beads, glass stems, and coloured beads have actually been discovered.

"If a glass-bead manufactury existed at Mogdishu, there is no reason why similar establishments should not have been erected elsewhere: although it is as well to restate the fact that while the existence of bead factories will explain the presence of special varieties of beads at these old ruins, it must not be concluded that they account for all such deposits."[1]

While it may be perfectly true that old graves contained necklaces of precious beads and were actually dug up for the purpose in the XIX. century, it stands to reason that if this had been an old practice, not a necropolis would have yielded any beads for centuries earlier. Obviously there must be some other explanation to the presence of large bead deposits in the soil at Benin and in Zanzibar, and the presence of complete apparatus for the manufacture of glass beads makes it certain that we are dealing with a commercial practice, most likely of Arabic origin. We have already seen that the more precious shell was blue and dates back

[1] F. B. Pearce, *Zanzibar, the Island Metropolis of Eastern Africa*, London 1920, p. 355 ff.

to a Chinese commercial custom. With the growth
of the glass industry the great advantage of manufacturing blue beads to take the place of the drilled shell
beads must have presented itself to the Chinese mind.
We actually have a documentary proof of the fact. In
1608 John Saris, in a letter from Bantam to the East
India Company, wrote: "I have many times certified
your worships of the trade the Flemings follow to
Soocadanna (Sukadana) which place yieldeth great
store of diamonds, and of their manner of dealing for
them for gold principally which comes from Benier-
massen (Banjarmasim) and blue glass beads which the
Chinese make and sell 300 for a ps of eight, and they
are there worth a mas a 100 which is 3/. s. and sometimes more sometimes less according as gold doth rise
and fall. I have delivered one of those beads unto
our General to show unto your worships, to the end
that if we shall trade there, we may have the like beads
brought out of England at a cheaper rate."[1]

But Chinese wares, in enormous quantities, have
been found at Zanzibar and the whole eastern littoral:
"Portions of similar Chinese property belonging to the
Ming dynasty have been found, it is understood, at
Zimbabwe, and certainly along the littoral of East
Africa. The variety of markings and pattern is very
great; and from the quantities which strew the beaches
and ruined sites, the importation of china ware to East
Africa during the later Middle Ages must have been
on an extensive scale.

"Much of the pottery found at various places on the
East African coast, and also at the ruins in Zanzibar and
Pemba, cannot be included with the older and rarer
specimens referred to above. It is of later date, and,
as will be seen from the list of the Victoria and Albert

[1] *Letters Received by the East India Company from its Servants in the East*,
London 1896, vol. I, p. 22.

Museum, belongs to the seventeenth and eighteenth
centuries.   In some instances this more recent ware
may have come from Persia.''[1]   There can, therefore,
be no doubt that the glass beads of Zanzibar, hence
of any other emporium in Africa, are due to the efforts
of the Persians and Arabians in popularizing Chinese
commercial customs among the savages.   But the
Arabs, as well as Marco Polo, were convinced that the
shells and porcelain were in some way related, and that
the porcelain had to weather in the ground for a long
time before it could be utilized.[2]   From this arose the
custom in Africa of considering glass or porcelain beads
of especial value, if they had weathered in the ground,
hence the preference shown by the Negroes to the
dimmed beads washed out from the soil, and the large
deposits of such beads in Arabic or European emporiums in Africa.

Duarte Pacheco does not speak of the Benin beads
as being of glass, but the Portuguese pilot distinctly
says that the aggry beads were not of glass, but of a
certain mineral.   In 1624 Braun said that the natives
considered *accarey* to be a precious stone, but that it
grew in the sea like a coral, and that it was of a sky-
blue color, but transparently sea-green.[3]   However,
Braun's opinion is merely based on hearsay and does
not tell us anything certain of the material of these
beads.   Balthasar Springer, in 1509, told of long blue
crystals which were current as money in West Africa.[4]
Similarly the Valentin Ferdinand Manuscript speaks of

---

[1] F. B. Pearce, *op. cit.*, p. 358.
[2] See p. 206 ff.
[3] G. Henning, *op. cit.*, p. 38.
[4] "Diss volck braucht noch nympt bei ynen gantz kein gelt sunder allein
seltzam auenturige Ding als Spigel Messingring lang blawe Cristallein
vnd der geleichen manigerlei was yn seltzam ist vnd ynen do hyn bracht
wirt Do geben sie ware vmb ware vnnd was sie haben vnd bei yn wechst
stuck vor stuck noch yrer liebe und zymlicher achtung der selben Ding,"
F. Schulze, *Balthasar Springers Indienfahrt, 1505–06*, Strassburg 1902, p. 37.

"contas matamungos e christalina."[1] "Crystal" may refer to glass, but since we know that the Venetians manufactured rock crystal beads before they took to those of glass, it is more likely that we are here still in the presence of stone beads. *Matamungo* is unquestionably of Hindu origin, of which the second part is Hindustani *manka*, Guzerati *manako* "bead, gem," and the first tells, no doubt, the material of which it was made. At the end of the XVI. century, beads were received both from India and Venice, for we read in Alvares d'Almada[2] of *"contaria da India"* and *"contaria, continha de Veneza."*[3] It is, therefore, apparent that the bead money for Africa originated in Asia, that is, principally Cambay, whence came the stone beads, but in the XVI. century soon gave way to the counterfeit Chinese and Venetian glass beads.

A study of the bead-trade in the XVI. century reveals its enormous importance in Africa. In 1618 the English factories still used agate and crystal beads,[4] by the side of a great quantity of coral beads from the Red Sea,[5] and glass beads are also mentioned.[6] Beads from Cambay were soon dispatched to Surat, as an experiment in the Madagascar trade.[7] Red and white Cambay beads[8] and carnelian beads from the same

---

[1] Franz Hümmerich, *Quellen und Untersuchungen zur Fahrt der ersten Deutschen nach dem portugiesischen Indien, 1505-6*, in *Abhandlungen der Kgl. Bayerischen Akademie der Wissenschaften, philosophisch-philologische und historische Klasse*, München 1918, vol. XXX, part 3, p. 82.

[2] A. Alvares d'Almada, *op. cit.*

[3] *Ibid.*, pp. 16, 30.

[4] "Bloodstones are difficult to get. 'Aggat or babagoria beades' can be furnished." W. Foster, *The English Factories in India, 1618-1621, A Calendar of Documents in the India Office, British Museum and Public Record Office*, Oxford 1906, p. 52.

[5] *Ibid.*, p. 131.

[6] *Ibid.*, p. 184.

[7] "Send 48 strings (24 corge) of beads suitable for barter in Madagascar, costing half a rupee per corge. Will procure a further supply if these are approved," *ibid.*, *1622-23*, p. 154.

[8] *Ibid.*, *1624-29*, p. 74.

place[1] remained popular, but the Cambay trade deteriorated rapidly.[2] At the same time the European beads were becoming more popular. At first much opposition was met with in Asia against the European amber beads,[3] while coral became "'the most staple and vendible commodity' that Europe produces."[4] At the same time the Portuguese made the small European glass beads popular.[5]

In Africa Dapper, in the XVII. century, once refers to rock-crystal (Bergh-Kristael)[6] as current on the river Gambia; occasionally he uses *kristal, kristallein*[7] alone, which may mean glass or coral, for he once himself adds the remark that instead of rock-crystal (Bergh-Kristal) they in his day rather used coral or beads.[8] Somewhat later, Barbot mentions rock-crystal as imported at James-Fort[9] and crystals at Goeree[10] and crystal beads at Sierra Leone,[11] but as in the latter place he also speaks of all sorts of counterfeit pearls and refers to false crystals imported by the French at Goeree, while elsewhere glass beads predominate to an overwhelming degree, we get a definite proof of the tremendous deteriora-

---

[1] *Ibid.*, p. 209. "Have just unexpectedly procured 216,550 red cornelian beads," *ibid., 1630-33*, p. 39.

[2] "Long red cornelian beads sent in the *Mary* for use in the next fleet. A further supply shall be provided for the *Jonas;* as for quality, Cambaia, where they are made, is so miserably decayed in those kind of artificers that we must take what we can have, if wee will hould ourselves to such a number as you command," *ibid., 1634-1636*, p. 62 f.

[3] *Ibid.*, pp. 131, 144, 173.

[4] *Ibid., 1637-1641*, p. 208.

[5] "Forward a quantity of long beads, round cornelian beads, and 'a small sort of glasse beads called by the Portugalls *contaria.*' The two latter kinds were found by the *Francis* to be much more desired than the long beads, 'which are not here (unlesse forebespoake) procurable without much difficulty, and those scarse worth the buying,' " *ibid.*, p. 289 f. "*Contaria* beads are also popular (at Madagascar), both there and along the coast of Sofala," *ibid.*, p. 296.

[6] O. Dapper, *op. cit.*, part 1, fol. 419.

[7] *Ibid.*, part 2, fols. 10, 126.

[8] *Ibid.*, part 1, fol. 411.

[9] J. Churchill, *op. cit.*, vol. V, p. 75.

[10] *Ibid.*, p. 44.

[11] *Ibid.*, p. 102.

tion in the bead material which had taken place in two hundred years in Africa. Barbot, like Dapper, definitely tells of *akori* as made at Benin from a blue coral,[1] which again shows a deterioration of the bead material, already mentioned by Braun, as compared with Duarte Pacheco's *cori*, which was still made from some stone.

In the XIV. century crystal jewels were taken from Italy to China,[2] obviously because they were manufactured there for export. In 1493 a Venetian document still speaks of the manufacture of glass crystal pipes (cannal vitrorum cristalinorum) at Murano,[3] but it is impossible to determine whether the reference is to rock-crystal or the glass substitute. In the XVII. c., as we have seen, we have frequently references to Venetian glass beads, but these are also manufactured in France,[4] especially in Rouen. It was apparently the Venetians who introduced the long pipes into the African trade, as the Negroes preferred to cut their own beads out of them, and the French glass factories continued this practice[5] as appears from philological considerations. In the Walloon region a pipe is called *buss* or *buzai*, and in Old French the word was *buse* or *buise*. The latter produced Dutch *beviese* "long Venetian bead." Marees tells of the Venetian *beviesen*, brought to the Guinea Coast by the Dutch,[6] which they break into four or five pieces and regrind.[7] These

[1] ". . *Accory*, or *blue coral* . The *blue coral* grows in branchy bushes, like the red coral, at the bottom of the river and lakes in Benin; which the natives have a peculiar art to grind or work into beads like olives," *ibid.*, p. 361; "the *Accory* is to be found no where but at Rio del Rey, and thence along to Camarones River," *ibid.*, p. 384.

[2] C. A. Marin, *Storia civile e politica del commercio de' Veneziani*, Vinegia 1800, vol. V, p. 261.

[3] G. M. Thomas, *Capitular des deutschen Hauses in Venedig*, Berlin 1874, p. 270.

[4] "They use glassbeads (glaze kralen), and other commodities, which the French bring to them, instead of money," Dapper, *op. cit.*, p. 703; "the French import . . . . . false crystal," J. Churchill, *op. cit.*, vol. V, p. 44.

[5] "Large beads from Rouen," *ibid.*, p. 349.

[6] *Op. cit.*, p. 274.

[7] *Ibid.*

long beads were popularized in England at least as early as 1579, when they were mentioned by Spenser in his *Shepherd's Calendar* under the name of *bugles*. The word *bugle* is due to a confusion of the French term *buise* with Old French *buisine* "trumpet, bugle." In Cotgrave[1] we find *"buisine, buzine, busine* a little pipe, conduct pipe, water pipe, bag pipe,"* while in Old French *buisine* is "trumpet, flute, pipe" and *buse* is also "some kind of trumpet." Hence the name of the musical instrument *bugle* was in England transferred to the Venetian glass-pipe bead.

We thus get a confirmation of the fact that the stone and coral beads of antiquity reëntered commerce in the Middle Ages as a substitute for money, the supremacy held by Cambay in the XVI. century passing over to the countries which manufactured glass counterfeits, China, Venice, France. In Africa, the old emporiums in the Benin country preserved a reminiscence of the early stone-bead money until the XVII. century, but as early as the XVI. century the glass beads usurped their place throughout the greater part of Africa, by the side of the two-valued shell-money.

---

[1] R. Cotgrave, *A Dictionarie of the French and English Tongues*, London 1632.

# CHAPTER IV.

## Wampum.[1]

Jacques Cartier, in 1534, described the shell-money of Canada as follows: "The most precious thing that they have in this world is *esnogny*, the which is white as snow, and they take it in the same river from the *cornibotz* in the manner which follows: When a man has deserved death, or when they have taken any enemies in war, they kill them, then cut them upon the buttocks, thighs, and shoulders with great gashes; afterward in the places where the said *esnogny* is they sink the said body to the bottom of the water, and leave it ten or twelve hours; then draw it up and find within the said gashes and incisions the said *cornibotz*, of which they make bead money and use it as we do gold and silver, and hold it the most precious thing in the world. It has the virtue of stanching blood from the nostrils, because we have tried it."[2]

The French texts write *esurgny, esnogny, enogny, esvogny*[3] as the name of the shell, and the correct form can be established from the still existing word in some of the Algonquin languages. We have Cree *soniyaw* "silver," *soniyawikamik* "bank," Otchipwe *joniia* "money, silver," *joniians* "shilling," where the meaning "silver" is due to an association with French "argent," which means

[1] For a full account read W. M. Beauchamp, *Wampum and Shell Articles Used by the New York Indians*, in *Bulletin of the New York State Museum*, No. 41, vol. 8, p. 327 ff. Here I deal only with origins.

[2] J. P. Baxter, *A Memoir of Jacques Cartier, Sieur de Limoilou*, New York 1906, p. 165 f.

[3] A. d'Avezac, *Bref récit et succincte narration de la navigation faite en MDXXXV et MDXXXVI par le capitaine Jacques Cartier aux îles de Canada, Hochelaga, Saguenay et autres*, Paris 1863, p. 58.

both "silver" and "money." Micmac *sooleawa*, Montagnais *shuliau* "money" is most likely a corruption of English "silver," while Abnaki *manni* "money" is obviously the corresponding English word. Cree *soniyaw* is found again in Long Island in 1642, when the Dutch are called by the Indians *Swanneke*,[1] that is, the "money people."[2] This is derived from *sewan, zeawant*: "This money consists of *zeawant*, which is nothing more than the inside little pillars of the conckshells, which the sea casts up twice a year. These pillars they polish smooth, drill a hole through the centre, reduce it to a certain size, and string the pieces on threads. The strings fill the place of gold, silver and copper coin."[3] "Their money is certain shells or horns found at the seashore, and these horns they rub on a stone as thin as they wish. Then they drill a hole through them and string them on a wire, or make of them strings a hand wide or more, and these they hang around the neck or body or through holes in their ears, or make caps for their heads of them, and there are two kinds of them, the white being the cheaper, the brownish-blue the better, and they give two white shells for one brown, and these are called by them *zeewan*, and they prize them as much as Christians prize gold, silver, and pearls."[4]

From these considerations it follows that *suogny* is nearly the form intended by Cartier, and that it has the general meaning of "money." We have already seen

[1] D. P. de Vries, *Korte historiael ende journaels aenteyckeninge van verscheyden voyagiens in de vier deelen des wereldts-ronde, als Europa, Africa, Asia, ende Amerika gedaen*, 's-Gravenhage 1911, p. 250.

[2] "*Sewan-hacky*, the name frequently applied by the Dutch to Long Island, was compounded from *sewan*, and the Delaware word *hacky*, or *hacking* 'the land,'" J. R. Brodhead, *History of the State of New York*, New York 1853, vol. I, p. 172.

[3] Extracts from a work called *Breeden Raedt aen de vereenighde Nederlandsche Provintien*, printed in Antwerp in 1649, translated from the Dutch original by Mr. C. in E. B. O'Callaghan's *The Documentary History of the State of New York*, Albany 1851, vol. IV, p. 128.

[4] De Vries, *op. cit.*, p. 243.

that Cartier several times referred to Brazil[1] in connection with Canada, hence we may expect him here,
too, to give the name current in Brazil for "money,"
which, no doubt, had been carried north before him.
Indeed, in the native language of Brazil we have çaang
"to experiment, prove, try," çaangaba "token, mold,
picture, signal, figure, form," while the Portuguese itself
has missanga "bead," from the Bantu word for "blue
currency,"[2] which shows that the Brazilian word was derived from the transference of the African word to European stamped money.    In the other Tupi languages
this çaang was taken to be a compound with the personal
prefix ç, producing a root aang, haang, and even haa,
with nearly the same meaning.   We have Guarani
haa, haangaba "signal, picture, image, medal, attempt,
resemblance," which again leads back to a meaning
"token."   Cartier calls the mussel from which the shell
is obtained cornibotz.   This is a real French name for
the mussel, the modern escargot, for which there are recorded escorobot, escarbot, écharbot.[3]

It is apparent from the account of the catching of the
mussels that we have here an exaggeration of the
African manner of obtaining them by means of a hide,[4]
except that a more gruesome practice of killing men
for the purpose is substituted.   That the whole story
is of African origin is further proved by the reference
to the stanching of blood with the shell, which is due
to a confusion with the account of the carnelian beads,
which were reputed to stanch the blood.   Thus Duarte
Pacheco says that the alaquequas, that is, the agates,
are called estancar sangue "blood stanchers."[5]

[1] See Africa and the Discovery of America, vol. I, p. 137.
[2] See p. 226.
[3] E. Rolland, Faune populaire de la France, Paris 1881, vol. III, p. 193.
[4] See p. 210.
[5] Op. cit., lib. I, cap. XXXI, p. 161, and Ibn-al-Baitār, op. cit., Nos.
1565, 1566.

In the beginning of the XVII. century we have fuller accounts of the beads used by the Indians in Canada. Lescarbot,[1] whose work appeared in 1609, that is, a little over seventy years after Jacques Cartier, shows what great changes had taken place in the use of beads among the Indians of Canada: "They are content to have *matachiaz* hanging in their ears and about their necks, bodies, arms, and legs.  The Brazilians, Floridians, and Armouchiquois make necklaces and bracelets (called *bou-re* in Brazil and *matachiaz* by us) from the shells of the large sea mussels, called vignols and resembling snails, which they cut and collect in a thousand pieces, then polish them on a sandstone and make them very small and, piercing them, make of them rosaries which resemble those that we call 'porcelain.' In these necklaces they alternate other beads, which are as black as the others are white, of jet or hard black wood which resembles it, which they polish and reduce as they wish, and all this is very gracefully done; and if things are to be esteemed according to the fashion, even as we have things done among our merchants, these necklaces, sashes, and bracelets of vignol or porcelain are finer than pearls (albeit I shall not be believed), and they are prized more than pearls, gold or silver, and what those of the Great River of Canada in the days of Jacques Cartier called *esurgni*, a word which I find it hard to understand and which Belle-Forest did not understand when he spoke of it.  Nowadays they do not have them, or have lost the trade, for they make great use of the *matachiaz* brought to them from France. . . At Port Royal and in the surrounding country, and near Terre Neuve and Tadoussac, where they have no pearls, nor vignols, the girls and women make *matachiaz* from fishbone or porcupine quills, which they tint black, white and vermilion, as

---

[1] M. Lescarbot, *op. cit.*, vol. III, p. 707 ff.

bright as possible, for our scarlet has nothing like the luster of their red color. But they prefer the *matachiaz* which come from the country of the Armouchiquois, and buy them at high prices. And since they get but little of it, on account of the war which the two constantly wage with each other, they bring to them from France the *matachiaz* made from small glass pipes mixed with tin or lead, which is sold to them by the fathom, for lack of an ell measure . . . Some of them have belts made of *matachiaz*, which they use only when they want to make a show or appear brave."

The shell-beads were not entirely abandoned, for twenty-three years later Sagard-Théodat found them still in use among the Hurons, under the name of *onocoirota*,[1] the modern *onekorha*. Sagard's *matachiaz* is the French *madache*, *matasse*, originally "silk stuff," but more commonly used in the sense of "string," that is, in our case "string of beads," which formed the unit of money value, in Africa as well as in America. It is interesting to find in Lescarbot's vocabulary of native words "needle" translated by *mocouschis*, "awl" by *mocous*,[2] obviously the same word, and referring to the imported steel implements, the latter used in the drilling of the shells. Not all the Algonquin languages possess the word. We have Otchipwe *migoss* "awl, bodkin," Delaware *muckoos* "awl, nail," Natick *mukqs* "awl," Narraganset *mucksuk* "awl blades." But a confusion with English "nail," which refers to the extremities of the body, produced Abnaki *m'kuse* "nail, claw, hoof," Natick *muhkos*, *muhkas* "nail, claw, talon, hoof." Trumbull[3] tries to derive all these from a root *uhquáe*

---

[1] F. G. Sagard-Théodat, *Le grand voyage du pays des Hurons*, Paris 1865, vol. I, p. 135, and G. Sagard-Théodat, *Histoire du Canada et voyages que les Frères Mineurs Recollects y ont faicts pour la conversion des infidèles*, Paris 1866, vol. I, p. 252 f.

[2] *Op. cit.*, vol. III, p. 667.

[3] J. H. Trumbull, *Natick Dictionary*, in *Smithsonian Institution, Bureau of American Ethnology*, Washington 1903, Bulletin 25, p. 168.

"at the point or extremity of," and this will be discussed further on.  Forty years before Cartier the
needle became known in the Carribean, through the
Spaniards, as Carib *acoúcha*, Arawak *akussa*, Galibi
*cacossa*, etc.,[1] and we shall see that the oldest reference to shell-money is found in the Spanish Darien,
hence in *migoss*, *mocouschis*, *muckoos*, all in regions
where shell-money is mentioned at an early time, we
must look for derivations of Spanish *aguxa*, that is,
modern *aguja* "needle."

We have already seen that the Dutch popularized
shell-money at Long Island.  In New England it was
unknown until introduced there by Governor Bradford
in 1627, but it took two years to familiarize the Indians
with its use:  "That which turned out most to their
profite in time, was an entrance into the trade of Wam-
pompeake;  for they now bought aboute 50ll worth of
it of them;  and they told them how vendable it was at
their forte Orania, [Aurania, now Albany] and did per-
swade them they would find it so at Kenebeck;  and so
it came to pass in time, though at first it stuck, & it
was 2 years before they could put of this small quantity,
till yᵉ inland people knew of it;  and afterwards they
could scarcely ever gett enough for them, for many
years togeather  .  .  .  And strange it was to see
the great alteration it made in a few years amonge yᵉ
Indeans themselves;  for all the Indeans of these parts,
& yᵉ Massachusetts, had none or very little of it;  but
yᵉ sachems & some spetiall persons that wore a little
of it for ornaments.  Only it was made and kepte
amonge yᵉ Nariganssetts & Pequents, which grew rich
& potent by it, and these people were poore & begerly,
and had no use of it.  Neither did the English of this
plantation, or any other in yᵉ land, till now that they
had knowledge of it from yᵉ Dutch, so much as know

[1] See vol. I, p. 50.

Plate 18

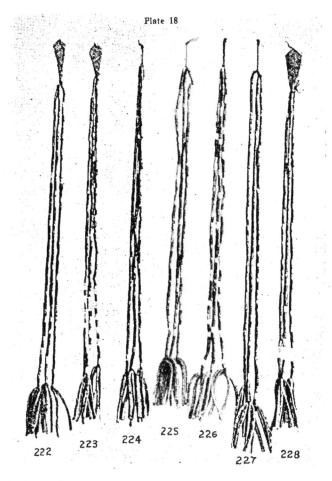

222 223 224 225 226 227 228

INDIAN BEADS, from W. M. Beauchamp's *Wampum and Shell Articles.*

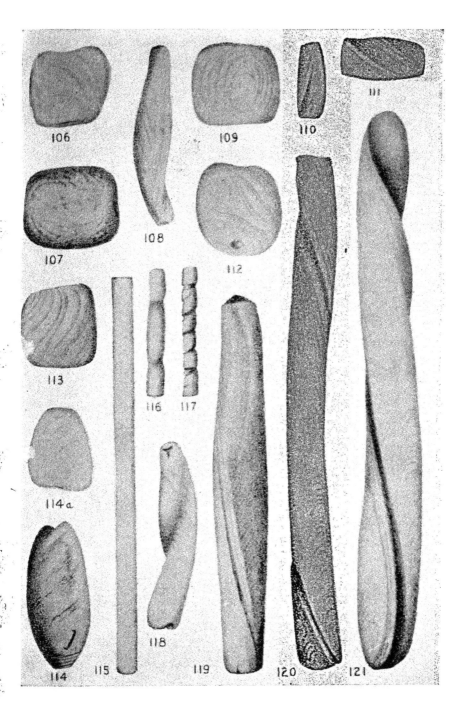

INDIAN LONG BEADS, from W. M. Beauchamp's *Wampum and Shell Articles*.

what it was, much less y$^t$ it was a comoditie of that
worth & valew.     But after it grue thus to be a comoditie in these parts, these Indeans fell into it allso, and to
learne how to make it; for y$^e$ Narigansets doe geather
y$^e$ shells of which y$^{ey}$ make it from their shors.     And
it hath now continued a current comoditie aboute
this 20 years, and it may prove a drugg in time.     In y$^e$
mean time it makes y$^e$ Indeans of these parts rich and
power full, and allso prowd therby; and fills them with
peeces, powder, and shots, which no laws can restraine."[1]     In the State of New York the shell-beads
dug up from the graves present the same distinction
between white and blue beads[2] as in Canada and Africa,
and, besides, we find here a large number of pipe beads,[3]
originally popularized in Africa by the Venetians.
Similar pipes have been found in the graves of the
Mound-builders,[4] which is significant for the dating of
these graves.

We have already seen that the Dutch and Indian name
*sewan, zeewant* for "money" is related to Cartier's
*esnogny* and some modern Indian names for "money,"
hence the assumed derivation from an Algonquin word
meaning "to scatter" is inadmissible.     The beads
themselves are recorded under *bi, pi,* plural *biak, peak,*
which, again, are related to the African and Chinese
words for "shell-bead."     The white bead was known
as *suckauhoek.*     This *biak, peak* is unfortunately not
recorded in many Indian languages, as representing a
rare connotation outside of the region where it was
found and distributed by the aid of white traders, but
none the less, it is found in scattered places throughout
both Americas.

[1] Beauchamp, *op. cit.,* p. 355.
[2] *Ibid.,* p. 332.
[3] *Ibid.,* p. 369 ff.
   *Ibid.,* p. 337.

It can, however, be shown, that the Canadian and New York wampum belts are related to the Brazilian wampum belt, which itself is of African origin. In his *La cosmographie universelle*, Thevet tells of "a certain kind of white necklaces made of very small cockle shells (vignotz), which they take in the sea and prize very highly. The beads which come to France, which are as white as ivory, are brought from this country, and the savages themselves make them, and the sailors buy them at a low price; and *from there came the first belts, which were ever seen in France as made of that material;* which they make so round, without file or other iron utensil, but only with rough stones, with which they cut and round them: with which stones, that are black and gray, they used to cut trees, and make wedges of them, before the Christians taught them the use of iron. When the beads were first brought to France, they thought that they were of white coral, and some said that it was porcelain. Call them what you may, I have seen them made of bones and fishscales of which the women over there wear bracelets as large as are those of soldiers over here."[1] From this we learn that the first wampum belts in Europe came from Brazil. Hans Stade similarly tells of the white rosaries made of a kind of sea-shell: "Of these the king had also some six fathoms length hanging round his neck."[2] "They wear an ornament, which they make out of large snail-shells; these they call *mattepue*. It is made like a crescent, to hang round the neck, and it is snow-white; they call it *bogessy*."[3] Léry gives a somewhat different account of the Brazilian bead necklace: "When after a long time they have polished on a piece of sandstone an infinity of small pieces of a large seashell called *vignol*, which they round out and make as

[1] *Op. cit.*, fol. 931 b.
[2] *Op. cit.*, p. 72 f. (cap. 28).
[3] *Ibid.*, p. 139 (cap. 15).

fine and round as a Tours dime, pierced through the
middle, they make necklaces of them called *boü-re*,
which, when they so wish, they put around their necks,
as we do in our country with gold chains.  This is
what, in my opinion, some call 'porcelaine' of which
we see our women over here wear belts, some of them
more than three fathoms, as beautiful as you may wish
to see, when I arrived in France.  The savages also
make necklaces called *boü-re* from a certain kind of
black wood, which, being almost as heavy and shining
as jet, is quite appropriate for it."[1]  "And so, to use
them for that purpose, they consider as very beautiful the small yellow, blue, green, and other glass buttons, strung like beads and called *mauroubi*, of which
we have brought such a large number to traffic with
them over there.  Indeed, as soon as we land in their
villages, or they come to our fort, to get them from us,
they present us some fruit or other native article, with
their speeches full of flattery, as they are wont to do,
bothering our heads, they incessantly keep repeating:
'*Mair, deagatorem amabé mauroubi*, Frenchman, you
are good, give me some of your glass button bracelets.'"[2]

Stade's *bogessy*, Léry's *boü-re* "necklace" are the
modern Guarani *mboi-rici* "bead necklace," preserved
in Tupi as *moyra*, while Léry's *mauroubi* is the Guarani
*mboi robi* "blue beads."  We thus get the Guarani
*mboi, poi* "shell-bead," which is obviously identical
with the African *abuy*, etc.  It is strange that the
French writers on Brazil, who so freely use *vignot*,
*vignol* for "a large shell," should not have known that
it is a French word.  Belon, before Léry, wrote:  "The
French call the beads made from large *vignols*, por-

---

[1] J. de Léry, *Histoire d'un voyage faict en la terre du Brésil*, Paris 1880,
vol. I, p. 126 f. (chap. VIII).

[2] *Ibid.*, p. 135 f.

celain beads.''[1]  These shells are found in enormous
quantities at Dieppe, hence it is most likely that the
French accounts referring to the shell-beads in Brazil
hark back to Dieppe accounts, and so may precede the
discovery of America by a century.  It is, therefore,
in the Norman country that the wampum belt, as a
precious ornament for European women, had its origin
and was by the Frenchmen transferred to Brazil and
Canada.

"Shell" and "bead" words are not often given in the
scanty vocabularies that have come down to us, and
only fragmentary information is possible here.  It is
not at all surprising that Brazilian *poi* should turn up
as *peag*, etc., in Canada, since again and again we will
find the close relationship of European and African
influence skipping from Brazil to the St. Lawrence.

The other Algonquin languages do not seem to have
a word corresponding to *bi*, *pi*, but the Canadian
languages of this group throw a bright light on the
relation of the shell-money to the French art of drilling.
Cree *mokisis* "bead" and *mikisi-yagan* "plate, porcelain," which has the meaning both of "chinaware" and
"shell-bead," Otchipwe *migiskan* "fish-hook" once more
show the relation to "awl, bodkin" and, at the same
time, help us to determine the origin of the Natick
words *uhquae*, originally "sharp point," *uhkos* "nail,"
*uhquan* "fish-hook" as either contaminations with some
other Algonquin roots, or, more likely, as derived
directly from a Spanish *aguxa*, *aguja* "needle," of
which all the others are derivatives.

We have a full description of shell-money in Virginia
in the beginning of the XVIII. century:  "The Indians had nothing which they reckoned Riches, before
the English went among them, except *Peak*, *Roenoke*,

---

[1] P. Belon du Mans, *Les observations de plusieurs singularitez & choses
memorables, trouvées en Grece, Asie, Judée, Egypte, Arabie, & autres pays
estranges*, Paris 1555, fol. 134a (cap. LXXI).

and such like trifles made out of the *Cunk* shell. These
past with them instead of Gold and Silver, and serv'd
them both for Money and Ornament. It was the
English alone that taught them first to put a value on
their Skins and Furs, and to make a Trade of them.

"*Peak* is of two sorts, or rather of two colours, for
both are made of one shell, tho of different parts; one
is a dark Purple Cylinder, and the other a white; they
are both made in size, and figure alike, and commonly
much resembling the English *Buglas*, but not so transparent nor so brittle. They are wrought as smooth
as Glass, being one third of an inch long, and about a
quarter, diameter, strung by a hole drill'd thro the
Center. The dark colour is the dearest, and dis-
tinguish'd by the name of *Wampom Peak*. The
English men that are called Indian Traders, value the
*Wampom Peak*, at eighteen pence per Yard, and the
white *Peak* at nine pence. The Indians also make
Pipes of this, two or three inches long, and thicker than
ordinary, which are much more valuable. They also
make Runtees of the same Shell, and grind them as
smooth as *Peak*. These are either large like an Oval
Bead, and drill'd the length of the Oval, or else they
are circular and flat, almost an inch over, and one
third of an inch thick, and drill'd edgeways. Of this
Shell they also make round Tablets of about four inches
diameter, which they polish as smooth as the other, and
sometimes they etch or grave thereon, Circles, Stars, a
Half Moon, or any other figure suitable to their fancy.
These they wear instead of Medals before or behind
their Neck, and use the *Peak*, Runtees and Pipes for
Coronets, Bracelets, Belts or long Strings hanging
down before the Breast, or else they lace their garments
with them, and adorn their Tomahawks, and every
other thing that they value.

"They have also another sort which is as current among them, but of far less value; and this is made of the Cockle shell, broke into small bits with rough edges, drill'd through in the same manner as Beads, and this they call Roenoke, and use it as the *Peak*.

"These sorts of Money have their rates set upon them as unalterable, and current as the values of our Money are.

"The Indians have likewise some Pearl amongst them, and formerly had many more, but where they got them is uncertain, except they found 'em in the Oyster Banks, which are frequent in this Country."[1]

Captain Smith gives the meaning "chain" to *roenoke* or *rawrenock;* hence there is, in all likelihood, no essential difference between this and wampum, except that the first was thought of as part of a necklace, while the second, being more carefully worked, was money proper. It is also clear that the shell-money was introduced into Virginia from the north by the traders acquainted with the Long Island or New England method of shell grinding and boring.   Thus we see that since the day of Jacques Cartier the shell-money was taken from Canada first to and near Long Island, and then to Virginia.   In the beginning of the XVI. century two streams of commercial enterprise are observable in the region of the Great Lakes, one emanating from Brazil, through the acquaintance of the French and, possibly, Portuguese traders along the St. Lawrence with the conditions prevailing in Brazil, and the other, an overland influence, obviously along the Mound-builders' route, from the Gulf of Mexico, whence the Spanish or Negro method of working shell-money was transferred to the region of the Great Lakes.

[1] R. Beverley, *The History and Present State of Virginia*, London 1705, Book III, p. 58 f.

Fortunately we get ten years earlier than in Cartier a documentary proof of the extension of the shell-money trade from Panama of Nicaragua at least toward Peru; thus the Carribean wampum trade is, at least as recorded, older than the one in the north. We have already seen[1] that in 1525 Indians from Peru exchanged a large number of commodities for shell-money off the coast of Nicaragua or Darien.[2] Uhle[3] says that all these articles mentioned were manufactured by the Chimus, and that the *Spondilus pictorum* and *Conus Fergusoni*, the shells found very near the shores of Lower California and Central America and abundantly deposited in graves at Trujillo[4] and Ancon,[5] are sufficient proof of a commercial relation between Peru and Central America. At Tiahuanaco a great number of shell-beads are found which must have come from the sea,

[1] See p. 78.

[2] "Este navío que digo que tomó, tenia parecer de cabida de hasta treinta toneles; era hecho por el plan y quilla de unas cañas tan gruesas como postes, ligadas con sogas de uno que dicen eneguen, que es como cáñamo, y los altos de otras cañas mas delgadas, ligadas con las dichas sogas, adonde venian sus personas y la mercaduría en enjuto porque lo bajo se bañaba. Traia sus mástiles y antenas de muy fina madera y velas de algodon del mismo talle, de manera que los nuestros navíos, y muy buena jarcia del dicho eneguen que digo, que es como cáñamo, y unas potalas por anclas á manera de muela de barbero. Y traian muchas piezas de plata y de oro por el ario de sus personas para hacer rescate con aquellas con quien iban á contratar, en que intervenian coronas y diademas y cintos y poniëtes y armaduras como de piernas, y petos y tenazuelas y cascabeles y sartas y mazos de cuentas y rosecleres y espejos guarnecidos de la dicha plata, y tazas y otra vasijas para beber; traian muchas mantas de lana y de algodon, y camisas y aljulas y alcaceres y alaremes y otras muchas ropas, todo lo mas de ello muy labrado de labores muy ricos de colores de grana y carmisí, y azul y amarillo, y de todas otras coores de diversas maneras de labores y figuras de aves y animales y pescados y arboledas; y traian unos pesos chiquitos de pesar oro, como hechura de romana, y otras muchas cosas. En algunas sartas de cuentas venian algunas piedras pequeñas de esmeraldas y cacadonias, y otras piedras y pedazos de cristal y ánime. Todo esto traian para rescatar por unas conchas de pescado de que ellos hacen cuentas coloradas como corales, y blancas, que traian casi el navío cargado de ellas." *Colección de documentos inéditos para la historia de España*, Madrid 1844, vol. V, p. 196 f.

[3] *La esfera de influencias del país de los Incas*, in *Revista histórica, órgano del Instituto Histórico del Perú*, Lima 1909, vol. IV, p. 22.

[4] *Ibid.*, p. 10.

[5] Reiss & Stübel, *The Necropolis of Ancon*, vol. III, plate 83.

and the question arises whether these do not belong to a later Inca period.[1] Thus we are once more confronted with the fact that the Chimu culture belongs to a later time than generally assumed. No wonder, then, that the Chimu graves contain representations of peanuts and other fruits which have been shown to be of African origin. According to the pilot's statement, Christianity was already known in 1525 off the coast of Peru,[2] and now, that we are sure that this report refers to the Chimus, we can determine the name *María Meseia*, obviously that of the Virgin Mary, from the Chimu language. In Chimu[3] *mecherräk* means "woman, doña," hence *María Meseia* literally means "Lady Mary," and the presence of Christianity off the shore of Peru is once more established. But if there was Christianity there, traders must have existed there before, and the relation of Peru to Panama or Nicaragua is simply the result of the influence of traders, either white or black, who emanated from that region, and we have seen that Negroes were settled in Darien before the first white settlement.

Indeed, Andagoya tells that in Careta, about thirty leagues from Darien, "shells were used as articles of

[1] "Auch ist nicht anzunehmen, dass der Titicaca See selbst solche Muscheln wie die, aus welcher Fig. 57 gearbeitet ist, darbietet. Das Material dürfte dem Ocean entnommen sein. Durch alle solche Umstände wird die Frage geweckt, ob hier nicht die Beweise einer Ketschuischen Werkstätte feinerer Arbeitsmateriale, statt einer einheimischen der Colla vorliegen. Sollte es eine von Ketschuas gehaltene gewesen sein, so wäre höchst auffallend deren Niederlassung auf dem Platze anderer älterer Denkmäler einer ganz anderen Kulturperiode, gewissermassen unter den Trümmern derselben," A. Stübel, W. Reiss und B. Koppel, *Kultur und Industrie südamerikanischer Völker*, Berlin 1889, vol. I, p. 52.

[2] "Hay una isla en la mar junto á los pueblos donde tienen una casa de oracion hecha á manera de tienda de campo, toldada de muy ricas mantas labradas, adonde tienen una imágen de una muger con un niño en los brazos que tiene por nombre María Meseia: cuando alguno tiene alguna enfermedad en alguno miembro, hácele un miembro de plata ó de oro, y ofrécesela, y le sacrifican delante de la imágen ciertas ovejas en ciertos tiempos." *Colección de documentos inéditos para la historia de España*, vol. V, p. 200.

[3] E. W. Middendorf, *Das Muchik oder die Chimu-Sprache*, Leipzig 1892.

barter with the inner lands, for they were not found anywhere except on the sea coast,"[1] and in the region nearby "there was a principal woman of this land who said that there was a belief among the chiefs (for the common people do not talk of these things), that *there is a beautiful woman with a child in heaven;* but the story goes no further."[2]   There is a great deal of confusion about this region, for *Careta* also appears as the name of a cacique near Darien, and both seem to be identical with *Quareca,* given by Gómara as the name of a province nearby, while Herrera records it as the name of a region.   In any case, it is right here that Gómara records the only Negroes in America, hence we once more get the close relation between the shell trade and semi-Christian Negroes, that is, those of Portuguese or French origin.

We are again brought back to the transference to America of African commerce, of which we have heard so much.   The bread roots, tobacco, wampum, all proceeded in their dissemination in America along the same roads.   The only question is to determine the date of the first contact.   There can be little doubt that in some things the African influence was exerted before Columbus, and that this influence could not have existed before the XI. century is plain from the fact that the many Mandingo words met with in connection with our words are of Arabic origin.   Most likely the Mandingos first reached America in the middle of the XV. century, with the Portuguese explorers, but should it be possible to prove that the French traders had reached America from the Guinea coast, where they were found already at the end of the XIV. century, the first contact of Africa and America may be set back another half a century.   Here we enter a

---

[1] P. de Andagoya, *Narrative of the Proceedings of Pedrarias Davila,* trans. and ed. by C. R. Markham (The Hakluyt Society), London 1865, p. 9.
[2] *Ibid.,* p. 15.

field of speculation only and must patiently wait for
further evidence, before the final judgment can be
passed.

The Chimus got their shells from Darien or Nicaragua, but they also received the impetus for the making
of the shell-beads from the same region, for we have
accounts in regard to the manufacture of such beads
in these regions. "In these islands (off the coast of
Nicaragua), there are some fishes which the Christians
call 'pié de burro,' which are like large and fat wafers,
and in them pearls are also found.  The sea people affirm
that it is the best fish of all.  From their conchs the
Indians make very fine and colored beads for their
necklaces and bracelets, which they call *chaquira*, and
which look like corals;  and they also make them murrey and white, and each color is perfect in the beads
which they make of these conches of the 'pié de burro,'
and they are quite hard;  these 'piés de burro' are as
large as a man's hand, and further down they are somewhat smaller."[1]   The same is told of the province of
Cueva in Castilla del Oro:  "From these large shells
they make certain small white beads, and others red,
and others black, and others murrey, and little pipes
of the same:  and they make bracelets in which they
mix with these beads others, and beads of gold which
are placed on the wrists and above the ankles and below
the knees for ornament, especially the women who
consider themselves highly and belong to the leading
class wear all these things on the limbs, as above mentioned, and about their necks, and they call these necklaces and such like things *cachira*."[2]

But we possess also another version of the pilot's
voyage toward Peru, by Oviedo, who received it
directly from the participants in the expedition from

[1] G. F. de Oviedo, *Historia general y natural de las Indias*, Madrid 1853,
vol. III, p. 110.
[2] *Ibid.*, p. 138.

which we learn that the Nicaraguan and Peruvian shell ornaments were identical with those used by the Portuguese in the Guinea trade: "We saw on the ocean side a ship of great size, which looked like lateen sails, and the captain and people voyaging in it were getting ready to fight, if it was necessary. And he bore down upon the boat and took it, and they found that it was a ship of merchants from those parts, who were going on their commercial errand, and in it were as many as twenty people, men, women, and children. This boat was constructed of heavy timbers strongly tied together with henequen ropes, with its quarterdecks, cabins, rudder, sails and tackle, and large stone blocks of the size of barber stones, which served in the place of anchors. They carried red conchshells, which there are in *Chaquira*, that is, strings of beads, such as are found in the Canary Islands, which are sold to the king of Portugal for Guinea, and for these the Indians give all the gold and silver and cloth which they carry for barter. They carried many black vessels and many garments of various colors, made of wool, shirts, finely-wrought colored mantles, white cloth with fringes, all new, for the trade, and dyed wool, wool dye, and many other delicate and fine things, from which it appeared that they were a clever people, but they look something like Berberisci. They told us the way they mined gold, and they said that they had sheep which they sheared every year, and that there were inhabited islands, and many pearls, and that they slept in beds with cotton sheets. They worship certain idols; their arms are lances, bows, and macanas, like those of the Indians of certain parts of Cueva, and in other parts they had no wars. They salt their fish, to keep it, as we do. The Indians are dressed in shirts, and the women in enaguas and shirts and mantles thrown under their arms, like the women of the Moors or in the Canary Islands.   They have assays with which to tell the gold, and scales to weigh it;  they worked silver and other metals, and knew it very well: and they carried a certain quantity of either, and they informed us that in their country there were many precious stones."[1]

Oviedo was not sure what the *chaquira* or *cachira* was, except that it referred to some kind of fine bead, and thought that it might be the name of the bead necklace. We learn more from Cieza de Leon, who says that in Peru they wear "a few ornaments, such as jewels of gold and very small beads, called *chaquira*.   In some provinces I have myself seen that the people put so high a value on these *chaquiras*, that they will give their weight in gold for them."[2]  "Few are the things they now make in comparison with the great and rich ornaments they made

[1] "É vido venir del bordo de la mar un navio que hacia muy grand bulto, que parescia vela latina, y el maestre é los que con él yban se aparejaron para pelear, si fuesse menester; é arribó sobrel navio é le tomaron, é hallaron que era un navio de tractantes de aquellas partes, que venian á hacer sus rescates, en el qual venian hasta veynte personas, hombres é mugeres é muchachos.

"La manera deste navio era de muy gruessos maderos reatados fuertemente con sogas rescias de henequen, con su alcáçar é retretes é gobernalles, velas é xarcias é potales de piedras grandes, tamañas como piedras de barbero, que sirven en lugar de áncoras.   Llevaban conchas coloradas, de que hay en Chaquira, *id est* sartales, como los de las islas de Canaria, que se venden al rey de Portugal para el rescate de Guinea; é por estas dan los indios todo el oro é plata é ropas que traen de rescate.   Traian muchos cántaros negros é mucha ropa de diverssas colores, de lana, é camisas é ayubas, é mantas de colores muy labradas, paños blancos con franja, todo nuevo, para contractar; é lana de colores, tinta en lana é otras muchas cosas sutiles é muy primas, en que parescia bien ser gente entendida.   Y eran de buena dispusicion de personas;  mas tienen alguna semejança de berberiscos. Decian la manera de cómo sacan el oro;  é decian que hay ovejas é que las tresquilan cada año, é que hay islas pobladas, é que hay muchas perlas, é que duermen en camas con sábanas de algodon.   Adoran ciertos ydolos: sus armas son lanças é tiraderas é macanas, como los indios de Cueva en algunas partes, é que en otras no tienen guerra.   Salan los pescados, para su mantenimiento, como nosotros.   Los Indios andan vestidos con camisas, é las indias con sus enaguas é camisas é mantas echadas debaxo del braço, á manera de moras ó canarias.   Traen toque para conoscer el oro é romana para pessarlo é pessar la plata labrada é otros metales, é conóscenlo muy bien: é traian cierta cantidad de lo uno é de lo otro, é dieron noticia que en la tierra avia muchas piedras de valor," *ibid.*, vol. IV, p. 121 f.

[2] C. R. Markham, *op. cit.*, p. 176 (chap. XLVI).

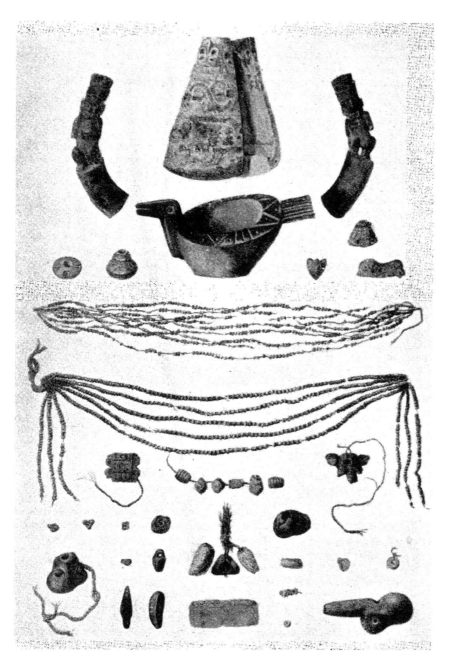

PERUVIAN BEADS, from Reiss and Stuebel's *The Necropolis of Ancon*.

in the time of the Yncas. They, however, make the
*chaquiras*, so small and accurately worked, by which
they show themselves still to be eminent workers in
silver."[1]  To this Garcilasso de la Vega says:  "Pedro
Cieza, in chapter XLIV, speaks at length of the wealth
found in those temples and royal chambers of the provinces of the Canaries as far as Tumipampa, which the
Spaniards call Tomebamba  .  .  .  outside of which
wealth there was a very great quantity of treasure in
pitchers and pots, and other vessels, and much clothing,
very rich and full of silver work and *chaquira*  .  .  .
The Spaniards name *chaquira* certain very small gold
beads, smaller than any glass beads, which the Indians
make with such skill and dexterity, that the best silver-
smiths whom I knew in Seville asked me how that was
done, because although so small the joints are soldered;
I found a few in Spain, and they marveled at them
greatly."[2]  Pedro Pizarro, in 1571, similarly wrote:
"There were mantles made of gold and silver *chaquira*,
which are certain very small beads, marvelous to look
at, because everything was full of these beads, without a
thread showing, like cloth of a closely woven net, and
these mantles were for the ladies."[3]

It follows from Garcilasso de la Vega that *chaquiras*
is not a native Peruvian word, but was introduced by
the Spaniards from Castillo del Oro. Here the form
*cachira* prevails over an enormous territory. It is
still found in Carib and Arawak, for we get Arawak
*kassuru* "bead," Carib "*cachourou* rassade, sont petits
grains de verre blanc, rond comme petites perles, on
l'apporte de Venise, au moins la plus grãde partie, les
Sauuages es en sont fort curieux en enfillent dans des
petites cordes de pitte, puis la tournent au lieu de la

---

[1] *Ibid.*, p. 404 f. (chap. CXIV).
[2] *Op. cit.*, parte 1, lib. VIII, cap. 5 (The Hakluyt Society).
[3] P. Pizarro, *Descubrimiento y conquista del Perú*, in *Colección de libros
y documentos referentes á la historia del Perú*, Lima 1917, vol. VI, p. 74.

iartiere la largeur de trois doigts, au tour du bras, entre l'epaule & le coude, au poignet au lieu de brasselets (outre les escharpes dont i'ay parlé cy-deuant) & cela paroist fort sur leur corps rougis: les femmes n'en sont pas moins curieuses que les hommes."[1]   In Campa we have *çhanquiro* "mussel," which is, no doubt, related to the Carib and Arawak words.

It is not difficult to show how all these arose in the gold trade of the Gold Coast of Africa.   De Marees tells of the *kakrauw*, small bits of gold, used by the Negroes in the trade, and originally introduced by the Europeans into Africa.[2]   Bosman[3] says:   "These Fetiches are cut into small Bits by the Negroes, about the worth of one, two or three Farthings.   'Tis a common Proverb, That you cannot buy much Gold for a Farthing, yet even with that value in Gold you may here go to Market and buy Bread or Fruit for your Necessities. The Negroe Women know the exact value of these Bits so well at sight, that they never are mistaken;   and accordingly they tell them to each other without weighing, as we do coined Money.   They are here called *Kakeraas*, the Word expressing something of very little value;   and the Gold it self is indeed very little worth: For we cannot sell it in Europe for above forty shillings the Ounce;   and yet it passes currant all over the Coast; and our Garrisons are paid their subsistence Money in it.   And for this they may buy all sorts of Edibles of the Negroes;   who mixing it with other Gold, bring it to us again;   and as soon as received, the Clerks are ordered to pick it out of the other with which it is mixed;   so that this Stuff seems to pass backward and forward without the least diminution, notwithstanding large quantities of it are annually sent to Europe by

---

[1] R. P. R. Breton and J. Platzmann, *Dictionaire caraibe-français,* Leipzig 1892, p. 99 f.
[2] *Op. cit.,* pp. 65 f., 197 ff.
[3] *Op. cit.,* p. 72 f.

the French and Portuguese, besides what we our selves spend: But the Negroes making them faster than we export them, they are like to continue long enough." At about the same time Barbot wrote: "These pieces of gold are by the Blacks cut into small bits worth one, two, or three farthings, used as coined money in the markets, to buy provisions, as bread, fruit, fish, flesh, etc. The Black women are so well acquainted with the value of those bits, which they call *Kakeraas*, or *Krakraas*, a word signifying a very little value, that they are never mistaken, and tell them to one another without weighing, as we do farthings or half-pence in England. And this sort of money is more generally found at Commendo, Mina, cape Corso, and the adjacent parts, than elsewhere. Those *Krakraas* are indeed worth very little, for that gold in any part of Europe, will not yield above forty shillings an ounce; and yet it passes current all over the coast, and the European garrisons are paid their subsistence in it, and can with it buy all sorts of eatables of the Blacks, who mix it with other gold, and carry it again to the European forts and ships."[1] "In former times those people had no other way of vending their commodities among themselves, than by bartering or exchange; but since the French first, and after them the Portuguese, taught them the way of cutting coarse gold into very small bits, by them call'd *Kra-kra*, to facilitate the buying and selling of small things, the Blacks have so well improv'd that sort of money, that now pretty large sums are paid in it."[2]

The etymology given by Bosman and Barbot is correct, for we have Asante *kakra* "little, small," *kakrawa* "little, very little," *kakawa* "the smallest, least, a kind of yellow precious bead," that is, in imitation of a gold

[1] J. Churchill, *op. cit.*, vol. V, p. 230 f.
[2] *Ibid.*, p. 269.

bead. This is not originally an African word, but Portuguese *caracol*, plural *caracoes*, "shell, trifle, small thing." The Spanish *caracol* has the same meaning, hence, as we have seen,[1] we get, in American, Galibi *caracoulis* "copper trinkets," *cacones* "trifles, trinkets," Carib *calluculi*, Accawai *corrocori*, Chayma, Cumanagote *carcuriri*, Cariniaco *cureuco* "trinkets, gold," Roucouyenne *caracouli* "silver." This word, from the form *chaquira*, is also found in Aymara and Kechua, geminated as *choque* and *cori* "gold." This brings us to the very important question whether all the Inca gold artifacts are due to *tangomao* initiative, a question which will have to be investigated in full. For the present this much is certain,—the tiny gold beads of Peru, the necklaces of Castillo del Oro are of African origin and belong to the same trade activity which produced the wampum belt. From Darien this activity extended down the coast as far as Peru, and to the north, in California, it resolved itself into a local point of distribution far inland of abalone and olivella shells.

[1] Vol. I, p. 51 f.

# WORD INDEX

*abdiga*, Kandin, 20.
*abduga*, Hausa, 20.
*abduya*, Tuareg, 20.
*abuy*, African, 216.
*acayetl*, Nahuatl, 143.
*accarey*, Benin, 244.
*accary*, African, 216.
*acoúcha*, Carib, 254.
ʻ*adai*, Somali, 21.
*agaga*, Ewe, 221.
*agūr*, Hebrew, 235.
*aguxa*, Spanish, 254, 258.
*ahuaramuto*, Uarao, 80.
*akorá*, Taimarona, 223.
*akorane*, Betsileo, 222.
*akorany*, Hova, 222.
*akori*, Benin, 240.
*akussa*, Arawak, 254.
*akūtan*, Landoma, 22.
*akwe*, Dahome, 221.
*akweho*, Dahome, 221.
*akweɉo*, Dahome, 221.
*akweno*, Dahome, 221.
*alaqueca*, Portuguese, 232.
*albafar*, Portuguese, 100.
*albafor*, Spanish, 100.
*aliupò*, Yaulapiti, 81.
*al-kawara*, Hausa, 223.
*allowa*, Hausa, 21.
*altabaca*, Spanish, 124.
*amacapulquauitl*, Nahuatl, 39.
*amacuahuitl*, Nahuatl, 39.
*amaju*, Brazilian, 81.
*amandyju*, Guarani, 81.
*amaniu*, Brazilian, 81.
*amano*, Cocama, 81.
*amanyju*, Brazilian, 81.
*amatl*, Nahuatl, 39.
*amatsitu*, Auetö, 81.
ʼαμβικισμόs, Greek, 94.
*ambix*, Latin, 90.
ʼαμβνκίƶω, Greek, 94.
ʼαμβνκισμόs, Greek, 94.
*a-misañga*, Quellimane, 226.
*amoniu*, Oyampi, 81.
*ampe*, Anti, 81.
*ampegi*, Anti, 81.

*amuijo*, Apiaca, 81.
*amulu*, Galibi, 81.
*amuniɉu*, Kamayura, 81.
*amydu*, Brazilian, 81.
*ankaora*, Taukarana, 222.
ʻ*aqīq*, Arabic, 224, 232.
ʻ*ataba*, Arabic, 19.
*atakxera*, Bakairi, 80.
*atakxira*, Bakairi, 80.
ʻ*atbah*, Arabic, 19.
*aualri*, Baniba, 80.
*auarli*, Baniba, 80.
*audiga*, Hausa, 20.
*ayupe*, Mehinaku, 81.
*ayupò*, Yaulapiti, 81.


*Bābāgūr*, Abyssinian, 235.
*bābāgūrī*, Guzerati, 232.
*bābāgūrī*, Turkish, 232.
*bad*, Hebrew, 7.
*bafeɉar*, Portuguese, 100.
*bafo*, Spanish, 100.
*baforada*, Portuguese, 100.
*bagūz*, Arabic, 7.
*baho*, Spanish, 100.
*bāhūr*, Arabic, 99.
*bakár*, Arabic, 99.
*balbal*, Arabic, 214.
*bam*, Hausa, 102.
*bara*, Sumerian, 7.
*baraš*, Arabic, 7.
*bargande*, Japanese, 183.
*barṣ*, Arabic, 7.
*bawaghori*, Guzerati, 232.
*bazz*, Arabic, 7.
*bella*, Sinhalese, 216.
βερβερι, Greek, 214.
*beviese*, Dutch, 247.
*beya*, Malay, 216.
*bi, biak*, Algonquin, 255.
*bia*, Siamese, 216.
βίκοs, Greek, 90.
*birs*, Arabic, 7.
*birš*, Arabic, 7.
*biya*, Malay, 216.
*boeɉies*, African, 217.

*boesjes*, Dutch, 218.
*bofar*, Portuguese, 100.
*bofarinheiro*, Portuguese, 99.
*bofe*, Spanish, 100.
*bofon*, LLatin, 99.
*bogessy*, Tupi, 256.
*boķôr*, Arabic, 99.
*boli*, Maldivian, 214.
*bolli*, Maldivian, 220.
*boly*, Maldivian, 214.
*βόμβαξ*, Greek, 10.
*bombyce*, Latin, 17.
*bosse*, French, 94.
*bouges*, French, 218.
*boü-re*, Tupi, 257.
*bousies*, English, 218.
*bout*, French, 94.
*bouton*, French, 94.
*buckoor*, Negro, 120.
*bufar*, Spanish, 100.
*bufarinha*, Portuguese, 99.
*bufarinheiro*, Portuguese, 99.
*bufo*, LLatin, 99.
*bufonerus*, LLatin, 99.
*bufonus*, LLatin, 99.
*bugle*, English, 248.
*bũḥār*, Arabic, 99.
*bũḥāriy*, Arabic, 99.
*buhoneria*, Spanish, 99.
*buhonero*, Spanish, 99.
*buise*, OFrench, 247.
*buisine*, OFrench, 248.
*bulbe*, Yiddish, 182.
*bumbo*, Hausa, 102.
*bummi*, Hausa, 102.
*bũṣ*, Hebrew, 7.
*bũṣâ*, Syriac, 7.
*buse*, OFrench, 247.
*busine*, OFrench, 248.
*buss*, Walloon, 247.
*βύσσος*, Greek, 7.
*buzio*, Portuguese, 210, 217.
*buta*, LLatin, 94.
*butta*, LLatin, 94.
*buttis*, LLatin, 94.
*buzai*, Walloon, 247.
*buzine*, OFrench, 248.

*çaang*, Tupi, 251.
*çaangaba*, Tupi, 251.
*cab*, Kiche, 53.
*caballo*, Spanish, 181.
*cachira*, Castilla del Oro, 264.

*cachourou*, Carib, 267.
*cacones*, Galibi, 270.
*cacossa*, Galibi, 254.
*c'aj-am*, Pokonchi, 54.
*calliomarcus*, Latin, 96.
*calluculi*, Carib, 270.
*c'am*, Kekchi, 54.
*c'am-al*, Kekchi, 54.
*canivet*, OFrench, 93.
*caracol*, Portuguese, 270.
*caracouli*, Roucouyenne, 270.
*caracoulis*, Galibi, 270.
*carbasus*, Latin, 12.
*carcuriri*, Chayma, 270.
*cascavel*, Spanish, 25.
*cassot*, French, 132.
*Castilla*, Spanish, 48.
*cauarli*, Mandauaca, 80.
*cax*, Maya, 49.
*caxlan*, Kekchi, 49.
*caxlan lem*, Kekchi, 49.
*caxlan oua*, Kekchi, 49.
*caxtil*, Nahuatl, 49.
*çhanquiro*, Campa, 268.
*chaquira*, Nicaragua, 264.
*χεθομένη*, Greek, 9.
*χεθόν*, Greek, 9.
*chicha*, Spanish, 114 f.
*chichi*, Nahuatl, 115.
*chichilia*, Nahuatl, 115.
*chichina*, Nahuatl, 115.
*χιτών*, Greek, 13.
*choque*, Aymara, 270.
*cnafa*, ASaxon, 93.
*çoço*, Nahuatl, 52.
*çoçoa*, Nahuatl, 52.
*cohore*, Moxa, 80.
*coj*, Chimu, 81.
*col*, Chimu, 81.
*contaria*, Portuguese, 245.
*continha*, Portuguese, 245.
*cori*, Aymara, 270.
*cori*, Benin, 237.
*coril*, Manicongo, 237.
*cornibotz*, OFrench, 249.
*corrocori*, Accawai, 270.
*cottamo*, Guaycurus, 80.
*coyllu*, Aymara, 73 f.
*curenco*, Cariniaco, 270.
*cynae*, Latin, 17.

*ḍarra*, Arabic, 22.
*dishniupan*, Gothic, 93.
*dragoman*, English, 112.

*écharbot*, French, 251.
*embocus*, LLatin, 89.
*embotar*, Catalan, 94.
*embotus*, LLatin, 88 ff.
*embudar*, Spanish, 94.
*embut*, OFrench, 89.
*embutz*, Provençal, 89.
*empa*, Coptic, 10.
*empai*, Coptic, 10.
*empombe*, Mozambique, 101.
*enogny*, Canada, 249.
*en-simbi*, Luganda, 222.
*eōru*, Kupa, 21.
*escarbot*, French, 251.
*escargot*, French, 251.
*escorobot*, French, 251.
*esnogny*, Canada, 249.
*esurgny*, Canada, 249.
*esvogny*, Canada, 249.
*etouab*, Coptic, 19.
*ettbbēu*, Coptic, 19.
*eupe*, Swahili, 20.

*fapa*, Sotho, 10.
*fap'a*, Pédi, 10.
*faraša*, Arabic, 7.
*fkotūn*, Bulonda, 22.

*gābal*, Hebrew, 11.
*gābar*, Hebrew, 11.
*gad*, Sumerian, 11.
*ganivet*, French, 93.
*gaur*, Hindustani, 236.
*gaura*, Sanskrit, 236.
*ǵaz'*, Arabic, 224.
*gazl*, Arabic, 22.
*gese*, Malinke, 22.
*gesē*, Kra, 22.
*gese-fute*, Soso, 22.
*geze*, Toma, 22.
*gid*, Sumerian, 11.
*gie*, Gio, 22.
*gil*, Sumerian, 11.
*ginbo*, Angola, 213.
*gorā*, Hindustani, 236.
*goraō*, Prakrit, 236.
*Gor Bāba*, Northern India, 236.
*gossypinus*, Latin, 17.
*gotun*, Arabic (oases), 21.
*grečikha*, Russian, 182.
*gri*, Neule, 240.
*guani*, Taino, 117.

*guanin*, Taino, 117 f.
*gungun*, Bagbalan, 22.
*Gūr-bābā*, Bhil, 235.
*guriyā*, Hindustani, 236.
*guṭikā*, Sanskrit, 236.

*haa*, Guarani, 251.
*haangaba*, Guarani, 251.
*ḥābal*, Hebrew, 11.
*ḥābar*, Hebrew, 11.
*ḥabaš*, Hebrew, 11.
*hamaniu*, Cocama, 81.
*hamba*, Bondei, 10.
*hañji*, Kannada, 8.
*ḥāpā*, Hebrew, 11.
*ḥāpāh*, Hebrew, 11.
*ḥāpap*, Hebrew, 11.
*ḥāpaš*, Hebrew, 11.
*ḥaraz*, Arabic, 224.
*harĕ*, Kannada, 8.
*hari*, Kannada, 8.
*ḥašbun*, Arabic, 17.
*ḥašiš*, Arabic, 114 f.
*hatti*, Kannada, 8.
*het en meni*, Egyptian, 9.
*ḥnau*, Coptic, 92.
*hnifr*, Icelandic, 93.
*ho-pei*, Chinese, 203, 222.
*hopeš*, Hebrew, 11.
*hosca*, Chibcha, 142.
*ḥotollo*, Peul, 21.
*ḥušbun*, Arabic, 17.

*ich-pocatl*, Nahuatl, 53.
*ich-taca*, Nahuatl, 53.
*ich-teco*, Nahuatl, 53.
*ich-tectli*, Nahuatl, 53.
*ich-tequi*, Nahuatl, 53.
*ich-tli*, Nahuatl, 54.
*ie*, Chibcha, 140.
*igovo*, Negro, 210.
*igovo*, Benin, 221.
*iguou*, Benin, 221.
*imbotare*, LLatin, 94.
*in-tsimbi*, Kaffir, 221.
*ipamba*, Tabwa, 10.
*īye*, Mano, 22.
*ix*, Maya, 53.
*ix-cax*, Maya, 53.
*ix-kanabal*, Maya, 53.
*ix-nabatun*, Maya, 53.
*ix-nuc*, Maya, 53.

*ix-pochina*, Nahuatl, 54.
*ix-tun*, Maya, 53.
*ix-tux*, Maya, 53.

*jam*, Chimu, 81.
*jariderli*, Caruzana, 80.
*jirbi*, Galla, 20.
*joniia*, Otchipwe, 249.
*joniians*, Otchipwe, 249.
*jop*, Chibcha, 141 f.

*kaan*, Maya, 54.
*kābal*, Hebrew, 11.
*kāban*, Hebrew, 11.
*kābar*, Hebrew, 11.
*kabath*, Maldivian, 208.
*kakawa*, Asante, 269.
*kakeraas*, Gold Coast, 268.
*kakra*, Asante, 269.
*kakrauw*, Gold Coast, 268.
*kakrawa*, Asante, 269.
*kal-gudan*, Bornu, 21.
*kal-gutan*, Kanuri, 21.
*kap*, Chinese, 12.
*kāpal*, Hebrew, 11.
*kāpar*, Hebrew, 11.
*kaparda*, Sanskrit, 222.
*kāpas*, Hebrew, 11.
*kāpat*, Hebrew, 11.
*kappu*, Kannada, 12.
*kara*, Kannada, 11.
*kārpāsa*, Sanskrit, 5, 12.
*κάρπασος*, Greek, 4 ff.
*kaṛpu*, Kannada, 12.
*Kartoffel*, German, 182.
*kašabel*, Coptic, 25.
*kassuru*, Arawak, 267.
*kathodnie*, Apinages, 80.
*kaṭṭān*, Arabic, 13.
*kauḍā*, Marathi, 222.
*kauḍi*, Hindustani, 222.
*kaurī*, Hindustani, 222.
*kavača*, Sanskrit, 12.
*kavadi*, Kannada, 12.
*kavadi*, Malayalam, 208.
*kavaḍi*, Kannada, 222.
*kavadiya*, Sinhalese, 208.
*kavi*, Dravidian, 12.
*kavidi*, Kannada, 12.
*kawara*, Hausa, 223.
*ketn*, Egyptian, 13.
*ketn meni*, Egyptian, 9.
*khorre*, Wolof, 223.

*kiah*, Chinese, 12.
*kid*, Sumerian, 11.
*kiḍ*, Kannada, 11.
*kil*, Sumerian, 11.
*kir*, Sumerian, 11.
*kittu*, Assyrian, 13.
*knaau*, Coptic, 92.
*Knabe*, German, 93.
*knap*, English, 93.
*knapp*, German, 93.
*knappr*, ONorse, 93.
*knau*, Coptic, 92.
*knave*, English, 93.
*kneif*, ONorse, 93.
*kneifen*, German, 93.
*knife*, English, 93.
*knifr*, OIcelandic, 93.
*knivus*, LLatin, 93.
*knob*, English, 93.
*Knopf*, German, 93.
*Knoph*, German, 93.
*κνούφιον*, Greek, 92.
*koḍā*, Guzerati, 222.
*koli*, Benin, 238.
*korandē*, Mandingo, 21.
*korandi*, Bambara, 21.
*korho*, Dyula, 21.
*korho-nde*, Dyula, 22.
*kori*, Bambara, 21.
*kotōdīn*, Malinke, 21.
*kotoka*, Makusi, 80.
*kotole*, Soninke, 21.
*kotollin-khare*, Soninke, 80.
*kotondo*, Bambara, 21.
*kouḍi*, Tulu, 222.
*koun*, Coptic, 92.
*koyondyī*, Toronka, 21.
*krakraas*, Gold Coast, 268.
*kristal*, Dutch, 246.
*ku*, Sumerian, 11.
*kudi*, Hausa, 223.
*kukuruza*, Russian, 182.
*kundēra*, Buduma, 22.
*kunkun*, Koama, 22.
*kunkuntu*, Gurma, 22.
*kuori*, Bambara, 21.
*kur*, Sumerian, 11.
*kurdī*, Hausa, 223.
*kuro*, Bambara, 223.
*kurpāsa*, Sanskrit, 12.
*kuru*, Sumerian, 11.
*kurūn*, Malinke, 223.
*kutan*, Arabic (oases), 21.
*kutandō*, Kalumga, 21.

*lançado*, Portuguese, 106 ff.
*lĕbŭš*, Hebrew, 12.
*lewu*, Udom, 21.
*libās*, Arabic, 12.
*libs*, Arabic, 12.
*līlu*, Puka, 21.
*lōlo*, Pika, 21.
*lolu*, Esitoko, 21.
*lōṭi*, Peul, 21.
*lubāra*, Assyrian, 12.
*lubašu*, Assyrian, 12.
*ludhu*, Tamazirt, 21.
*luḷḷo*, Hausa, 21.
*luḷo*, Goali, 21.
*lulu*, Nupe, 21.
*lumaca*, Italian, 211 f.
*lu-simbi*, Nyamwesi, 222.

*madache*, French, 253.
*māḥ*, Egyptian, 10.
*mahe*, Coptic, 10.
*mahi*, Coptic, 10.
*maïd*, Somali, 21.
*manako*, Guzerati, 245.
*manholu*, Carib, 81.
*manhulu*, Galibi, 81.
*manka*, Hindustani, 245.
*manni*, Abnaki, 250.
*mashanga*, Swahili, 225.
*μαστάριον*, Greek, 90.
*matachiaz*, Canada, 252.
*matamungo*, Portuguese, 245.
*matasse*, French, 253.
*mattepue*, Tupi, 256.
*mauroubi*, Tupi, 257.
*mauru*, Galibi, 81.
*mazari*, Hausa, 22.
*mbai*, Coptic, 10.
*mbamvu*, Kongo, 102.
*mbiya*, Kongo, 221.
*mboi-rici*, Guarani, 257.
*mboi-robi*, Guarani, 257.
*mbombo*, Angola, 102.
*me-ca-tl*, Nahuatl, 54.
*mecherräk*, Chimu, 262.
*meḥi*, Egyptian, 10.
*meni*, Egyptian, 9.
*metl*, Nahuatl, 49.
*m'hi*, Egyptian, 10.
*miḍarrah*, Arabic, 22.
*mien*, Chinese, 9.
*migiskan*, Otchipwe, 258.
*migoss*, Otchipwe, 253.

*mikisi-yagan*, Cree, 258.
*misanga*, Fiote, 226.
*missanga*, Portuguese, 226, 251.
*m'kuse*, Abnaki, 253.
*mocous*, Canada, 253.
*mocouschis*, Canada, 253.
*mokisis*, Cree, 258.
*moneyu*, Trumai, 81.
*mpai*, Coptic, 10.
*mpamba*, Swahili, 10.
*mpempa*, Coptic, 10.
*m'sanga*, Fiote, 226.
*muckoos*, Delaware, 253.
*mucksuk*, Narraganset, 253.
*muhkas*, Natick, 253.
*muhkos*, Natick, 253.
*muiniju*, Emerillon, 81.
*mujinha*, Kimbundu, 81.
*mukqs*, Natick, 253.

*negbie*, Neule, 221.
*newū*, Ekantulufu, 21.
*nibble*, English, 93.
*nip*, English, 93.
*njimbu*, Kimbundu, 213.
*nsañga*, Quellimane, 226.
*nsungu*, Kongo, 226.
*nzimbu*, Kikongo, 213.

*och-pana*, Nahuatl, 54.
*odonti*, Akra, 22.
*okondo*, Fan, 22.
*olulu*, Sobo, 21.
*ōro*, Isoama, 21.
*osca*, Chibcha, 141 f.
*'oṭbe*, Saho, 20.
*'oṭbi*, Afar, 20.
*ὀθόνιον*, Greek, 5.
*otocuare*, Cumanagota, 80.
*otoquat*, Chayma, 80.
*oudega*, Bagirmi, 20.
*ōŭrō*, Okuloma, 21.
*owo*, Yoruba, 221.
*ōwu*, Aku, 21.
*owuh*, Yoruba, 21.

*pai-tié*, Chinese, 8.
*pai ts'z*, Cantonese, 205.
*paj*, Kakchiquel, 48.
*paj-am*, Pokonchi, 48.
*pakhta*, Persian, 8.

# SUBJECT INDEX

*Ablution* words for "cotton" in Arabic and the African languages, 21.

*Acosta* and the banana, 73 f.

*Africa*, "cotton" words in, 18 ff.; and the Arabic "purification" words for "cotton," 18 ff.; and the Arabic "ablution" words for "cotton," 21; agriculture of, in Peru, 63; fruits from, in Ancon graves, 75; and wine, 101 ff.; universality of smoking in, 188; cowries in, 209 f.; beads imported from Cambay to, 226 ff.; beads in North America originate in, 251; commerce in America from, 263; origin of American culture in, 263.

*Agate* trade of Cambay, 235.

AGGRY BEADS, 237—248.

*Aggry* beads, their history, 237 ff.; in Benin, 238 ff.; supposed to grow in the sea, 244.

*Albiruni* on cowries, 208.

*Alchemy* and the distilling cap, 92 ff.

*Alcyonium* and smoking, 85 ff.

*Algonquin* languages and "bead" words, 258.

*Alloy* of gold in Africa and in America, 118 f.

*Almagro* on cotton in Peru, 78 f.

*America* visited by Negroes before Columbus, 116 ff.

*Ancon*, mummies at, 72; graves of recent origin, 73 f.

*Andagoya* on bead money, 262 f.

*Arabic*, "cotton" words in, 7; word for "tree" basis for Pliny's *gossypium*, 17; influence in Africa in "cotton" words, 18 ff.; "purification" words for "cotton," 19.

*Archaeology* has no means for determining history of cultivated plants, 185; its fallacy in applying Egyptian and Babylonian data to America, 195; must be checked by history and philology, 196 ff.

*Arriaga* and reburials in Peru, 75 ff.; and guano, 77 f.

*Arrian* mentions cotton in India, 5.

*Assyria*, cotton in, 3.

*Awls* in North America, 253 f.

*Bābāgūrī* from Cambay, 229; name for onyx at Cambay, 232; and Solomon's stone, 235; see *Solomon's stone*.

*Baessler* and reburials in Peru, 71.

*Bahrein*, cotton in, 4.

*Banana* in Peruvian graves, 73; spuriousness of native variety of coyllo in Peru, 73; and Garcilasso de la Vega, 73 ff.

*Bantu*, "cotton" words in, 10.

*Barbosa*, his account of the Cambay beads, 227 f.

*Barbot* on crystals in Africa, 246; on gold beads in Africa, 269.

*Barnabé Cobo* and reburials in Peru, 69 f.

*Barros* on cowries in Africa, 209 f.

*Basket-makers'* culture and tobacco pipes, 196 ff.

*Beads* and Columbus, 25; imported into Africa from Cambay, 226 ff.; red, from Cambay at Sofala, 230 f.; blue, called "coris," 237 f.; opinion of their origin, 238; coral, 238; artificial, made in Europe for African trade, 239; of Arabic manufacture, 240; blue, in Benin, 240; at Zanzibar, 240 ff.; manufactured in China for Arabic trade, 243; from Cambay in Madagascar, 245; from India and Venice in Africa, 245; the African trade in XVI. c., 245 f.; their deterioration in Africa in the last two centuries, 246 f.; manufactured at Venice, 247; substitute for money, 248; stanch blood, 249; names for, in North America, 249 f.; names in Brazil, 251; obtained in America as in Africa, 251; among Indians of Canada, 252; at Long Island, 254

CPSIA information can be obtained
at www.ICGtesting.com
Printed in the USA
LVHW041612200123
737528LV00011B/866

9 781360 139432